Wh   ut

Pro Truth

This book should interest anyone concerned with the implications of the post-truth era for the functioning of democracy. This era is characterized by the absence of the conditions in the public sphere for members of our democracy to determine the truth as verifiable statements about reality. Far too many seem to have abandoned evidence and fact-seeking and have instead committed to what Tsipursky and Ward call "tribal epistemology." *Pro Truth* encourages citizens to celebrate a commitment to truth-telling and reject spreading inaccurate, false, and misleading information. Ultimately, this book (and the Pro-Truth Pledge) is one of the most innovative solutions to the problems posed by the post-truth era I have encountered. The book outlines strategies for bolstering truth-telling and strategies for building a larger movement that will have implications for our democracy for decades to come.

Stephen K. Hunt, PhD, Professor at Illinois State University, Executive Director of the ISU School of Communication

This book reminds us how we all suffer when there is a lack of orientation to the truth, and how mindful we must be to overcome our biases and bad habits. In trying to solve problems in groups, we often concentrate on fighting and trying to prevail for our cause. But the book urges us to shift that perspective to one of "searching for truth together," turning ourselves from a goal of prevailing over others to one of finding optimal solutions in agreement with them. We learn how our instincts can mislead us, and how we can expand our experience and information through that reorientation towards truth above our prejudices and biases. This book is sorely needed in these times, and the authors have given us one of the best prescriptions for what ails our post-truth society. As someone who has worked in both politics and the field of fighting fakery, I was overjoyed to find a project like the Pro-Truth Pledge. The pledge addresses the psychology behind the information mess we're in, and borrows tactics from behavioral science that we can use to help get us out of it.

Felicia Winfree Cravens, 20-year veteran of Texas conservative activism, founder of the Houston Tea Party Society, and founder of Unfakery, which helps conservatives learn better how to avoid fakery that was targeted at them

The truth matters, a lot. Important decisions are made every day that have profound consequences for our health, our national security, our financial security, our climate, and more. When the truth is discounted or denied in those decisions, everyone is harmed. The Pro-Truth Pledge is an important step to ensure that the truth is considered when important decisions are being made.

Edward Maibach, PhD, Distinguished Professor of Communication and Director of the Center for Climate Change Communication at George Mason University

During my six successful bids for election to the Maine State Legislature in a closely divided district, I've seen a steep decline in truth-telling as the power of social media and the influence of Orwellian double-speak has flooded the public forum. It was refreshing in the 2018 elections to take the Pro-Truth Pledge, subjecting myself to the power of crowd-sourced accountability, and to invite my opponent and others to join me.

Seth Berry, Maine State Representative, Past Majority Leader and Assistant Majority Leader

I am an initial endorser of the Pro-Truth Pledge. Unless we change the whole system to one based on honesty and honest accountability, we're dead. This is our lives and the lives of all our children we are talking about. A more fragmented gradual approach short of making, keeping and enforcing the Pro-Truth Pledge is doomed to failure.

W. Brad Blanton, PhD, founder of Radical Honesty Enterprises, and author of seven books, including *Radical Honesty: How to Transform Your Life by Telling the Truth*

Few things are more important than truth. And few ways are more effective at focusing our politics on truth than simply talking about it. The Pro-Truth Pledge is an important step.

Rob Sand, Iowa State Auditor

Civic duty makes democracy work. The notion that citizens must contribute to the common good has been at the heart of democracies. Today, our civic duty is to resist the "post-truth" society. When deliberate falsehoods can be described as "alternative facts," when certain politicians claim that "there is no such thing as fact anymore" or that "truth isn't truth," then we must recognize that as a threat to liberal democracies. The Pro-Truth Pledge is one way in which we can express that civic commitment.

Stephan Lewandowsky, PhD, Chair of Cognitive Psychology at the School of Experimental Psychology, specializing in studying misinformation, fake news, and post-truth politics

I love the concept of the Pro-Truth Pledge. It is a simple method of aligning the entire globe around a commitment of collaboration, while letting individuals come up with the great ideas.

Dhruv Ghulati, Founder and CEO, Factmata

Skeptical Science has been actively countering misinformation about climate change since 2007. Our values are matched by the values of the Pro-Truth Pledge—commitment to truth and facts, a skeptical, evidence-based approach to understanding the world, and a resolve to proactively educate the public and counter misinformation. But the problems facing climate change—misinformation and science denial—also face all facets of society. A well-functioning democracy requires a well-informed populace in order to function.

John Cook, PhD, Founder of Skeptical Science, Professor at George Mason University

Everyone thinks they have "The Truth." As a former victim of delusionary ideological "Truth," I now know the importance of stepping back and applying skepticism not just to the claims of others, but to my own beliefs as well. This is a very difficult task, but Tsipursky and Ward's eye-opening *Pro Truth* teaches us precisely how to do it: by consciously pledging ourselves to respect objective evidence, no matter where it leads.

Dan Barker, author of Life Driven Purpose and Mere Morality, Co-host of Freethought Radio and Freethought Matters, Co-President of the Freedom From Religion Foundation, Co-founder of the Clergy Project

This book presents a model for behaviors that encourage civility in our rapidly-decaying contemporary public sphere, and I myself took the Pro-Truth Pledge because I am committed to presenting information in a way that ensures that integrity is maintained in our public discourse.

Lorenzo T. Neal, Conservative Christian senior pastor of the New Bethel African Methodist Episcopal Church in Jackson, Mississippi, and host of the radio show Zera Today with Pastor Lorenzo Neal

Pro Truth

A Practical Plan for Putting Truth Back into Politics

Pro Truth

A Practical Plan for Putting Truth Back into Politics

Gleb Tsipursky and Tim Ward

CHANGEMAKERS
BOOKS

Winchester, UK
Washington, USA

JOHN HUNT PUBLISHING

First published by Changemakers Books, 2020
Changemakers Books is an imprint of John Hunt Publishing Ltd., No. 3 East Street,
Alresford, Hampshire SO24 9EE, UK
office@jhpbooks.com
www.johnhuntpublishing.com
www.changemakers-books.com

For distributor details and how to order please visit the 'Ordering' section on our website.

Text copyright: Gleb Tsipursky and Tim Ward 2019

ISBN: 978 1 78904 399 0
978 1 78904 400 3 (ebook)
Library of Congress Control Number: 2019941677

All rights reserved. Except for brief quotations in critical articles or reviews, no part of this
book may be reproduced in any manner without prior written permission from the publishers.

The rights of Gleb Tsipursky and Tim Ward as authors have been asserted in accordance with the
Copyright, Designs and Patents Act 1988.

A CIP catalogue record for this book is available from the British Library.

Design: Stuart Davies
Cover: Wayne Straight

UK: Printed and bound by CPI Group (UK) Ltd, Croydon, CR0 4YY
US: Printed and bound by Thomson-Shore, 7300 West Joy Road, Dexter, MI 48130

We operate a distinctive and ethical publishing philosophy in
all areas of our business, from our global network of authors to
production and worldwide distribution.

Contents

Also by Gleb Tsipursky

The Truth Seeker's Handbook: A Science-Based Guide
Never Go With Your Gut: How Pioneering Leaders Avoid
Business Disasters and Make the Best Decisions
The Blindspots Between Us: How to Overcome Unconscious
Cognitive Bias and Build Better Relationships

Also by Tim Ward

Nonfiction:
The Master Communicator's Handbook (with Teresa Erickson)
Indestructible You: Building a Self that Can't be Broken (with
Shai Tubali)
The Author's Guide to Publishing and Marketing (with John
Hunt)

Literary travel:
Zombies on Kilimanjaro: A Father/Son Journey Above the
Clouds
Savage Breast: One Man's Search for the Goddess
Arousing the Goddess
The Great Dragon's Fleas
What the Buddha Never Taught

This book is dedicated to all who choose to uphold the truth in our politics and public discourse:

To private citizens who speak the truth about public matters, even when the truth goes against their preferred political goals, and who withdraw support from political leaders who lie, including those leaders whose policies they support.

To politicians of all parties who uphold the facts, despite the constant temptation of taking the easy route of winning short-term victories through deception.

To journalists, editors and producers who take seriously their responsibility to hold public figures accountable for the truth, who clearly distinguish factual reporting from opinion, avoid misleading and "clickbait" headlines, and never mistake false equivalence for balance.

Foreword

by Rick Shenkman

On the shelf behind me as I write this in my office are three door-stopper books on history and political science. All have this one thing in common: they purport to explain human behavior. Some of the books bear a recent publication date. One goes back to the 1950s. Henry Steele Commager's *The American Mind*, published in 1950, claims to describe how Americans think. Francis Fukuyama's *The Origins of Political Order* is all about the various ways human beings have organized themselves "from prehuman times to the French Revolution." Yuval Noah Harari's *Sapiens* immodestly brags on its cover that the book offers nothing less than a "history of humankind."

Whew! That about covers everything, doesn't it? How we think and how we do politics and the history we've made.

In an experiment I picked them up one by one to see if the indices contain the word "truth." I found that none of them do.

This can't be because the authors didn't highly esteem the truth. It's self-evident that they did. Each author aspired to write the truth as they saw it. But not one saw fit to discuss the truth as a category of knowledge in and of itself. They wanted to tell the truth but not explain what they meant by "the truth."

All took for granted that their readers would understand that the aim was to tell a story based on facts and that the facts, arranged in a convincing narrative, would give the readers meaningful insights. That is, the truth.

But what do we mean by the truth? This, it turns out, is a question these authors did not bother to ask. Yet it's never been more vital that we do so now when truth is under attack by post-truth politicians eager to confuse the public with lies. In today's world we must think hard about what we mean by the truth and

1

how we are constantly importuned to turn away from the truth when it proves inconvenient.

Human beings have never exactly revered the truth, to be sure. As Harvard evolutionary psychologist Steven Pinker has written, what we want is not for the truth to prevail, but that our version of the truth does so. But today a virtual war on the truth requires us to be on our guard 24/7 lest the lies overwhelm us. This is our new reality.

An intriguing movement is underway to address this problem. It's the Pro-Truth Pledge project established by Gleb Tsipursky, one of the co-authors of this book. The goal is to encourage citizens to follow 12 rules of truth-telling in the hope that this will help establish a society where the truth is honored. I hope it succeeds. We need an army of people committed to the truth. Steven Pinker has signed up. So has Jonathan Haidt. And so I have. Maybe you will too.

Rick Shenkman is the bestselling author of seven books, including Political Animals: How Our Stone-Age Brain Gets in the Way of Smart Politics. *He is also the founder of the History News Network and an Emmy-award-winning investigative reporter.*

Preface

by Tim Ward

Dr. Gleb Tsipursky and I share a fundamental belief that truth is essential for democracy. I found Gleb online in 2018 while researching a book I wanted to write on this topic. Gleb's Pro-Truth Pledge struck me as an inspiring, practical way for citizens to work together to put truth back into politics. When I discovered he had a draft of his own book already written on this exact subject, I abandoned my plans, and agreed to collaborate with him. I took on revising his chapters and adding my own perspective and ideas as a former journalist, and public communications expert. Since the substance of the book is his analysis of post-truth politicians from the perspective of a behavioral scientist, and the behavioral techniques that can help us resist their lies and promote truth, we agreed to keep his singular narrative voice throughout the book. I've never been so happy to play second fiddle.

At heart, Gleb and I are both pragmatists. So, you won't find a deep philosophical discussion in this book on the nature of truth. By "truth" we simply mean verifiable facts about the world that any reasonable observer can perceive through their senses. If I tell you I ate a bowl of oatmeal at the Tastee Diner on Norfolk Road in Bethesda, Maryland, at 10 a.m. on April 29, 2020, any reasonable observer at these coordinates in space and time could verify whether or not I was telling the truth. Because our world is vastly complex, this definition includes as "true" the consensus of experts such as scientists, as they have observed and studied aspects of reality in detail that the rest of us have not. It's important to remember, though, that science does not hold any of its truths to be absolute. Science constantly questions and re-evaluates the evidence. In so doing science gives us robust working models of how the world works. Its openness to revision is what helps us correct our errors, so that our knowledge evolves.

Belief, on the other hand, does not require rational observation and consensus. Belief does not need to be proven. It is, if you like, an inner Truth with a capital "T." This includes the eternal Truths of religious faiths, but also the many particular beliefs individuals may hold about the world and their place in it. These differ widely from person to person. Democracies *embrace* this difference. Freedom of belief is the essence of a free society. Only oppressive, fundamentalist regimes dictate what their subjects must believe.

Belief thus holds a different place in politics than small "t" truth. Our beliefs define our values, and people with common values tend to group together into political parties. But, crucially, in a democracy, people with very different beliefs can come together and agree upon a set of facts verifiable through their eyes, ears, and other senses. Having a set of common facts enables citizens and their politicians to discuss, debate, negotiate, compromise, and ultimately pass wise legislation that affects their lives. That's the genius of democracy: it allows people of different beliefs to collaborate for the common good. When it works, this makes democracy the best political system in the world. It only works, however, when citizens value truth (with a small "t"). If politicians and leaders devalue truth, trust between groups that hold different values gets eroded, and democracy declines.

People then look to others who share their beliefs—their "tribe"—as the only ones they feel they can trust. Those from other tribes they come to view as enemies ready to undermine and attack them. Too easily this leads to *tribal epistemology*—a perverse situation in which people believe that whatever their side says is true, and whatever the other side says is false. Facts based on evidence no longer matter. The only metric for truth is loyalty to one's own side. So, if Democrat Al Gore says climate change is a threat, Republicans must rally around it being a hoax. If Donald Trump says building a wall on the Mexican border will reduce illegal immigration, Democrats must declare that a wall is immoral. There's no thinking here, no investigation of reality, just a knee-jerk reaction against whatever the other side says.

This is the precipice upon which the United States and some other democracies stand today. As trust erodes, will we slide down that slippery slope? Or can we take a step back, onto the firmament of truth?

Acknowledgments

Gleb Tsipursky:
Many people dedicated to the truth made this book possible. I'd like to start by acknowledging the other leaders who serve on the Board of Directors of Intentional Insights and thus shape the overall strategy of the Pro-Truth Pledge project: Bentley Davis (who also oversees the website), Steve Monge (who manages the accounting and finances) and Agnes Vishnevkin (who coordinates the back-end operations and, as my wife, put up with the many, many hours I spent writing this book). I'd also like to recognize those who serve on the Advisory Board of Intentional Insights, including Felicia Winfree Cravens (who founded the Houston Tea Party Society), Lorenzo Neal (a conservative Christian pastor), Stephan Lewandowsky (top cognitive scientist on addressing fake news), Michael Tyler (a business leader), Brad Blanton (who leads the Radical Honesty movement), and Rick Shenkman (bestselling author on emotions and politics and founder of the History News Network). Besides them, numerous other activists made this book possible; in particular Jeffrey Dubin and Wayne Straight provided extensive commentary on early versions of this book.

Tim Ward:
Thanks to my colleagues John Hunt, Dominic James and Maria Barry at Changemakers Books and John Hunt Publishing for their enthusiastic support of this project. In addition, thanks to the production team: Andrew James Wells as editor, Stuart Davies for design, Nick Welch for cover design, and Mollie Barker for editing and proofreading. I would also like to thank a few friends who have inspired me. First, Dr. Chris Haney, who shares my passion for cognitive biases and endless capacity for discussing them. Second, Dean Self, who never shies away

from challenging my own biases in our political conversations. Third, Drs. Losang Rabgey and Tashi Rabgey, the sisters who run Machik.org; they are my role models for speaking truth to power, as they tirelessly seek to create a better future for the people of Tibet.

I would also like to thank four people in my life who helped me respect and strive for truthfulness. My father Peter, a political journalist whose visceral disgust of politicians who abused the public trust has stuck with me to this day. My mother, Jane, who told me her truth, and showed me that I could trust others with mine. My wife, Teresa, who made me want truth to be a cornerstone of our relationship; in so doing I have come to love her deeply, and also better know myself. My son, Josh, who made me want to be a good example and strive to live my life with integrity.

Introduction

Our Moment of Truth

Oxford Dictionary named "post-truth" the 2016 word of the year, defining it as "circumstances in which objective facts are less influential in shaping public opinion than appeals to emotion and personal belief." In explaining why it chose this adjective, Oxford Dictionary pointed to the successful tactics used by Donald Trump's campaign in the 2016 US presidential election, and by the "Vote Leave" side of the Brexit campaign in the UK that year.

So, are we living in a post-truth world? No, not yet at least. The best evidence for this is the number of people around the world—myself included—who felt appalled by the misinformation spread during those campaigns, and worse, that those who spread lies won in two of the most mature democracies in the world. We fear that if enough politicians win by lying and suffer no consequences, politics will degenerate into a "race to the bottom," where truth is irrelevant and the best liar wins.

Just as alarming, not all who voted for Trump were duped by the lies he told. In fact, plenty of conservatives voted for Trump in spite of the lies, holding their noses and voting for the standard conservative policies he proposed, such as cutting taxes for corporations and high earners, putting conservative judges in federal courts, and eliminating regulations. As Trump delivered on many of these promises after the election, the sentiment has emerged among many—not all—that if his post-truth methods were what it took to get elected, then perhaps it was worth it. At least some voters for Brexit followed the same reasoning after their victory. In this book, I remain neutral on the policies, respecting that intelligent people take different sides on these issues, although I will mention that I have donated to and voted for both Republican and Democratic politicians in the past and intend to do so in the future. Instead I focus on the destructive consequences of making it okay for politicians to lie with impunity.

If politicians can win by telling lies, then they do not need to care about serving the true interests of the citizens. Without a norm of truthfulness as a basic check on the behavior of politicians, they can steal taxpayer money and collude with corporate interests to line their own pockets. Worse, they can use lies to keep power in an authoritarian manner by: stuffing ballots and stealing elections, arresting those who oppose them on trumped-up charges, and murdering journalists or other opponents who try and expose their lies. These abuses of power are not dystopian fantasies. They are taking place today in many powerful nations the world over, including some that used to be democracies. This is why it is frightening to see the early stages of this process happening in the UK and US. For generations, these nations have been held up as models of government the rest of the world could aspire to, and served as a light of hope for dissidents living under authoritarian regimes. That light has dimmed, as dictators of these regimes can now point to our leaders' post-truth tactics, and say there is no difference between us and them.

I am particularly passionate about the role of truth in politics because when I was a child, my family lived inside the Soviet Union, in the Republic of Moldova. My parents sought to escape from the destructive lies and deceptions that dominated the political and civic conversations in that part of the world by coming to the US in 1991, when Moldova was freed from Russian domination. So, for me, it has been incredibly depressing to see misinformation and post-truth politics on the rise in my new home.

People who value truth in this post-truth moment may be tempted to despair; they wonder what they could do to make a difference. Many books and articles have been published trying to explain the Trump phenomenon. Such texts can be helpful to understand where we are, but they do not really explain what can be done to prevent the downward spiral of deceit and its accompanying corruption and creeping authoritarianism. While this book does offer an analysis—one informed by relevant research in psychology, behavioral economics, political science, history, and communication—it has at the heart of it a pragmatic plan for creating a pro-truth movement.

I take Donald Trump as the case study of this book to explain how post-truth politicians mislead and manipulate voters. I also place Trump's success in the broader context of other post-truth political activities, such as the "Vote Leave" campaign in Brexit, as well as powerful and formerly democratic countries that have fallen further under the influence of post-truth politicians, such as Vladimir Putin's Russia and Recep Tayyip Erdogan's Turkey. Let me be clear: the use of these leaders as examples is not a critique of the political platforms of any particular party, but rather to highlight the kind of damaging behavior pursued by post-truth politicians. The choice to focus on Trump is in part because, as a US citizen, I watched the 2016 election take place in my own front yard. It's also because the office of President of the United States has such a powerful impact on the rest of the world. I believe it's a mistake to think of Trump as a "black swan" event—something so singular as to be virtually unpredictable. Post-truth politicians rise up time and again. While I do not condemn Trump and the others—neither as people, nor for their policies—I do shine a light on the kind of post-truth tactics they use, and how these tactics undermine democratic politics. This book is non-partisan—trans-partisan, actually—in that truthfulness in politics is a value that serves democracy, and so deserves to be honored and protected by all political parties.

Beyond analysis, this book offers a plan of action for the many people who are determined to resist post-truth politics.

The plan provides a blueprint for a Pro-Truth Movement that has already begun, offering readers a chance to join a rapidly growing global army of advocates across the political spectrum determined to advocate for truth in politics. I myself have chosen to redirect my energy and time from my academic pursuits to go into a leadership role in this young movement, practicing what I preach and using my scholarly expertise to analyze and direct on-the-ground activities to fight lies and promote truth in the US and abroad. You will thus get more from this book than a behavioral scientist's analysis. You'll get the practical experience of a civic activist in the trenches.

My activities included organizing a March for Truth and similar events in my area and across the country and beyond: giving over 350 interviews to conservative and liberal talk shows and reporters in the US, Canada, UK, Ireland, Australia, India, Germany, Singapore, and many other countries; publishing over 400 pieces in top US newspapers, conservative and liberal (*New York Daily News, The Dallas Morning News, The Plain Dealer*) and other venues (*Time, Scientific American, Salon, Psychology Today*); coordinating volunteers on a host of projects related to truth-seeking; and serving as the volunteer president of a 501(c)3 educational nonprofit, Intentional Insights, which is devoted to promoting truth and rational thinking (my co-author and I are donating a third of the royalties from this book to this organization).

Holding truth above party politics can lead to some tensions in friendships and relationships. It would be an understatement for me to say it has been a bumpy ride. I have faced a slew of hateful words and actions from those opposed to truth-oriented activism, and had a number of friends and family, as well as professional colleagues, turn away from me when I spoke hard truths that they did not want to hear because it did not align with their political ideology. But standing up for truth in politics is exactly what our world needs to move forward. We have to cross party lines and unite with those who may not share our political preferences but value the truth, in order to have any hope of reversing the tide of lies and fighting post-truth politics.

So please imagine with me a world where millions of people join a Pro-Truth Movement that bridges political divides, bringing together liberals and conservatives, business leaders and nonprofit leaders, clergy and secular activists, and ordinary people from all walks of life. Imagine volunteers organizing at all levels—international, national, regional, and local—to promote truthful behavior in all areas of public discourse. Imagine these volunteers working side by side with staff from truth-maintenance organizations, who coordinate these volunteers and are paid for by the donations of checkbook activists who have more money than time, to hold politicians, journalists, and other public figures accountable, celebrating truths and condemning lies.

It may be hard to envision this happening in our current post-truth moment in time. The incentives in our political system and people's psychological predispositions, as this book will make clear, will only lead to the situation growing worse if we do not intervene. Still, consider that in the early years of the environmental, women's rights, civil rights, and marriage equality movements the situation grew worse before people united and took action. The early activists in these movements knew that, to paraphrase a Chinese proverb, to remove a mountain one must start by carrying away small stones. Using the best practices from these successful movements, along with behavioral science research, will enable pro-truth activists to carry away large boulders from the mountain of post-truth politics instead of just small stones, and this book provides the groundwork and guidelines for doing so.

That's the purpose of this book: to better equip readers like you for this task, and to provide you with a platform to align your individual efforts with our common purpose.

The book begins with the question: Why should we care about truth in politics? I dissect the lies of post-truth politicians, and offer strategies we can use to protect ourselves from being deceived. I then explore the corrosive effect of post-truth lies in mainstream and social media, and how the erosion of trust creates a "tragedy of the commons" in our politics. Next, I introduce the Pro-Truth Pledge, and describe how it changes our behavior toward truth. The pledge can help reverse the trend and turn the tide against post-truth politicians and the normalization of lies. At the time of publication, the pledge has been signed by approximately 10,000 individuals from all over the world. Additionally, over 650 politicians have signed it, including members of the US Congress and state legislatures, Democrats and Republicans alike, as well as other politicians around the globe. (For the current list, see: https://www.protruthpledge.org/public-figures-signed-pledge/). I include in the pledge chapter compelling evidence, published in peer-reviewed journals, that the pledge works. But the pledge is the tip of the iceberg of the broader Pro-Truth Movement itself, which unites a community of people committed to upholding truth in politics and saving democracy around the globe. The remaining two chapters describe new approaches for holding political conversations with people who hold irrational beliefs, and for holding constructive conversations across the political divide. You will then find a glossary of important terms used in the book, followed by a complete list of references. To supplement the book, additional chapters on becoming a pro-truth activist are available online as a free download, if you have been inspired to join us.

Will history record the victories of Trump and Brexit as the start of a post-truth era? Or will 2016 mark a turning point, a moment of truth, that gave birth to a movement and re-established the US as a light for democracy around the world? If we can grasp this moment, then perhaps we can transform this post-truth moment into a pro-truth era. The choice is up to you.

The Pro-Truth Pledge

I Pledge My Earnest Efforts To:

Share truth

Verify: fact-check information to confirm it is true before accepting and sharing it

Balance: share the whole truth, even if some aspects do not support my opinion

Cite: share my sources so that others can verify my information

Clarify: distinguish between my opinion and the facts

Honor truth

Acknowledge: acknowledge when others share true information, even when we disagree otherwise

Reevaluate: reevaluate if my information is challenged, retract it if I cannot verify it

Defend: defend others when they come under attack for sharing true information, even when we disagree otherwise

Align: align my opinions and my actions with true information

Encourage truth

Fix: ask people to retract information that reliable sources have disproved even if they are my allies

Educate: compassionately inform those around me to stop using unreliable sources even if these sources support my opinion

Defer: recognize the opinions of experts as more likely to be accurate when the facts are disputed

Celebrate: celebrate those who retract incorrect statements and update their beliefs toward the truth

Fig. 0.1 The Pro-Truth Pledge

Chapter 1

Why Should We Care About Truth in Politics?

Many people shuddered when Donald Trump's senior adviser Kellyanne Conway described the Trump administration's false statements as "alternative facts" in a January 22, 2017 interview on NBC's *Meet the Press*. She was defending the deceptions of Sean Spicer, the White House Press Secretary, about Trump's inauguration in his first White House press briefing on January 21. For instance, Spicer stated that Trump drew "the largest audience to ever witness an inauguration, period," despite the aerial photos and other evidence showing that Barack Obama's inauguration drew significantly bigger crowds.

This incident drew wide condemnation. Brian Fallon, Hillary Clinton's former Press Secretary, called for Spicer to resign in a January 23 interview with CNN. Prominent columnists, such as Jill Abramson (January 24, *The Guardian*), condemned Conway for appealing to "alternative facts." Even the usually apolitical Merriam-Webster dictionary tweeted on January 22 that "A fact is a piece of information presented as having objective reality." Internet memes satirizing "alternative facts" spread quickly (see Figure 1.1).

Despite this widespread condemnation, Conway defended her statement in an interview published on March 18, 2017 in *New York Magazine*, saying that

Fig. 1.1 "Alternative Facts" meme (courtesy of Skeptic Skull and instagram.com)

she has "spoken 1.2 million words on TV," and that whoever wants to "focus on two here and two there, it's on you, you're a f—ing miserable person, P.S., just whoever you are."

Well, many folks, including myself, fall under Conway's definition of "miserable person," because we are allergic to lies uttered by prominent public figures, especially lies defending other lies. It's not a partisan matter: many of us despise lies equally by either Democrats or Republicans.

For instance, in a March 17, 2008 speech at George Washington University, Hillary Clinton lied about her March 1996 trip to Bosnia: "I remember landing under sniper fire. There was supposed to be some kind of a greeting ceremony at the airport, but instead we just ran with our heads down to get into the vehicles to get to our base." Yet an article on March 21, 2008 in the *Washington Post* reported that in reality, Clinton was greeted by smiling officials, and a ceremony at which an 8-year-old Muslim girl read a poem for her. The *Post* even found a video showing that Clinton got a kiss from the girl—hardly a sniper fire situation.

Reading that article inspired a strong visceral response in me about Clinton's lies. Many people share my intuitive reactions to deceit, because they have both an emotional distaste for lies and an instinctive recognition of the dangers of lies in politics. They care about the truth first and foremost, regardless of their personal values—liberal, conservative, or centrist. However, those passionate about the truth tend to be outliers, as illustrated by Jonathan Haidt, in his 2012 *The Righteous Mind: Why Good People Are Divided by Politics and Religion*. He describes extensive research that shows what values are most prized by mainstream liberals, such as justice, fairness, and equality, and conservatives, including purity, safety, and security. Truth is not among the top values for either group. This helps explain why so many do not intuitively recognize the harm done by deception to democratic institutions, whether in the US or around the globe. Moreover, they resonate more with appeals to emotions rather than facts, as shown by research such as in the 2000 *Emotions and Beliefs: How Feelings Influence Thoughts*.

How do we communicate convincingly the dangers of post-truth political tactics, whether perpetrated by Trump or others, to people who do not have a visceral concern about truth in politics? Just wagging a finger and calling out such lies, as many intellectuals and public commentators have done in the past and are currently doing, clearly has not worked to prevent such deception. We tend to overestimate the extent to which other people share our opinions and predispositions, a typical thinking error that behavioral scientists call the *false consensus effect*, well described in a 1987 review article by Gary Marks and Norman Miller. However strange it may seem to readers of this book or those intellectuals and public commentators, plenty of people do not see an inherent problem when politicians they support lie to gain political credibility.

Thus, while it is necessary to highlight political deceptions, it is not sufficient for the people who do not have an intuitive aversion to lies. Instead, we need to demonstrate clearly why such lies are harmful to the long-term interests of our countries and our political institutions. We need to show people why they should care—deeply and viscerally—about truth in politics, for the sake of their own political and personal goals. This is by no means a new venture. George Orwell's novel *1984* painted a grim future for humanity, based on his vision of a power-hungry party ruling through the power of lies. Orwell wrote: "Not merely the validity of experience, but the very existence of external reality was tacitly denied by their philosophy. The heresy of heresies was common sense...The party told you to reject the evidence of your eyes and ears. It was their final, most essential command." Many journalists found an alarming resonance between quotations from *1984* and remarks like this one President Trump made during his speech at the Veterans of

Foreign Wars national convention in Kansas City on Tuesday, July 24, 2018: "Just remember what you're seeing and what you're reading is not what's happening..."

One Way to Tell the Truth, Many Ways to Lie

Before talking about the importance of truth, we need to start with definitions. By "telling the truth," I mean conveying an *accurate* portrayal of the *relevant* features of reality that any *reasonable person* might want to know about the topic. Implicitly, this definition includes *not intending to misinform*. It's pretty simple.

Now let's ground that statement with some examples of what *not* telling the truth looks like. Say you decide to get a used car, and the salesman introduces himself as Truthful Tom. You point to a car, and ask him to tell you about it. What scenarios might result?

Scenario 1: Tom answers: "Oh, it's a great car. Let's sign the deal now." Most of us will suspect that Truthful Tom's *vagueness* does not sound very truthful. He didn't list the relevant features of the car that he might expect any reasonable customer to want to know. But the description "great" is such a generality it can hardly be pinned down as a lie. Maybe Tom truthfully means, "great for me if I can sell it to you at this price"?

Scenario 2: Tom answers: "This is a car for true patriots. I can tell you love your country, so this is the right car for you. Let's sign the deal now." In this scenario, Tom is deceptively appealing to emotions via flattery, and is again not describing what is relevant to you, the buyer. This particular kind of flattery is called a *glittering generality*, an emotionally appealing phrase that is so closely associated with highly valued concepts and beliefs that it carries conviction without supporting information or reason. The appeal to love of country (or desire for peace, freedom, glory, honor, and so on) so dazzles you and affirms your beliefs that you fail to notice the lack of other salient information.

Scenario 3: Tom gives you the relevant details any reasonable customer might want to know about the car, and answers your questions. He tells you accurately that the car was serviced regularly. However, he did not know and thus failed to mention that the car had a problem with the transmission. That problem is a relevant piece of information. Normally, we would say Tom is simply wrong, not lying. But in this scenario, Tom had previously instructed the showroom's mechanic not to tell him if there were any engine problems. When she tried to tell him, he would cut her off or walk out of the room, arguing that such information would only hamper his job of selling cars. So Truthful Tom is not simply wrong, he is *willfully ignorant*.

Scenario 4: Tom knows about the problem with the transmission and does not tell you about it. Tom committed what is known as a *lie by omission*, meaning deliberately withholding relevant information and thus deceiving you.

Scenario 5: Tom was told about the transmission problem but rather conveniently he forgot about it. So, he doesn't mention it to you, even though he had the information and should have told you. In this case, Tom engaged in *confabulation*, making false statements due to incorrect memories about the past without a deliberate intent to deceive.

Scenario 6: Tom knows about the transmission problem, but rather than admitting it, he distorts the truth through exaggeration (or hyperbole), telling you that everybody who owns this model of car is happy with it (when in reality, some owners are happy, and some are not). By overemphasizing the degree of customer satisfaction, Tom thinks he's not lying, *just* exaggerating, and indeed not all exaggeration is meant to deceive. But in this case, *deceptive hyperbole* is clearly his purpose.

Scenario 7: Tom tells you about the faulty transmission, but uses jargon that he knows only car specialists would recognize. Tom is deceiving you through *obfuscation*. He's not actually lying, but deliberately making the information unclear and confusing to you.

Scenario 8: You directly ask whether there is a problem with the transmission and Tom tells you it's just fine. Truthful Tom is directly lying. We call this a *blatant lie*. Experienced liars have one specific trick to make blatant lies more convincing: they use vivid details to make their fiction seem real. Tom might elaborate on his lie by saying, "In fact, I was with Olga the mechanic when she was inspecting the vehicle, and I recall her telling me, 'Tommy, this transmission is in great shape!'"

Scenario 9: Tom lies to you about the transmission, but in the service center documentation you find Olga's inspection report that declares the transmission is faulty. You confront Tom. He responds that the service center people are dishonest and always lie. "That Olga, she makes mistakes like this all the time. Frankly, I think management are going to fire her later this week."

Tom asks you to trust only him as the source of truth about the car. This is the type of behavior characteristic of post-truth car salespeople. In extreme forms it is known as *gaslighting*, meaning manipulating someone into questioning their own sanity through denying the truth of reality. Comedian Richard Pryor immortalized gaslighting in the story of his wife catching him "in the act" with another woman. He denies his blatant infidelity, asking his wife, "Who you gonna believe, me or your lying eyes?"

These nine scenarios help reveal that there is a spectrum of truth and lies, with tactics like vagueness, glittering generalities or obfuscation being closer to truthful, while blatant lies and gaslighting are more definitively lies (we list them all for you at the end of the chapter). This spectrum helps explain why fact-checkers typically have a scale of evaluating claims, whether the *PolitiFact* 5-scale system that ranges from "True" to "Pants on Fire," or the *Washington Post* fact-checking system that goes from 0 to 4 Pinocchios. Statements made by politicians can be farther or closer to the truth, depending on how they align with an accurate depiction of the reality of a specific policy or decision as it is relevant for voters.

Another important element to consider in whether we label something as a deception, or simply a wrong statement, is the question of intent. Dictionaries define lying as being intentionally misleading. Someone can fail to tell the truth and be wrong yet not be lying. However, it can be hard to determine intent. Imagine you bought the car from Tom and found out later that it had a faulty transmission. How do we know what Tom knew and did not know? How do we know whether he was willfully ignorant, lying by omission, blatantly lying, or just plain mistaken? It's not easy in a one-time encounter.

Often, we need to make our own numerical estimate of intent—a likelihood-of-truthfulness scale—based on prior evidence and reasonable assumptions. If Tom assures you that the car was serviced regularly, he probably had documentary evidence of it being serviced. How likely is it that the service mechanic forgot to put the information about the problem with the transmission into the service report? Not very likely—that's a pretty major fault on the service mechanic's part. Moreover, the mechanic is financially incentivized to be truthful, because the mechanic would get paid for repairing the car. When greed combines with competence, you have a very low likelihood of failing to report a problem. How likely is it that Truthful Tom hid his knowledge of the problem for the sake of selling the car? Highly likely, since he is incentivized to sell the car, and lying would help him achieve his goal. For Tom, greed and competence combine to induce him to deceive. So, you might weigh Tom's words together with your past experiences with car salespersons and decide there's a 7 out of 10 chance he was attempting to deceive you about the faulty transmission.

Similarly, we need to be especially careful and suspicious when politicians make ostentatious, yet verifiable, statements favorable to their reputation and/or their political interests, such as about the size of their inauguration crowd or landing under sniper fire. We need to create a norm for politicians to back up such claims with credible evidence that would convince a reasonable person of any political persuasion. If we ask for such evidence and they fail to provide it, we can safely dismiss their statements as wrong, until proven otherwise. If they do not provide evidence, but continue to insist that they are right, then we should condemn them as being intentionally misleading— the dictionary definition of "lying." If someone lies repeatedly, and keeps doubling down on their deception, then we can shift our baseline perception to consider that person a systematic liar who may even be engaged in gaslighting, which is worse because it involves extensive psychological manipulation intended to make the victims doubt reality and accept an alternative version forced on them by the perpetrator.

The term *gaslighting* comes from the 1938 play *Gas Light*, which was made into two movies in the 1940s, most famously starring Charles Boyer and Ingrid Bergman. It's a thriller about a recently married rich woman who thinks she's going insane. Items disappear in her house, or suddenly appear in different places than where she put them. Among other things, the gas lights all over the room flicker weirdly from time to time, but no one else seems to see it. What the woman doesn't know is that her husband keeps leaving the house and then sneaking back in through the attic. He moves things around in the house in order to convince her she is going crazy. She finally realizes that the flickering lights are someone walking around in the attic. In the end, his nefarious scheme unravels and she saves herself.

If we can better categorize a politician's level of deceptiveness (from generally truthful to blatant liar and gaslighter) we can more easily tune our ears to the appropriate level of skepticism. This is one aspect of *probabilistic thinking*, where we assign probabilities to our understanding of reality, and change our estimates based on new evidence we acquire. For instance, a politician who lies repeatedly can be safely labeled a blatant liar. When there is clear prior evidence of their lack of credibility, we can probabilistically dismiss any self-favorable statements by these people as lies unless they provide verifiable evidence upfront.

Finally, an evaluation of the truth must consider what constitutes credible evidence. While we often deal with clear-cut situations, such as the nine scenarios with Truthful Tom described above, in other cases we have to deal with more complex situations of incomplete information coming from multiple sources, each with its own biases. To help us orient toward the truth, we can rely on credible fact-checking websites and/or on the scientific consensus.

An easy way to determine the quality of fact-checkers is to outsource the evaluation to others who have strong motivations to pick the best fact-checkers. For instance, a number of fact-checkers around the globe have passed vetting by the Poynter Institute's International Fact-Checking Network and are listed as "verified signatories" on its website. This strong external standard is a good tool for verifying quality fact-checkers.

In other cases, fact-checking websites have not evaluated certain claims, but the claim will be opposed by scientific research. Since science is the best of all methods we as human beings have found to determine facts about the world and to predict the outcomes of our actions, it deserves trust as an excellent guide to public policy, as described by Jonathan Baron in a 2014 paper presented at an Annenberg Public Policy Center conference. The *scientific consensus* refers to the collective judgment of the community of scientists within a field. Such consensus involves broad—although not necessarily unanimous—agreement. We can see evidence of such consensus through statements by scientific institutes and associations, such as the October 21, 2009 statement from 18 associations on the reality of human-caused climate change, or the result of meta-analysis studies (evaluations of a series of other prominent studies) that come to a clear determination, such as the 2014 study by Luke Taylor et al. showing no relationship between vaccines and autism.

The Dangers of Deception for Democratic Decision-Making

Ideologically Informed Deception
Let's consider the danger lies pose when making decisions in the political sphere. To make a wise decision so as to reach our political goals, we need to know the relevant facts on the ground. For instance, to decide what car to buy from Truthful Tom, any reasonable customer would want accurate information about the price, the car's current condition and history, and any warranties. To make a decision about any political policy, a reasonable citizen requires the facts about the impact of that

policy on our society, with a list of costs and benefits in material and human terms. But politicians can be motivated to ignore or distort information based on their ideology.

As a hypothetical example, let's take a politician, Anti-gun Annie, proposing a federal gun-control law, say a 48-hour waiting period before purchasing a gun. Anti-gun Annie describes the aim as reducing gun-related deaths due to "heat-of-the-moment" urges. To evaluate her proposal, we as citizens would want to know the costs of this legislation in terms of its burden on gun buyers and stores, and the costs of implementing the legislation for the government through increased monitoring. We would also want to know the expected benefits in terms of decreased deaths. After all, presumably the vast majority of us want to reduce deaths, and also avoid unnecessary burdens and costs for both business and government.

According to a 2013 Institute of Medicine report, that year there were 33,636 fatal shootings in the US. Anti-gun Annie gives that number—which is accurate—and then claims that thousands of deaths would be prevented by the waiting period. How can we know whether a claim of "deaths prevented" is accurate or not? If we go by our gut feelings, many would intuitively feel that yes, if folks don't buy guns, they will likely not commit crimes of passion, while others will deny that notion. We do have substantial evidence that states with strong gun-control laws, which often include waiting periods, have much lower gun-related homicide and suicide rates, as shown in a 2013 paper by Eric Fleegler et al., but it seems that the waiting period by itself does not do much to prevent deaths. For example, we have research from a 2000 article by Ludwig and Cook showing that the federal waiting period that was part of the 1994 Brady Handgun Violence Prevention Act resulted in fewer firearm suicides overall, but did not result in fewer deaths overall (homicide and suicide combined). It turned out people found other means of committing suicide. Research by Fredrick

Vars in 2014 found a sharp increase in suicide risk within the first week of gun purchase, but did not evaluate whether the people would have committed suicide using other means. So, we have evidence of lower gun-related *suicide* statistics associated with a waiting period, but no substantive evidence of reduced overall deaths. It looks like Annie fell into what's called the *fallacy of the single cause*: she jumped to the conclusion that an outcome (fewer gun-related deaths) had a single, simple cause (a cooling-off period), when in reality many causes might be required to produce the desired outcome.

Yet when Anti-gun Annie was presented with evidence that undermined her position, she rejected the information and refused to examine it further (*willful ignorance*). Instead she doubled down. In her heart, she said, she knew that a waiting period was key. She told cherry-picked stories of people buying guns and then killing themselves or others, as if these were typical cases (*deceptive hyperbole*), and appealed to voters' emotions toward shooting victims: "As a compassionate society, we must pass this act to save lives!" (*glittering generalities*). Finally, she called the researchers frauds, and falsely claimed the gun lobby had funded their research. Now she was *gaslighting*.

Eventually, she pushed through her waiting period: harming gun buyers and stores, and forcing taxpayers to fund the implementation of this measure, while not bringing about an actual reduction of deaths. This is the kind of negative outcome that results from *ideologically informed deception*, where an ideologue pushes through her favored agenda despite the actual evidence. The likely outcome: unnecessary burdens on the gun industry and gun buyers, increased costs of implementing and policing the new rule by the government, and the same amount of deaths, although somewhat fewer suicides by guns.

This case study represents an example of how, if voters are vulnerable to emotional appeals, and do not rely on the facts on the ground, everyone suffers. Citizens need to care about and know the reality of political affairs, at least in broad terms, to make wise decisions regarding which politicians and policies to support.

Here are two well-known, real examples of ideologically informed deception: 1. Pro-Brexit politicians claimed in 2016 that leaving the EU would "give the National Health Service the £350 million the EU takes every week." This *obfuscation* was admitted to be false by those leaders after the UK voted to leave the EU, though it lingered on in social media. 2. The Trump administration claimed in early 2019 that "there's a growing humanitarian and security crisis at our southern border," a crisis that could only be resolved by building a multibillion-dollar border wall. There were too many lies to count during the ensuing government shutdown, but the US border authority's own data on illegal border-crossing apprehensions showed a marked decline of illegal immigration from fiscal year 2000 (more than 1.6 million apprehensions) to 2018 (overall apprehensions below 400,000). The average southern-border patrol agent apprehended 14 single adult migrants during all of 2018 (*U.S. Border Patrol Monthly Apprehension* (FY 2000–FY 2018), from www.cpb.gov). Although the number of migrants spiked in spring 2019, at the end of 2018, exaggerating this situation as an immigration crisis was something between *deceptive hyperbole* and a *blatant lie*. To frame it as a humanitarian crisis (appealing to our sense of compassion) was a *glittering generality*. To persist in the face of the border authority's facts was willful ignorance at best, and gaslighting at worst.

Deception and Corruption

Corruption, a natural bedfellow of political deception, is another negative outcome of post-truth politics. In a post-truth political situation, politicians win office by competing for who tells the best lie. If voters don't mind or don't notice the lies, politicians have no incentive to represent the actual concerns of the citizenry once elected, including concerns for how tax dollars are spent or for government dealings with business. Failing to condemn "alternative facts" thus leads to a scenario where politicians can take bribes right and left for giving favorable contracts to businesses, and divert our tax dollars into their pockets. After all, without the truth about the influence of money in politics, citizens cannot evaluate who is corrupt. They thus cannot use their votes to address the biggest fear of US citizens. According to the 2016 Chapman University Survey of American Fears, corruption rests at the top with 60.6 percent, above terrorist attacks at 41 percent and even above not having enough money for the future at 39.9 percent.

Let's consider how corruption and deception play out in another hypothetical example. Greedy Garry has been a senator for 12 years and is running for re-election. Serving on the Senate Committee on Energy and Natural Resources, he has been cutting undercover deals right and left with energy businesses. For instance, Garry enabled a solar power company to get a huge tax credit of $7 million in exchange for opening a plant in his state and transferring $500,000 to a Cayman Islands bank account under his wife's name. He ensured that his friend won a federal contract to build an oil pipeline in his state, despite his friend's bid being far from the cheapest—and next year, his friend bought him a $100,000 yacht for his birthday, despite not having given Garry birthday presents previously.

When the newspapers got wind of Greedy Garry's activities and published stories about them, Garry denied the allegations with *blatant lies*. While newspapers presented the objective facts, Garry went for emotions. He claimed the deals were "real winners for the state" (*vagueness*), that he worked hard every day to provide jobs for the people of his state, because the people's welfare was all he cared about (*lying by omission* about his payoff). He instead accused the papers of trying to ruin the livelihood of those workers who now worked in the solar power plant and on the oil pipeline (*gaslighting*). He cherry-picked stories of previously unemployed mothers who got jobs and could support their families thanks to his deals. His winning campaign ad featured a mother and her crying girl ripping apart a newspaper whose headline blasted Greedy Garry.

Given our recent turn toward post-truth politics, we can expect more and more Greedy Garrys at all levels of our political system. Even worse, other politicians may look at the successes of Greedy Garry, and conclude they might as well adopt his strategies of lying and accepting bribes, because they work and he gets re-elected anyway.

Deception and Authoritarianism

Most dangerous of all, post-truth politics paves the path for authoritarianism. Just as successful appeals to emotions over facts can destroy checks and balances on political corruption, if politicians can win by lying, they can use lies to gain power and hold it indefinitely.

Here's another hypothetical example: Power-hungry Patty was elected US President four years ago, and is running for re-election. Her original election was mired in controversy. A couple of weeks prior to the election, when polls showed Patty losing, she called the election rigged, and riled up her supporters for demonstrations leading up to the election. Patty ended up winning the election through a slim victory in the Electoral College, while losing the popular vote by nearly 2 million votes. She blamed her loss on millions of illegal votes cast for her opponent, and launched an investigation into voter fraud, which didn't turn up any evidence of fraud, but received wide press coverage. Most of her supporters ended up believing that Patty indeed won the popular vote, but that the judicial system was rigged against her.

Patty also appointed an attorney general, Legal Larry, well known for aggressive voter suppression tactics. Along with

Patty, Larry promoted the myth of widespread voter fraud in US elections, especially in Patty's election to the presidency. This myth is common in US politics despite having no evidence behind it. In fact, extensive evidence from many studies of US elections shows minimal voter fraud, as seen in a thorough meta-analysis in a report from the Brennan Center for Justice at New York University School of Law. Patty, Larry, and other members of Patty's post-truth administration ignored the reality for the sake of promoting their political agenda. When newspapers and experts, along with members of Patty's own party, called out Patty for her lies about the election, Patty ignored or denounced them. Many of Patty's supporters who did not care about the truth trusted Patty.

Would you be surprised to learn that when Patty lost her re-election, she did not concede? Instead, she claimed her opponent actually won due to massive voter fraud, with millions of illegal ballots swinging the election. Although no evidence existed for such fraud, Patty had Larry launch a thorough investigation of the ballots. Larry's control of the Department of Justice enabled him to trump up some initial fake evidence of voter fraud. Although newspapers and experts questioned this evidence, Patty used it to press her case. Moreover, Patty's supporters believed her, and launched large demonstrations to support her power. With her control of the administrative and judicial resources associated with the presidency, and the rallies of her supporters, Patty pressed the Electoral College to vote for her instead of her opponent. In four more years, Patty used the same tactics to transfer power to her chosen successor, Patty Jr. This is how the United States transitioned from a democracy into an authoritarian state.

While many non-American readers of this book might easily recognize this scenario as a common one for how democracies transform into authoritarian states, it may be hard for my fellow Americans to do so, as we lack the experience of authoritarianism in our country. After all, we have never had a dictator take power here. An authoritarian regime in the US would be what Nassim Taleb calls a *black swan event*, an unimaginable and very impactful event that radically transforms our society (*The Black Swan*, 2007). Examples of black swans include the 2008 fiscal crisis, the September 11 terrorist attacks, and Pearl Harbor. Fortunately, we can change a black swan into what Taleb terms a grey swan — an imaginable radical event, one that we can prepare for and address in advance, so that we are not hurt nearly as badly if the negative event happens.

One of the best techniques for transforming a black swan into a grey swan is to compare our situation to other historical and contemporary contexts. While the word "post-truth" is a recent invention, appeals to emotions over objective facts leading to an authoritarian takeover have a long history in democracies, as Michael Signer describes in his 2009 book, *Demagogue*. A *demagogue* is a dictator who initially rises to power with support from the public. The term originated in ancient Greece, when democratic city-states such as Athens occasionally witnessed the rise of political figures who appealed to emotions over facts and manipulated the masses at the expense of the well-being of the city as a whole. The demagogue Cleon, for example, was depicted by historical accounts as charismatic, eloquent, and skilled at appealing to the masses — presenting an image of himself as rough and unpolished, despite being an aristocrat. He pursued military actions that harmed Athens (according to the historical consensus) by exaggerating the military resources of Athens, and minimizing the strength of its rival, Sparta. More recent examples of demagogues who came to power through democratic elections, largely by misleading voters, include Benito Mussolini in Italy, Adolf Hitler in Germany, and Hugo Chavez in Venezuela. A number of contemporary authoritarian leaders who rose to dominance through post-truth tactics include Recep Tayyip Erdogan in Turkey, Robert Mugabe in Zimbabwe,

Viktor Orban in Hungary, Daniel Ortega in Nicaragua, Vladimir Putin in Russia, and Silvio Berlusconi in Italy.

The US has its own examples of people widely termed demagogues by historians, such as the Republican senator Joe McCarthy and the Democratic senator Huey Long. They gained significant power, though not the presidency, through a combination of emotional appeals and lies, and the US suffered much harm because of their deceptions. However, because they never became authoritarian rulers—although McCarthy came dangerously close—Americans find it hard to imagine the US transitioning to authoritarian rule. To counteract this complacency, we have to keep these examples in mind. Then we can turn the black swan (authoritarianism can never happen in the US) into a grey swan (it almost happened with McCarthy, and has happened recently in other democracies). This will motivate us to fight to preserve our political system from the corrosive effects of "alternative facts"—revealed in this chapter as a whole spectrum of deceptions.

In summary, this chapter has made the case that politicians who tell lies erode democracy, damage society, and hurt us all.

Fig. 1.2 Don't Spread Lies (design by Ed Coolidge for Intentional Insights)

While memes that mock "alternative facts" (such as the one cited at the beginning of this chapter) will motivate people like me who have an intuitive distaste for lies in politics, they are not effective at changing the mind of the average citizen. To arouse national concerns about truth in politics, we need to highlight how we are all harmed by the negative consequences of political deception through: 1) poor decision-making by elected officials; 2) corruption; and 3) authoritarianism. To better motivate people to care, instead share memes like the one shown in Figure 1.2.

How to Arouse Concern About Truth in Politics

To demonstrate the effectiveness of arousing concern about truth in politics, I went on conservative radio shows with hosts such as Scott Sloan, Dwight Lilly, and Larry Stevenson, all Republican activists. I chose Republicans, as Trump is our first post-truth president and he is a Republican, making it more challenging to communicate with Republicans who would intuitively be disinclined to criticize their own party. The reasoning I used in my conversations appealed to what the hosts and their listeners cared about—poor decisions, corruption, and authoritarianism. We had very productive conversations during which we agreed on the dangers of post-truth politics and the importance of not taking any claims at face value, instead demanding credible evidence. In my post-show informal discussion with him, Lilly said that our conversation had really made him think, and, he told me, "that's a dangerous thing."

Given that these hosts have a wide following among Republicans, the approach I outlined seems quite promising for getting them to care emotionally about fighting post-truth politics. The key is to determine what the people you seek to influence do care about, and show them how "alternative facts" will, in the end, destroy what they value. Doing so will enable us to form an alliance across the political spectrum to fight for truth in politics, in letter and spirit, for the sake of preserving our democracy and preventing us from sliding down into corruption and authoritarianism.

Become a Human Lie Detector

A lie only works when it fools people. If you can identify a lie, it loses its power. If citizens call out politicians on their lies and make lying a reason not to vote for them, this will help us tilt the balance toward truth in politics. To sharpen your skills at detecting political lies and the damage they can do, use independent fact-checking sources, and then familiarize yourself with the nine types of untruth categorized in this chapter. Consciously practice distinguishing which kinds of lies are told by which political figures. Become like a birdwatcher for liars. By noticing the different kinds of liars, and the frequency of their lies, you can distinguish between the marginal and most heinous offenders. This puts you in a position to make truth a value you can act on as a citizen. Rather than simply believing "all politicians lie," your more observant view gives you a scale by which to judge them. This will guide you better when you cast a vote or discuss the worthiness of candidates with others. If you attend town hall events, you can call out a lie more accurately: "Rep. Annie, your last answer seemed a lie by omission. Could you please tell us if there are statistics that back up your answer?" Wouldn't you love to see a questioner do this on TV, in the face of a dissembling politician?

Here's a short summary of the kinds of lies identified at the beginning of the chapter. Remember, there are other kinds of lies you can identify and add to this list:

Vagueness: a vague statement that can't be pinned down as a lie, but gives an overall misleading sense.

Glittering generality: an emotional appeal to valued concepts (such as love of country) that distracts from a lack of relevant supporting information.

Willful ignorance: sharing incorrect information by purposefully choosing not to learn or understand the relevant facts.

Lie by omission: deceiving by deliberately omitting relevant information.

Confabulation: making false statements due to incorrect memories, without a deliberate intent to deceive.

Deceptive hyperbole: distorting reality by deliberately exaggerating or minimizing some aspect of it.

Obfuscation: deliberately making the information unclear and confusing without actually lying.

Blatant lie: knowingly spreading false information.

Gaslighting: when confronted by evidence you lied, attacking the veracity of the truthful source (or purposefully causing someone to doubt their accurate perceptions of reality).

Important Terms Referenced in This Chapter

Black swan event: an unimaginable and very impactful event that radically transforms our society. The mental error is that because these events are rare, we mistakenly think they are impossible, and fail to plan for them; the solution is to anticipate rare events, thus turning them into 'grey swans' that we can plan for.

Demagogue: a dictator who initially rises to power with support from the public.

False consensus effect: a tendency to overestimate the extent to which other people share our opinions and predispositions.

Single cause fallacy: assuming that a single, simple cause created an outcome, when in reality the outcome may have happened due to a number of causes.

Probabilistic thinking: assigning probabilities to our understanding of reality, rather than thinking in black and white, true or false terms.

Ideologically informed deception: where an ideologue pushes a favored agenda despite the actual evidence.

Chapter 2

The Behavioral Science of Political Deception: The 2016 US Election

You know, to just be grossly generalistic, you could put half of Trump's supporters into what I call the basket of deplorables. Right? The racist, sexist, homophobic, xenophobic, Islamophobic—you name it...but that other basket of people are people who feel that the government has let them down, the economy has let them down, nobody cares about them, nobody worries about what happens to their lives and their futures, and they're just desperate for change... Those are people we have to understand and empathize with as well.
—Hillary Clinton

This quote from Hillary Clinton's speech on September 9, 2016 in New York City angered many Trump supporters. Facing criticism, Clinton issued a statement the next day: "I regret saying 'half'— that was wrong." Still, Clinton's words represent the thinking of many liberals about Trump's supporters. For instance, the *New Republic*, a prominent liberal magazine, published an article in June 2016, "Are Donald Trump's Supporters Idiots?" Despite the provocative title, the author argued that Trump's supporters are not idiots, but are conscious, self-aware "white racists [who] see themselves as benefitting from Trump's proposal to shore up the old racial status quo." The author also stated that "racism is evil, but it is not idiotic from the point of view of racists."

The well-known liberal comedian Jon Stewart, in an appearance on *CBS This Morning* on November 17, 2016, even criticized fellow liberals who painted Trump supporters with a broad brush:

There is now this idea that anyone who voted for him has

to be defined by the worst of his rhetoric. There are guys in my neighborhood that I love, that I respect, that I think have incredible qualities who are not afraid of Mexicans, and not afraid of Muslims, and not afraid of blacks. They're afraid of their insurance premiums. In the liberal community you hate this idea of creating people as a monolith. Don't look at Muslims as a monolith. They are individuals and it would be ignorance. But everybody who voted for Trump is a monolith, is a racist. That hypocrisy is also real in our country.

Senator Bernie Sanders, a prominent liberal, also spoke out. He said at a rally on March 31, 2017: "Some people think that the people who voted for Trump are racists and sexists and homophobes and deplorable folks. I don't agree." Earlier, in a November 11, 2016 op-ed for the *New York Times*, Sanders argued that Trump's supporters were "expressing their fierce opposition to an economic and political system that puts wealthy and corporate interests over their own." Still, such criticism of Trump voters as motivated mainly by racism continues among liberals, for example in an article in *The Intercept* on April 6, 2017, entitled "Top Democrats Are Wrong: Trump Supporters Were More Motivated by Racism Than Economic Issues."

These arguments implicitly assume that voters are rational creatures who choose a candidate based on a self-aware, intentional desire, whether to proclaim their opposition to an economic and political system that puts wealthy and corporate interests over their own, to paraphrase Sanders, or to shore up the old racial status quo, as the *Intercept* article implies. In reality, much recent research shows that voters often act based on intuitions and emotions, rather than careful and thoughtful evaluation of reality. To be clear, I am not agreeing with Jonathan Chait's claims in *New York Magazine* in a May 11, 2016 article, "Here's the Real Reason Everybody Thought Trump Would Lose." Chait castigates the intelligence of Republican voters for nominating Trump: "as low as my estimation of the intelligence of the Republican electorate may be, I did not think enough of them would be dumb enough to buy his act." He further added that "to watch Donald Trump and see a qualified and plausible president, you probably have some kind of mental shortcoming."

Such criticism shows a lack of understanding of how the human mind works, and fails to understand Trump's skillful manipulation of his base. Certainly, many people voted for Trump because they truly supported his approach—whether economic or racist. Others did so because Trump and his allies succeeded in selling them falsehoods. Indeed, our intuitive thinking patterns, barring training in critical evaluation of reality, predispose us to believe comfortable lies over uncomfortable truths.

Truth Versus Comfort

What do I mean by a "comfortable lie"? Obviously, people think that whatever they believe is true. But the way evolution has sculpted our brains sometimes fools us into mistaking information that makes us feel comfortable for information that is true. By "comfortable," I mean feelings of security, confidence and ease—feelings that we get when presented with information that fits our worldview, that is, our beliefs about how the world really is. Similarly, when confronted with information that conflicts with our worldview, we feel uneasy, sometimes even threatened by it.

Post-truth politicians feed people false information that fits their sense of reality so well that it feels true to them, but in fact, it is a comfortable lie. It *feels* true, because it has been crafted for exactly that purpose. For example, a zealous Trump supporter might find it uncomfortable that Trump lost the popular vote in 2016, and thus lacked a mandate to implement his policies. This supporter might more willingly accept the misinformation spread by Trump and his surrogates that 3 million illegal votes were cast for Clinton, and that Trump really won the majority—

because that would fit the worldview that Trump and his policies would be good for the country. Meanwhile, a Clinton supporter might feel so uneasy that Trump won the election that he or she would seek any explanation that lessened their discomfort. For example, that Trump's campaign secretly colluded with Russians to win (even though intensive investigation of these allegations by the Mueller Report did not find sufficient evidence to merit prosecution).

Think of it like this: the deceptions of post-truth politicians are like fishing lures. A lure is specially designed to fool a fish's brain so it can't see the deadly hook in what looks to be its favorite meal. The fish is not stupid. It is just following a billion years of evolution. Similarly, comfortable lies don't work only on the weak and the foolish. In ways modern science is only beginning to understand, our brains are built with features that make us all susceptible to certain kinds of mental errors and blindspots known as *cognitive biases*. Researchers have discovered literally hundreds of these biases in human psychology, and every person suffers from them to some degree. It's important to note, though, that there's no morally negative connotation in the term "bias." In this sense it only means a distortion. It does not mean a prejudice or preference, as in a bias toward a favorite sports team, or a bias against an ethnic minority. For example, if your car always pulls to the left when you drive, you could say it has a leftward bias. Or if you wear glasses for distance, you could say your eyes have a nearsighted bias. In neither case is there an ethical judgment—though it would still make sense to opt for a wheel alignment or pair of glasses.

While we do not know the exact origins of cognitive biases, recent scholarship (for instance in an article entitled "The evolution of cognitive bias" in the 2005 *The Handbook of Evolutionary Psychology*) suggests different biases evolved long ago as adaptations that were in some way useful for tribes living in certain environments. For instance, in an environment of prosperity and safety, people who have an *optimism bias* and believe things will go well would advance their tribe's situation. But, in an environment of scarcity and threat, those with a *pessimism bias,* the belief things will go poorly, might come to the fore and prove the tribe's salvation.

The bad news is that these biases are filtering our experience without our conscious awareness. They work automatically in our unconscious mind. Whether buying a car (as in Chapter 1), evaluating a new business deal, or a potential romantic partner, our cognitive biases too often lead us astray in costly ways. The good news is that by learning more about how these biases affect us, we can develop *debiasing* strategies to protect ourselves. Driving offers a good analogy. What do you do when you want to change lanes as you drive along the highway? You shoulder-check. Why? Because in driver's ed they teach that drivers have a blindspot between the side-view and rear-view mirrors. A car in that blindspot could cause an accident if you tried to change lanes into its path. By anticipating this dangerous blindspot, we can consciously develop a habit of looking over our shoulder before we change lanes. As a result of this simple routine, countless accidents are avoided and lives saved. You can think of debiasing techniques as like shoulder-checks that help us detect and avoid the costly errors caused by our blindspots.

Four Cognitive Biases at Work in Politics

While there are myriad cognitive biases at work in politics, I want to explore with you in this chapter four of the biggest ones that Trump exploited with particular effectiveness in the 2016 election. By better understanding these as strategies of political deception, you will find yourself less likely to fall under their spell. Think of a deceiving politician as like a magician performing tricks. If you know how the trick is done, if you can catch the sleight of hand, or the distracting flourish, you won't be fooled by the magic!

Rosy Retrospection

Rosy retrospection refers to our tendency to remember the past as much better than it actually was, as explored by Terence Mitchell et al. in a 1997 *Journal of Experimental Social Psychology* article. Studying people prior, during, and after they took a tour of California on bicycles, the scholars found that during the event, many described unpleasant conditions, such as bad rain and exhaustion. However, looking back after the vacation, people provided substantially more positive evaluations of their travels. Similarly, many people remember their childhood with warmth, and forget all the negative aspects of being a child. The same applies to any past period of our lives, frequently leading those suffering from rosy retrospection to imagine that our circumstances have declined over time.

Trump's central message was "Make America Great Again," or #MAGA on Twitter. Borrowing this phrase from Ronald Reagan's 1980 presidential campaign, Trump promised to bring back "the good old days," focusing on secure and well-paying jobs, and revising trade agreements "unfair" to the US. For instance, Trump condemned the North American Free Trade Agreement (NAFTA) as the "worst trade deal ever" in terms of job loss for the US during his first presidential debate with Hillary Clinton. As *PolitiFact* found in a September 29, 2016 analysis, Trump's claim "fails on a couple of points. First, in terms of impact on the economy, the prevailing consensus among economists is that NAFTA has largely been a wash. Not everyone agrees, but most say, by and large, the treaty created about as many jobs as it cost."

Likewise, a number of liberals express suspicion that Trump's slogan represented coded language for going back to a time when minorities of all sorts "knew their place," as described in *Mother Jones'* January/February 2017 issue, in an article titled "Trump Didn't Invent 'Make America Great Again.'" Trump made numerous statements falsely disparaging minorities: For instance, in his speech announcing his presidential campaign, he stated, "When Mexico sends its people, they're not sending their best...They're bringing drugs. They're bringing crime. They're rapists. And some, I assume, are good people." The *Washington Post* fact-checking column gave this statement, and related ones made by Trump, its worst rating of Four Pinocchios, in a July 8, 2015 article, "Donald Trump's false comments connecting Mexican immigrants and crime." As the reporter pointed out, in fact first-generation immigrants commit fewer crimes on average than native-born Americans.

In a January 17, 2017 piece in *The Guardian*, "Can Trump really make America great again?", the newspaper evaluated what Trump's supporters thought MAGA meant. Indeed, they did want a strong focus on jobs and revising "unfair" agreements. Supporting the perspective of coded language, a number expressed support for rolling back various forms of inclusivity and pluralism, and harsher policing of immigration. Despite making many demonstrably false statements, Trump succeeded in convincing his base that he represented the only hope of solving these problems by "Making America Great Again."

Similarly, Brexit was characterized by more older voters favoring their vision of an earlier UK. A story in *Time* on June 24, 2016, "The U.K.'s Old Decided for the Young in the Brexit Vote," describes how polls indicated that less than 20 percent of those between 18 and 24 supported the "Leave" position, while among pensioners, 59 percent supported "Leave." This breakdown is somewhat sharper, but overall similar to the vote for Trump in the US presidential campaign. According to *USA Today*, in a November 9, 2016 piece called "How we voted—by age, education, race and sexual orientation," only 37 percent of those aged 18–29 voted for Trump, while 53 percent of those over 65 voted for Trump.

The politicians campaigning for Brexit painted an image of an earlier UK characterized by a strong economy, and blamed immigrants for mooching off the welfare system of the UK. However, these claims turned out to be exaggerated, according to an article in the *Daily Beast*, "Brexit Voters Had the Wrong Idea About Immigration and Unemployment," on June 26, 2016. For instance, one of the immigrant groups targeted for abuse by the "Leave" side—Poles—actually have less unemployment than native-born citizens of the UK. So, a simplistic painting of immigrants as moochers was false, yet presented an image that older UK citizens felt was real, as it conformed with their longed-for UK of the past, which they saw through rose-colored glasses.

Similarly, Vladimir Putin appealed to a base of voters who wanted to turn back the clock to a more powerful, dynamic Russia, invoking memories of Soviet military might and economic prosperity, while ignoring the human rights violations and suppression of freedoms in Soviet times. A typical claim made by Putin is represented by the title of an article in *Russia Today*, a Russian government-controlled media channel, on September 23, 2016: "Putin: USSR Could Have Been Reformed, There Was No Need to Destroy It." A December 2016 article in *National Geographic*, "Why Many Young Russians See a Hero in Putin," describes how Putin called the fall of the Soviet Union "the greatest geopolitical catastrophe" of the twentieth century, and relates that, according to polls, 58 percent of those in Russia want a return to the Soviet order, with Stalin seen favorably by 40 percent.

Horns Effect

The cognitive bias known as the *horns effect* (as in, horns of the devil) refers to the following thought pattern: when we dislike one aspect of something (a person, party, country), we let this dislike negatively color other aspects of that thing, as related by Scot Burton et al. in a 2015 *Journal of the Academy of Marketing Science* article. For instance, if we find someone to be unattractive physically, our minds will tend to devalue that person's competence in other areas, as shown by Sidney Katz in a 1995 article in *Down to Earth Sociology*. Similarly, students asked to measure the quality of the curriculum presented by teachers were strongly influenced by their perceptions of the teachers' charisma or the lack thereof, despite the fact that the curriculum itself had nothing to do with the style of presentation by the teacher, as described in Mark Shevlin et al.'s 2000 article, "The validity of student evaluation of teaching in higher education: love me, love my lectures?"

The name "horns effect" evokes a related bias, *the halo effect*. In this bias, when we positively evaluate one thing about a person, we tend to make positive evaluations about other unrelated characteristics of the person. Trump used the halo effect to glowing advantage: he convinced his supporters that because he had a reputation as a successful businessman, he would be a successful president. The fact that running a government requires quite a different skill set than running a business didn't seem to bother them.

Trump used the horns effect to great effect (pun intended) against his political opponents, through name-calling. For example, toward Ted Cruz in the Republican primaries: "In the case of Lyin' Ted Cruz. Lyin' Ted. Lies. Ooh, he lies. You know Ted. He brings the Bible, holds it high, puts it down, lies" (from an Indianapolis rally on April 20, 2016, as reported in a *Politico* article that day: "Trump revives his 'Lyin' Ted' attack on Cruz"). Trump powerfully associated something generally perceived as negative—lying—with Cruz, thus blackening Cruz's reputation as a whole. Such nicknames served as a staple for Trump during the primary campaign against Cruz and other Republicans: "Little Marc" Rubio; "Low-energy Jeb" Bush. And of course, in the general election campaign, "Crooked Hillary." His supporters made not only memes out of these nicknames, but also posters and signs (see Figure 2.1).

Fig. 2.1 Trump supporters with a sign criticizing "Crooked Hillary"
(courtesy mccauleys-corner, flickr.com)

I'm sure you have encountered this tactic in your own life. It's schoolyard bullying. Like a bully, Trump's name-calling is not random. He hits real weaknesses in his victims. Elizabeth Warren *did* once make claims to Native American ancestry. So, when Trump mocked her as "Pocahontas," it stung, and her attempts to defend herself (including taking an DNA test) just heightened the negative attention. Likewise, polls in early 2016 revealed that many voters, including Democrats, doubted Clinton's honesty. This tactic puts the victim in a double bind. If they ignore the attack, it sticks. If they engage, they merely keep the media focused on their weakness. Meanwhile, the sheer nastiness of verbal bullying raises our emotional antenna. Regardless of whether or not we like or dislike the victim, the attack triggers a cluster of automatic thinking reflexes. Millions of years of evolution in social groups makes us more attuned to things that are negative, emotional, and potentially threatening. Plus, when something is repeated often enough, our brain processes the information as if it comes from many different sources, so unconsciously we start to believe it is true. The media thus magnifies the horns effect through relentless coverage of

Trump's tweets. My co-author, Tim, recalls discussing Clinton's campaign in 2016 with a Korean economist living in Asia. He said, "Well, there's just something about her that I don't trust." But he couldn't say exactly why he felt this way. The horns effect for Clinton had spanned the globe. Finally, as in the image above, it's easy to fall prey to the *bandwagon effect*, in which people do something primarily because other people are doing it, regardless of their own beliefs. This was the horns effect multiplied by all these other biases at work.

Trump's opponents tried to turn the tables against him, but they did not have Trump's success in making nicknames stick. Clinton's campaign, together with the Democratic National Committee, came up with the term "Dangerous Donald." This lame attempt proved singularly ineffective, and was widely criticized, even by Clinton's own party! So, why does name-calling work for Trump and not for others? Let's recall the school bully again. There is a nastiness in ridiculing someone for their flaws. We saw it most blatantly in Trump's mocking of a disabled journalist during the campaign. That menacing negativity creates a sense of emotional drama that makes these kinds of attack impossible to ignore. But when the smart kid in school tries to fight the bully with name-calling, it simply seems laughable, because his or her attempts do not come from a place of authenticity—even when the authenticity is that of a nasty bully. Other post-truth leaders with a similar menacing negativity use similar strategies effectively. Putin, for example, ridiculed protesters in Moscow for wearing a white ribbon to symbolize their opposition to his regime. In a 2011 TV interview, Putin called these white ribbons "condoms" (*The Guardian*, "Vladimir Putin mocks Moscow's 'condom-wearing' protesters," December 15, 2011).

There is one tactic that might work against Trump's use of the horns effect. It's what works against school bullies: forming a united front. In this case, it would mean leaders from both parties calling out his bad behavior whenever he describes opponents with malicious names. Without repeating the slur, describe the tactic as bullying, and condemn Trump for its use. The media could also do this, and it would be much more productive than endlessly repeating the insults.

Group Attribution Error

Blaming large groups for the behavior of a few members is a classic mistake of the human mind, identified by scholars as the *group attribution error*. This error involves taking one person's attitudes and behavior to represent accurately the opinions of a group to which this person belongs.

For instance, a study showed that if you observe a community that implements a water conservation law, you will tend to assume that all members of that community align with that law — regardless of how they really feel. The same study (by Scott Allison and David M. Messick published in 1985 in the *Journal of Experimental Social Psychology*) found that we tend to attribute more homogeneity to members of groups different from our own. In other words, the more distant other people are from us, the more similar to each other they seem to us. Another study, by Diane Mackie and Scott Allison in the same journal in 1987, showed that the more threatening we perceive a certain group to be, the more similar to each other we perceive its members to be. The latter finding shows that the horns effect reinforces the group attribution error.

Trump widely appeals to this combination of group attribution error and horns effect. One example is a December 7, 2015 press release by the Trump campaign "calling for a total and complete shutdown of Muslims entering the United States" to prevent terrorism in the US. After becoming President, Trump issued an executive order to ban all citizens of Iraq, Iran, Libya, Somalia, Sudan, Syria, and Yemen from traveling to the US, with the aim of preventing terrorism. Yet an analysis by the conservative Cato Institute, published on January 25, 2017, bears the title "Little National Security Benefit to Trump's Executive Order on Immigration." It describes how citizens from those countries have not killed any Americans in terrorist attacks on US soil for the last three decades. As the report concludes, "a rational evaluation of national security threats is not the basis for Trump's orders, as the risk is fairly small but the cost is great. The measures taken here will have virtually no effect on improving US national security." Trump's comments on Mexicans fit the same pattern.

Similarly, in the United Kingdom, Brexit "Leave" campaign advocates riled-up anti-immigrant sentiments to accomplish their political agenda. For example, Nigel Farage unveiled an anti-immigrant poster a week before the vote, which was reported to the police for inciting racial hatred, according to *The Guardian*'s June 16, 2016 article, "Nigel Farage's anti-migrant poster reported to police" (see Figure 2.2).

Fig. 2.2 Nigel Farage with his poster (courtesy of *The Guardian*, June 16, 2016)

In France, far-right Marine Le Pen condemned Muslims and more subtly criticized Jews, as related by *The Atlantic* in an April 17, 2017 story, "How Marine Le Pen Relies on Dividing French Jews and Muslims." Putin rode to power in 2000 in part by blaming Chechens for a series of apartment bombings in

1999, and presenting himself as a forceful leader by invading Chechnya to supposedly put a stop to these bombings. However, some evidence shows that Russian security services may have actually committed the bombings and scapegoated Chechens (see *National Review*, "The Unsolved Mystery Behind the Act of Terror That Brought Putin to Power," August 17, 2016). Regardless of the reality, Putin succeeded in his efforts to attribute blame to Chechens as a group for the bombings, a classic example of group attribution error and horns effect combined.

Confirmation Bias

All new information that goes against our current beliefs causes us emotional discomfort. Our minds naturally tend to reject such information, instead looking for and interpreting information in a way that provides us with comfort by conforming to our existing beliefs. Scholars term this thinking error the *confirmation bias*, as described by Raymond Nickerson in a 1998 article in the *Review of General Psychology*, and another piece by Charles Lord et al. in the *Journal of Personality and Social Psychology* in 1979. This phenomenon subverts our ability to evaluate reality accurately. Research on the confirmation bias in regard to political beliefs by Charles Taber and Milton Lodge published in 2006 in the *American Journal of Political Science* shows that people tend to accept uncritically political information that favors their current beliefs. They express skepticism only toward data that goes against their beliefs. Just imagine how powerful the confirmation bias is when it comes to politics: reinforcing one's existing beliefs, regardless of the evidence!

Confirmation bias among Republicans served Trump well, as he attacked any source of information that did not present a flattering perspective of him. Consider Trump's statements about former FBI Director James Comey (as reported in an *NBC News* article on May 10, 2017, "Here's a Timeline of Trump's Statements on Comey"). On October 31, 2016, Trump praised him for having "a lot of guts" for reopening the investigation into Clinton's emails, and on April 12, 2017, Trump said "I have confidence" in Comey. Yet on May 9, 2017, Trump fired Comey, apparently with the primary motive of easing the pressure from Comey's investigation into Trump and his allies potentially colluding with Russia to subvert the US presidential election (as reported by the *New York Times* in its May 19, 2017 article, "Trump Told Russians That Firing 'Nut Job' Comey Eased Pressure from Investigation"). Trump fired Comey in part based on a memo written by his deputy attorney general Rod Rosenstein, whom he praised in an interview on NBC News on May 11, 2017, "Trump Interview with Lester Holt: President Asked Comey If He Was Under Investigation." Specifically, Trump said about Rosenstein: "He's highly respected—very good guy, very smart guy. The Democrats like him. The Republicans like him." Yet just over a month afterward, on June 16, 2017, Trump tweeted, "I am being investigated for firing the FBI Director by the man who told me to fire the FBI Director! Witch Hunt."

Did these previously credible, trustworthy people suddenly transform into nasty witch-hunters? No, of course not. They kept doing their jobs in an ethical and competent manner. The thing that changed was that both Comey and Rosenstein became more involved in the investigation into the Trump–Russia connection, leading Trump to lash out at them. This represents part of Trump's broader general trend of attacking all information that is unfavorable to him, to strengthen the confirmation bias response in his supporters and get them to perceive only him as the authoritative source of knowledge.

Polls demonstrated the power of the confirmation bias in this instance. How do you think Republicans would respond to Trump's explanations for firing Comey compared to the general population's responses? What percent would believe Trump's narrative, versus the narrative of the Democrats, immediately after the firing, when no further information for the cause of the firing was available? Take a guess before reading the next paragraph.

A poll taken on May 10–11, 2017 by YouGov, a credible polling agency, shows that only 24 percent of Republicans believed that Trump's actions had to do with the FBI's investigation, compared to 47 percent of the total poll respondents. Most of you were probably not surprised; it's pretty intuitive that Republicans would give Trump more benefit of the doubt. However, over the next two weeks, extensive evidence emerged that Trump first pressured and then fired Comey to block the FBI's investigation of Trump's administration over possible collusion with Russia.

Another poll by a credible agency, Rasmussen Reports, was released after these events, on May 24, 2017. Take a guess at the changed percentage figures both for Republicans and the general population before reading onward. The general population had a significant update, with 60 percent of all who took the poll now believing that the firing had to do with Comey's investigation of the administration. So, we have about a 25 percent increase, from 47 percent to 60 percent, toward where the truth lies, according to the evidence. However, the same poll showed that still only 24 percent of Republicans believed that this firing had to do with Comey's investigation of the administration. Clearly, the evidence that emerged over these two weeks moved the general population to update their perspective on Trump's actions as stemming from a desire to hinder the FBI's investigation. Republicans, suffering from confirmation bias, failed to update their beliefs. Let me clarify that there is no reason to suppose that in a similar situation Democrats would have responded differently. Confirmation bias affects us all.

In other global contexts, post-truth politicians similarly portrayed themselves as the only source of truth, and demonized anyone who criticized them. For instance, in Russia, once Putin came to power at the turn of the millennium, he focused much effort on seizing control over the mass media, according to an

April 21, 2015 story in *The Atlantic*, "How the Media Became One of Putin's Most Powerful Weapons." The article discusses how Putin came to dominate the news infrastructure in Russia, citing his words at a 2013 annual news conference: "There should be patriotically minded people at the head of state information resources, people who uphold the interests of the Russian Federation." By closely managing the information available for consumption, Putin made sure that it was very hard to get any information that went against his perspective, thus playing into the confirmation bias of his followers while denying those who might otherwise oppose him the opportunity to get information to confirm their opposition. This control over the media plays a huge role in Putin's ability to command his high popularity ratings. Erdogan in Turkey used similar methods, as reported in a piece in *Foreign Policy* on August 12, 2015, "How President Erdogan Mastered the Media."

To conclude, many castigate Trump's followers as "deplorable" racists, misogynists, and homophobes, and others argue that they instead are simply alienated and disheartened by their economic conditions. But presenting his followers in this light fails to recognize that we as human beings are not intuitively rational, in neither our political engagement nor other areas of life. Trump's victory paves the way for other politicians to adapt his manipulative strategies for their own needs.

While Trump's model will likely encourage mostly conservative politicians, there is nothing inherently conservative about it. Erdogan, for example, pursues left-wing economic policies and criticizes the market system (as described in "Erdogan's War on the Market Economy," published by *Al-Monitor* on December 12, 2016). Any politician may use psychological manipulation over facts to achieve their goal of swaying their followers to elect them. After all, politicians win not by telling the truth, but by getting elected. Telling the truth is useful only so far as it gets them elected, and if lies and manipulations help politicians get elected, then they will have a clear incentive to make such appeals to get their followers to believe them.

Become a Rational Voter and Avoid the Traps of Political Deception

Think of this book as a training manual for your brain. Specifically, my goal is to share with you the mental tools that will equip you to be aware of our in-built thinking errors and notice when you are being psychologically manipulated by politicians. If you know the magician's tricks, you won't so likely be fooled by them. You can then call out their manipulations, and flag these abuses so that others can be aware of them too. In other words, you will become a rational voter and a force for truth.

Fig. 2.3 Become a Rational Voter (designed by Charles Cassidy and Alexis Wenceslao for Intentional Insights)

Important Terms Referenced in This Chapter

Debiasing: with motivation and training, we can learn to detect and avoid the costly errors of our mental blindspots and cognitive biases.

Optimism bias: the belief things will turn out well.

Pessimism bias: the belief things will turn out poorly.

False consensus effect: the tendency to overestimate the extent to which other people agree with what we think.

Expressive voting: accepting all that a favored politician says as true because we would be uncomfortable doing otherwise (using our "gut" rather than our head).

Emotional contagion: the ability of charismatic leaders to "infect" their followers with their emotions (most influential when combined with expressive voting).

Cognitive biases: problematic thinking patterns that can easily lead us into error.

Rosy retrospection: our tendency to remember the past as much better than it actually was.

Horns effect: when we dislike one aspect of a whole, we let this dislike color other aspects of that whole. This dislike may apply to a person, an ethnicity, a political party or a nation.

Halo effect: when we positively evaluate one thing about a person (or ethnicity, political party, or nation), we tend to make positive evaluations about other unrelated characteristics of the person (or ethnicity, political party, or nation).

Bandwagon effect: when people do something primarily because other people are doing it, regardless of their own beliefs.

Group attribution error: assuming one person's attitudes and behavior accurately represent the attitudes and behavior of a group to which the person belongs.

Confirmation bias: the tendency to look for and interpret new information in a way that conforms to our existing beliefs, and ignore or reject new information that goes against our current beliefs.

Chapter 3

The Illusory Truth Effect

"I was totally against the war in Iraq. You can look at *Esquire* magazine from '04. You can look at before that."

Donald Trump made this statement at a forum on national security in New York City on September 7, 2016. It's true that in an interview in *Esquire* magazine more than a year after the war began, in August 2004, Donald Trump said some negative things about the Iraq war. Yet looking "before that," the media easily found a September 2002 Trump radio interview with Howard Stern. In that interview Trump was asked whether he supported the impending invasion of Iraq. He replied "Yeah, I guess so." Thus, Trump's statement that he was "totally" against the war was a lie. From a political perspective, the lie served Trump. According to a Quinnipiac Poll in May 2015, about 59 percent of respondents believed that going to war in Iraq in 2003 was the wrong thing to do. By falsely claiming that he was "totally against" the war, Trump appealed to the majority, while Clinton was stuck with her pro-war vote in the Senate.

Numerous media venues and fact-checkers, such as CNN, *The Washington Post*, *The New York Times*, *PolitiFact*, *Los Angeles Times*, *Snopes*, *Politico*, *The Atlantic*, and many others, called Trump out on this lie. After all, an important role of mainstream media is to serve as a referee in our public sphere, blowing the referee's whistle when a high-profile lie on an important national issue comes to light. Yet instead of following the long-established "rules of the game" and backing down when caught, Trump doubled down on his deception. This was no one-time exception: it followed a pattern that's characteristic of a post-truth politician. The day after uttering his lie at the forum in New York, Trump gave a speech in Cleveland where he said:

"Iraq is one of the biggest differences in this race. I opposed going in and I did oppose it, despite the media saying no...I see the lies last night that Donald Trump was always in favor of the war in Iraq, and that's why I have to do this, because the media is so dishonest, so terribly dishonest. I just had to set the record straight because there's so much lying going on."

This example was only one of many instances where Trump made false claims, was called out by the media, and responded not by recanting but by attacking the media's credibility. You might ask, how can this possibly work? Repetition is the answer. It creates a powerful form of deception called the *illusory truth effect*.

The Science of the Illusory Truth Effect

The *illusory truth effect* is a mental error that causes us to perceive something to be true when we hear it repeated frequently and persistently. Regardless of whether a statement is false or true, the more we hear it, the more likely we are to believe it. The scientific research supporting the *illusory truth effect* is quite robust, as shown by an analysis of 51 academic studies on this phenomenon published in *Personality and Social Psychology Review*. According to research by Hal Arkes et al., the illusory truth effect applies both to statements of minor importance (such as "some spiders have 12 eyes"), important social evaluations (such as whether vaccines cause autism), and political issues (such as whether Trump "always opposed" the Iraq war). These research findings would not be news to Adolf Hitler. In *Mein Kampf* he wrote: "Slogans should be persistently repeated until the very last individual has come to grasp the idea."

Perhaps the most shocking finding is that "Knowledge does not protect against illusory truth"—the title and topic of a peer-reviewed article published in the *Journal of Experimental Psychology* in 2015. Previously, most scholars had assumed that the illusory truth effect resulted from people being unaware of factual reality. Yet the 2015 study demonstrated that repetition of falsehoods increased the perception of how true a claim was, even for claims that people *already knew were false*. In this study by Lisa Fazio et al., participants rated 176 statements for truthfulness, using a scale labeled "1 – definitely false; 2 – probably false; 3 – possibly false; 4 – possibly true; 5 – probably true; and 6 – definitely true." The experimenters found that some study participants correctly answered the question "What is the name of the short pleated skirt worn by Scots?" (a kilt). The subjects then rated the truth of the statement that a "sari is the name of the short pleated skirt worn by Scots," giving it a low-truth rating. Those subjects were then asked to read a number of statements, including that a "sari is the name of the short pleated skirt worn by Scots." After some time passed, they were asked to again rate the truth of that statement. Surprisingly, despite knowing that the pleated skirt is called a kilt, not a sari, they still rated the truth value of the sari statement as *higher* than they did initially. The sobering conclusion: *repetition chips away at our certainty, even about things we know for a fact.*

Did you ever wonder why you see an ad on a TV show repeated over and over again in a single episode? Research published in the *Journal of Advertising* shows that the advertising industry motivates people to buy products by repeating claimed benefits, rather than by providing strong evidence that the product *has* the claimed benefits. Sheer repetition creates the impression advertisers want to leave on our minds, just as dripping water in a cave creates a stalactite. Here's a short list of evidence-free advertising claims you have probably heard before. As you read the list, notice whether or not you have a general sense of positive feeling for each product, regardless of whether or not you even tried it (with thanks for suggestions from Facebook supporters of the Pro-Truth Pledge for offering up these examples):

- L'Oréal: Because You're Worth It

- Gillette: The Best a Man Can Get
- Red Bull: It Gives You Wings
- De Beers: A Diamond Is Forever
- BMW: The Ultimate Driving Machine

The illusory truth effect is magnified by advertisements that prime consumers to trust their feelings, rather than their reason. In view of this, it's no wonder that Trump encouraged his followers to rely on their instincts, as in a January 30, 2013 tweet, where he proclaimed: "go with your gut." Indeed, there are situations where going with your gut is the best option. For example, you might consider it a waste of time to do a thorough analysis of which of several roughly identical cleaning products works best. So, sure, go with your gut for minor decisions, even if your gut has been manipulated by an advertising campaign. But for selecting a president? That deserves rational considerations.

The illusory truth effect was recently studied in the specific context of fake news stories. Danielle Polage at Central Washington University ran an experiment where participants read fake news stories which the researchers depicted as true. After five weeks, these same participants were tested again by reading the same fake stories. Not surprisingly, these repeat participants rated the stories as more truthful than participants who read the fake stories for the first time. Additionally, some repeat participants formed false memories about the stories' origins, forgetting that the stories originated from the experiment. Thus, repeating fake news stories not only leads people to perceive these stories as true; it can also obscure in their minds the original source of the stories. For example, people might misremember that they learned about a news story through social media, which are notoriously plagued by fake news, and believe the story came from watching the more credible nightly news on TV.

This drastic impact of the illusory truth effect relates, in large part, to *processing fluency*, a concept referring to how easily our minds process information. The more often we hear a statement, the less effort it takes to process it. The less effort it takes to process, the more comfortable with it we become. The more comfortable we become, the more truthful the statement seems to us on a gut level. As discussed in Chapter 2, we find that the problem stems from a fundamental mistake our brains tend to make, of equating comfort with truth.

Trump's Illusory Truths

Given Trump's background in marketing and advertising, it's plausible that he is consciously aware of the illusory truth effect. However, whether consciously or not, he certainly takes advantage of this hard-wired error in people's thinking. Trump's post-truth political approach consists of combining repetition and deceit to his advantage. Here are just three examples.

The "Birther" Movement

Perhaps it is not surprising that Trump has adopted these tactics, given his success as a leader of the "birther" movement. He gained political prominence by repeating lies about President Obama not being born in the United States, and allegedly being a secret Muslim. These lies continued to gain credibility after Trump repeated them again and again on well-known shows, such as Fox News' *The O'Reilly Factor* on March 30, 2011. Even after Obama made public his long-form birth certificate, Trump persisted in his false claims, and found an all-too-willing audience of believers. In a feat that still defies political gravity, on September 16, 2016 Trump held a press conference where he declared, "Hillary Clinton started the birther movement, but today, I am ending it." He never apologized for perpetuating the lie. Surveys since the election show that despite Trump's reversal, significant numbers of Republicans still believe Obama was not born in the United States (see for instance a YouGov poll of 1,500 adults in December 2017 that found 51 percent of Republicans in the survey held that false belief).

NAFTA

Another example from the 2016 election is Trump's deceptive and repeated statement that the North American Free Trade Agreement (NAFTA) "is the worst trade deal maybe ever signed anywhere, but certainly ever signed in this country." Trump falsely claimed that NAFTA cost Americans millions of manufacturing jobs. As a political marketer, Trump aimed to appeal to the voters of the Rust Belt states such as Ohio, Pennsylvania, Michigan, and Wisconsin who have suffered from manufacturing automation and outsourcing. As discussed in Chapter 2, his claims have been disproved by prominent economists who have thoroughly studied NAFTA and know far more about its impact than Trump or any other politician. But despite being condemned by mainstream newspapers, fact-checkers, economists, and non-partisan researchers for lying about NAFTA, Trump stubbornly repeated his claims, while attacking the media and experts who disputed them.

After winning the election, Trump used his threat to tear up NAFTA to negotiate a new agreement, signed by the US, Mexico and Canada on November 30, 2018, entitled USMCA. At the signing, Trump called USMCA a "truly groundbreaking achievement" that would be "the envy of nations all around the world." In reality, the general consensus of economists is that USMCA was more of a tweak to NAFTA. The *Economist* magazine wrote in October 2018: "Although the new pact does contain improvements to NAFTA, taken as a whole it is a step backwards for free trade. As a result, it will harm America." (As this book goes to publication, the deal has yet to be ratified by Congress).

To recap Trump's use of the illusory truth effect over NAFTA:

1. Declare NAFTA the worst trade deal ever.
2. Negotiate minor changes.
3. Declare the new deal "a truly groundbreaking achievement."

It's important to notice the positive feeling generated by the final claim, that the agreement will be the "envy of nations all around the world." That positive feeling is the advertiser's flourish that on a gut level increases our comfort about the final claim.

North Korea

Trump's use of the illusory truth effect since the election follows a similar three-part pattern:

1. North Korea is a rogue nation and nuclear threat to the US that previous presidents have never dealt with. Trump then antagonized President Kim Jong-un on Twitter, calling him "Little Rocket Man," raising fears of imminent conflict.
2. Trump holds a summit in Singapore with Kim, on June 12, 2018.
3. The next day Trump declares on Twitter: "Everybody can now feel much safer than the day I took office...There is no longer a nuclear threat from North Korea."

Note again the positive emotion created by the illusory truth of the third step: everyone can now "feel much safer." In January 2019, when national intelligence agencies testified that North Korea remained a nuclear threat, and would not likely give up its nuclear weapons, Trump attacked them on Twitter, writing: "Perhaps Intelligence should 'go back to school.'" The second summit between Trump and Kim in February 2019 ended abruptly with no deal, and the resumption of North Korea's missile program.

The Narrative Fallacy

So far, we have examined the illusory truth effect in terms of single claims. The emerging trend from the above examples shows how a pattern can also trigger the effect. We keep hearing the same story over again: Things are terrible; Trump makes a change; things are now the best they have ever been in all human history! Trump tells, again and again, the story of him winning—and America feeling *great* about it. He even primed his supporters for this during the 2016 campaign, saying repeatedly that if he was elected, "We're gonna win so much you may even get tired of winning." The power of this story comes from repetition of the pattern, and the positive feeling imparted to those who believe it. That makes it all the easier to dismiss the critics who point out the lies as people who hate America: because they are enemies of the gut *feeling* evoked by Trump's relentless stories of winning. By sticking to one story and keeping it simple, Trump enhances our *processing fluency*, as discussed above. Compare him to wonky politicians like Clinton who seek to engage the public in complicated policy lectures.

Trump's story-telling also takes advantage of a cluster of other cognitive biases.

First, the *narrative fallacy*. The narrative fallacy is our tendency to fit whatever information we have available into a story that makes intuitive sense. See what you make of this story: *It's Valentine's Day. John holds a red rose. He is sitting alone at a table for two in a restaurant. It's now ten o'clock. There are tears in his eyes.* You can't help but tell yourself the story that John has been stood up on a date. Why that story? Perhaps because of your own experience with roses, or from our culture's countless movies and books that make romantic patterns like the jilted lover familiar. (This is known as the *availability heuristic*, a mental shortcut that inclines us to rely on immediate examples that come to mind when evaluating a specific topic, concept, method, or decision.) But perhaps John's fiancée has just agreed to marry him; she's gone to the bathroom and left him alone and full of joy. Or what if he's a rose salesman meeting a client at 10 a.m., and his allergies are bothering him?

I imagine as you read these alternative scenarios, you considered them possible, but maybe a bit annoying. Perhaps you even said to yourself, "Yes, but 'John the jilted lover' is still the most *likely* story." Three other biases have kicked in. First, the *primacy effect*: When presented with a lot of information, we tend to remember *best* what we are exposed to *first*. The *primacy effect* often leads to *anchoring*, a cognitive bias where an individual relies too heavily on an initial piece of information (the "anchor") when making decisions. In other words, once we make an initial judgment about what something means, we tend to get fixed on it, and it's hard to change our minds.

Back on the African savannah, these cognitive biases helped our ancestors sort information and remember what was important for their survival. But today, they can be used to manipulate us into believing lies. Trump tells stories that are simple, familiar, and emotionally powerful (like "winning!"), creating a compelling emotional narrative out of a few details. He tells these stories *first and fast*, often getting them out on Twitter or at rallies. This triggers the primacy effect and sets an anchor in our unconscious mind. The media then reports these tweets *ad nauseam*, making them unconsciously more convincing by the power of repetition. Even as the media produces new facts that disprove the narrative, the facts fall flat against the power of illusory truth combined with the narrative fallacy.

Before moving on, it's worth mentioning one additional and significant story that Trump tells again and again: the story of himself as a victim. This persecution narrative has served him well. Whenever a critic questions his lies or objects to his policies, rather than defend the facts of the issue, he shifts the narrative to focus on the "haters." Philip Rucker, White House bureau chief for the *Washington Post*, wrote an article about this titled "The president as the persecuted: Donald Trump's strategy of self-victimization" (June 4, 2018). Rucker writes:

> Unfair is one of his [Trump's] favorite words, and he has used it in 69 tweets. He calls the federal investigation into Russian interference in the 2016 presidential election a rigged witch hunt. He accuses the FBI of infiltrating his campaign with spies. He insists the media is running a sophisticated disinformation operation to discredit him...In President Trump's telling, which can often be more imaginary than real, he is a victim—a long-suffering, tormented victim.

Does Trump's strategy work? One indication is a June 2017 online poll by the conservative *Washington Times* newspaper. The poll asked a simple question: "Is Donald Trump the victim of a media witch hunt?" Of the approximately 11,000 readers who responded, 84 percent said "yes." (Of course, this self-selective poll most likely attracted Trump supporters, and is not the same as a random-sample statistical analysis.)

The Illusory Truth Effect Around the Globe

Trump's actions are a case study in how post-truth politicians around the globe have exploited the illusory truth effect for their own gain.

Vladimir Putin claimed multiple times that protesters against his authoritarian-government style in Russia were paid to do so, a strategy aimed to delegitimize them. During his December 15, 2011 annual televised question-and-answer session, he said the following about the widespread protests that followed the parliamentary elections, which international observers widely condemned as rigged: "I know that students were paid some money" to protest. He also attributed such payments to foreign powers, and placed blame on then-Secretary of State Hillary Clinton for these actions, as part of supposed American efforts to weaken Russia. Putin provided no evidence to support his oft-repeated claims, and the state-controlled media in Russia, unsurprisingly, did not challenge his assertions.

Similarly, the Vote Leave campaign in the UK Brexit referendum falsely claimed that the UK was sending £350 million per week to the European Union, and that this money could instead go to the UK National Health Service if the Vote Leave campaign won. This claim played a vital role in the Vote Leave message. It was painted on the side of the Vote Leave campaign bus. The political motivation behind this lie was a desire to convince voters that leaving the EU would enable the country to spend more of its money domestically, especially on health care. Britain's statistics watchdog, the UK Statistics Authority, made a public statement revealing that the Vote Leave campaign was "misleading and undermines trust in official statistics" with their false claim. The strong rebuke was reported in numerous media venues, but the Vote Leave campaign continued to repeat the lie—until after they won the referendum. Shortly after that, Vote Leave leaders backed away from the claim. Nigel Farage, one of the most prominent leaders of the campaign and leader of the UK Independence Party, gave an interview on *Good Morning Britain* immediately after the vote, where he said that promising to spend that money on the National Health Service "was one of the mistakes that I think the Leave campaign made."

Yet in the run-up to the final Brexit decision, a study released

Fig. 3.1 From Vote Leave's Facebook page, February 2019

in October 2018 by King's College London found that 42 percent of respondents still believed the claim, while just 36 percent thought it was false and 22 percent were unsure. As of February, 2019, the Vote Leave Facebook page still leads with the lie (see Figure 3.1).

British citizens who were motivated to vote for Brexit because they wanted increased funding for health care will be sorely disappointed when it never materializes. In this case, counting the painful economic costs of falling for the illusory truth effect, and determining not to fall for it again, is the only silver lining in the bleak Brexit cloud.

In conclusion, the way that Donald Trump and other politicians from around the globe have used repetition to convince citizens that lies are true makes clear the devastating power of the illusory truth effect. Democracies around the world are vulnerable to post-truth politicians who will learn from the success of Trump, Putin and the Vote Leave campaign and will exploit the illusory truth effect to achieve their goals and corrode their democracies. Many citizens who vote for these politicians will likely come to regret their decisions.

How Can We Fight the Illusory Truth Effect in Politics?

In Chapter 2 I invited you to think of any post-truth politician as being like a magician. One who uses the illusory truth effect as effectively as Trump could be equated to the Wizard of Oz. Recognize that creating powerful illusions is the trick of the post-truth politician's trade. This will put you in the mindset of appropriate skepticism. Then when you see them in action you will be alert for the illusion of truth. In the movie *The Wizard of Oz*, Dorothy and her companions are dazzled and terrified by the wizard's spectral, gigantic, floating head, the smoke and fire, the booming voice. Dorothy's dog pulls aside a curtain to reveal a little old man at the side of the hall pulling levers and speaking into a microphone. "Pay no attention to the man behind the curtain!" booms the giant head. But the illusion has been punctured. This is what we have to do. Pull the curtain aside and puncture the illusion. CNBC used exactly this analogy in a story on Trump's first 100 days of government ("Pay attention to the man behind the curtain: Trump is no wizard of government," CNBC, April 28, 2017).

But how do we pull the curtain aside, especially given that to some extent we depend on our political leaders to give us information that is not readily available? Here are five things you can do:

1. *Notice the repetition of claims without information.* This is the hallmark of any attempt to cast the illusion of truth. For example, after the 2016 election Trump repeatedly and falsely claimed that over 3 million people had voted illegally for Hillary Clinton, so actually he won the popular vote.

2. *Question why there is no information to back up the claim.* Simply ask yourself: if there were convincing information, wouldn't the politician use it? If Trump had possessed any evidence of voter fraud, wouldn't he have used it to make his case? In fact, Trump set up a White House Commission in 2017 to find evidence of voter fraud; it found no evidence. In January 2018 Trump disbanded the commission, while continuing to claim that voter fraud cost him the popular vote.

3. *Reverse the statement: what if the opposite were true?* Apply the following aphorism, known as *Hitchen's Razor*: "That which can be asserted without proof can be dismissed without proof." Like a razor, this simple statement shreds the curtain of illusory truth. When you hear a post-truth politician make a claim without evidence, say the opposite to yourself. For example, in the case of voter fraud above, you would say to yourself: "In the 2016 election, the votes

were counted accurately." Then ask if there is evidence to support this statement. In the voter fraud case, an Internet search will lead you to many studies, such as this one from the Brennan Center for Justice: "Studies Agree: Impersonation Fraud by Voters Very Rarely Happens." It is important to phrase the question neutrally. Don't say: "There was no voter fraud in the 2016 election." If you say that, you actually keep the false claim of fraud alive in your mind, which feeds the illusory truth effect. It's like the old mental trick: "Don't think of a pink elephant." The rosy pachyderm appears despite all efforts to keep it out of your mind.

4. *Ask: if the claim were a lie, how would it benefit the liar?* Having shredded the curtain, ask whether or not the wizard frantically working the levers stands to benefit from you believing the lie. For example, the 2016 election results showed that Clinton received 2.87 million more votes than Trump, a margin of 2.1 percent. This number clearly undermined any claim for a popular mandate for Trump's new presidency. He stood to gain a lot by creating the illusion of massive voter fraud. This step is important, because it helps you connect the lie with the purposeful intent to deceive. In our personal lives, when we realize someone lied to us like this, we typically have a strong emotional reaction of disgust or aversion. The emotion protects us from naively trusting the liar in the future. You could think of this final step as like a tearing down of the wizard's curtain. From this point on, you will be watching whenever he or she works the levers.

5. *Tell others what you have discovered.* Take it upon yourself to share with others how you were able to pull the curtain aside. As the public gets better informed about the illusory truth effect, post-truth politicians will feel the cost every time they are exposed.

A word of caution: remember, the illusory truth effect is powerful and it works on your unconscious "gut level" thinking. It takes persistent effort in order to think through each false claim. Post-truth politicians like Trump are masters at implanting a false idea that shapes how your mind views the world. Like participants in the kilt-or-sari experiment, the illusory truth effect can too easily make you question your confidence about reality. As a test, using the scale of 1–5, from strongly disagree to strongly agree, check these claims of Donald Trump:

- Criminals form a large proportion of illegal migrants crossing the southern US border.
- Iran violated its nuclear treaty and is currently developing nuclear weapons.
- Climate change may not be human-caused, and the climate may change back.
- The United States pays 70 percent or more of the costs for NATO—more than its fair share.

If you rated anything higher than a 1, then you are not aligned with the majority of experts, and most likely a victim of one of Trump's illusory truth effects. Granted, in the Iran case, there are prominent voices such as John Bolton who consider Iran a real threat. But the January 2019 combined US intelligence assessment stated Iran was not developing nuclear weapons. So, ask yourself how probable it is that your intuitive gut feeling is better than the US intelligence agencies investigation. The NATO case, however, leads us to one important variation on the illusory truth effect that must be covered.

Paltering: Using the Truth to Cover a Lie
A quarter can block out the sun. Just close one eye and hold the coin to the sky, the right distance from the other eye. In the same way, skillful liars can use a small truth to cover a big lie.

The term for this is *paltering,* and according to a *Harvard Business Review* article from October 2016, this kind of lying is common in business. Certainly, it is practiced in politics to enhance the illusory truth effect. An example is Trump's NATO claim, which he stated explicitly at a press conference after a NATO summit in Brussels, on Thursday, July 12, 2018. According to a *Politico* article published that day, he said: "The United States was paying for anywhere from 70 to 90 percent of (NATO), depending on the way you calculate." That sounds like a fact, right? NATO's 2017 budget report shows total defense spending of all NATO members at about $957 billion. The United States spent about $686 billion in total. That's about 72 percent of the total. But what the article points out is that the vast majority of US defense spending is *not* spent on NATO-related costs but on other priorities; for example, aircraft carriers in the Pacific, troops in Afghanistan, supporting the Pentagon, humanitarian disaster relief around the globe. There's no way to figure out exactly what percentage of the military budget goes toward the protection of Europe, but it's clearly significantly less than 70 percent. NATO does have a cost-sharing arrangement with its members to cover common expenses, such as staff, equipment, and certain defenses based in Europe. The US, as the largest economy, pays 22 percent of those joint costs ($550 million for 2017). Of course, you will never hear Trump use that 22 percentage to argue America pays more than its fair share for NATO. Instead, he has successfully anchored us on a real-but-misleading 70 percent figure that is the wrong one to apply to NATO.

Naturally, it is easier to practice these defenses from the illusory truth effect against politicians who hold positions or represent parties you oppose. You already have some initial skepticism toward their claims, so their attempts to appeal to your emotions will more likely fall flat. To become a powerful pro-truth advocate, learn to practice these techniques with the politicians you favor. Listen critically, especially when they wrap strong emotions around claims without evidence. If you have the courage to expose the illusory truth from your own side, you not only strengthen your resilience against lies; ultimately you will make the party that you support stronger too, by discouraging lies and promoting truth.

Important Terms Referenced in This Chapter

Cognitive biases: problematic thinking patterns that can easily lead us into error.

Illusory truth effect: a mental error that causes us to perceive something to be true when we hear it repeated frequently and persistently, regardless of whether it is objectively true, or whether or not we are presented with evidence supporting it.

Processing fluency: the more comfortable we become with a statement through hearing it repeatedly, the more truthful it seems to us on a gut level.

Narrative fallacy: our tendency to want to fit whatever information we have available into a story that makes intuitive sense to us.

Availability heuristic: a mental shortcut that inclines us to rely on immediate examples that come to mind when evaluating a specific topic, concept, method, or decision.

Primacy effect: when presented with a lot of information, we tend to remember *best* what we are exposed to *first*.

Anchoring: the tendency to rely too heavily on an initial piece of information (the "anchor") when making decisions. Once we make an initial judgment about what something means, we tend to get fixed on it, and it's hard to change our minds.

Hitchen's Razor: an aphorism useful for resisting claims made without evidence: "That which can be asserted without proof can be dismissed without proof."

Paltering: using a small truth to cover a big lie.

Chapter 4

The Decline of Mainstream Media's Influence

"How the heck can voters think Donald Trump is more honest than Hillary Clinton?" was the headline of a November 2, 2016 article in the *Washington Post*'s "The Fix," one of the most prominent political columns in the US, written by Chris Cillizza. In the column, Cillizza goes over a number of lies told by Trump, such as his false claim of opposing the war in Iraq from the start, or the lies about seeing thousands of Muslims cheering on rooftops in New Jersey on September 11, 2001. He then describes how the well-regarded fact-checking column of the *Washington Post* gave Trump a rating of Four Pinocchios or "totally false" on 63 percent of the 91 Trump statements checked by the column. By comparison, most candidates get between 10 and 20 percent of their checked statements rated as Four Pinocchios, and Clinton fell right in the middle, with 14.2 percent. Cillizza goes on to express confusion and concern that the *Washington Post*–ABC News tracking poll that came out just before the article, surveying likely voters on October 30–31, showed that respondents saw Trump as more trustworthy and honest than Clinton by an eight-point margin (see Figure 4.1).

The problem, according to Cillizza, stems from people's mistaken perceptions of Trump as more honest than Clinton due to the candidates' communication styles. Cillizza at the same time defends the reporting of mainstream newspapers, TV networks, and radio. Cillizza wrote that while it's easy to scapegoat mainstream media for failing to fact-check and call out Trump's lies, the media actually do so quite frequently. To quote Cillizza, "The problem here isn't the media. The problem is that people stick very hard to their own preconceived notions—

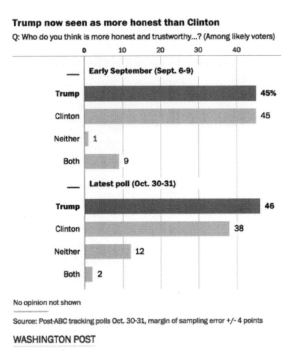

Trump now seen as more honest than Clinton

Q: Who do you think is more honest and trustworthy...? (Among likely voters)

Early September (Sept. 6-9)

- Trump: 45%
- Clinton: 45
- Neither: 1
- Both: 9

Latest poll (Oct. 30-31)

- Trump: 46
- Clinton: 38
- Neither: 12
- Both: 2

No opinion not shown

Source: Post-ABC tracking polls Oct. 30-31, margin of sampling error +/- 4 points

WASHINGTON POST

Fig. 4.1 Poll results from *Washington Post*–ABC News tracking poll on October 30–31, 2016 (image courtesy of the *Washington Post*'s "The Fix," November 2, 2016)

evidence to the contrary be damned." He goes on to nuance this statement by slamming new media sources: "One place where the media can be blamed is in the rise of partisan media outlets that offer confirmation bias galore to people who see the world through a particular partisan lens."

Cillizza's response to Trump is typical of most mainstream media commentary on the matter of Trump's and Clinton's honesty, and other qualities needed for a presidential candidate. No wonder that Trump received fewer endorsements by major newspapers than any major party candidate in American history. Just 2 regional newspapers—the *Las Vegas Review-Journal* and the *Florida Times-Union*—endorsed Trump, compared to Clinton's 57, according to the American Presidency Project. Moreover,

Clinton received endorsements from newspapers that generally endorse Republican candidates, such as the *Dallas Morning News*, the *Arizona Republic*, the *San Diego Union-Tribune*, the *Cincinnati Enquirer*, the *Houston Chronicle*, and the *Columbus Dispatch*. Other newspapers, such as *USA Today*, asked their readers to vote for anyone but Trump. In fact, the Libertarian candidate, Gary Johnson, received twice as many endorsements from major newspapers as did Trump.

In these endorsements, Trump's prolific lies served as one of the biggest issues determining the anti-Trump bent of the newspaper editorial boards. Yet such articles still had not changed people's perceptions of Trump being more honest than Clinton on the eve of the election, as the *Washington Post*–ABC News tracking poll (Fig. 4.1) showed. Neither did all of the newspaper endorsements stop Trump from being elected president, though they might have made a dent in Trump's support.

What explains this apparent inability of the mainstream media to make a sufficient impact on the electorate's beliefs and actions? What is the tie-in to the broader context of transformations in mainstream media and our society as a whole? And is Trump really all that different in the extent and nature of his lies than Clinton or other politicians?

Is Trump Really Different from Other Politicians?

We'll start with the last question first. Certainly, plenty of presidents have lied in the past. "I did not have sexual relations with that woman, Miss Lewinsky," according to Bill Clinton's statement in January 1998. Sure you didn't, Clinton—tell us another one. "If you like your health care plan, you can keep it." No we can't, Barack Obama. That statement was rated as "Lie of the Year" by *PolitiFact* for 2013. To look back a little farther in history, Lyndon Johnson interrupted TV broadcasts on August 4, 1964, to make the false claim that two US ships in the Gulf of Tonkin had come under unprovoked attack in international waters by North Vietnam. This lie paved the path for the Vietnam war, according to Edwin Moïse's 1996 *Tonkin Gulf and the Escalation of the Vietnam War*.

Republican presidents lied, too. "The Iraq regime continues to possess and conceal some of the most lethal weapons ever devised," according to George W. Bush on March 18, 2003, the day before he took military action in Iraq. However, a study by the Center for Public Integrity and its affiliated group, the Fund for Independence in Journalism, found that, "The Bush administration led the nation to war on the basis of erroneous information that it methodically propagated." The study identified 935 separate false statements by the administration, according to Charles Lewis's 2014 book, *935 Lies: The Future of Truth and the Decline of America's Moral Integrity*. Remember too: Ronald Reagan lied about the Iran–Contra affair. On November 13, 1986 he said he did not trade arms for hostages (he did). Richard Nixon is perhaps the most glaring example of a president who lied, in his case to cover up the criminal efforts of his political staff to wiretap political opponents in the infamous Watergate scandal. "I am not a crook," said Nixon (he was).

Nonetheless, when called out by the media, experts, and investigations, these political figures have generally backtracked on their deceptions. On November 7, 2013, Obama apologized for his deceptive statements about people being able to keep their plan. In August 1998, Bill Clinton stated: "I know that my public comments and my silence about this matter gave a false impression. I misled people, including even my wife." On March 4, 1987, Reagan apologized that "what began as a strategic opening to Iran deteriorated, in its implementation, into trading arms for hostages." Bush stated in a December 1, 2008 interview with Charlie Gibson on ABC News that the "biggest regret of all the presidency" was incorrect intelligence that Iraqi President Saddam Hussein had weapons of mass destruction. Nixon had to resign under threat of impeachment when his cover-up was publicized.

Moreover, these leaders kept their lies within certain proportions. As mentioned above, most politicians get Four Pinocchios from the *Washington Post* Fact Checker column between 10 and 20 percent of the time. Trump got Four Pinocchios 63 percent of the time, over four times as much as the average politician (see Figure 4.2).

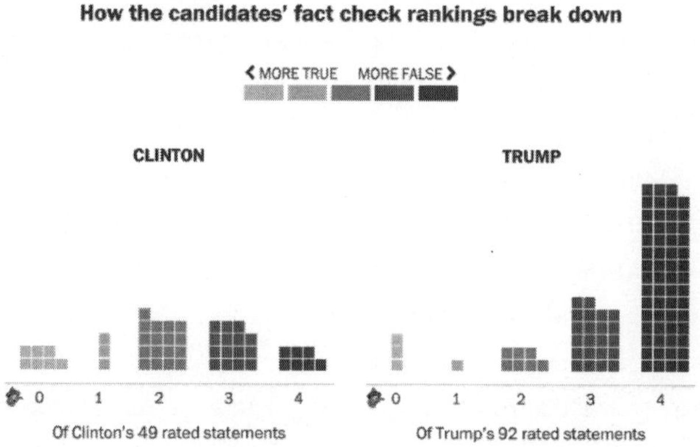

How the candidates' fact check rankings break down

<MORE TRUE   MORE FALSE >

Fig. 4.2 The *Washington Post* Fact Checker comparison of Clinton and Trump on November 3, 2016 (courtesy of the Washington Post https://www.washingtonpost.com/graphics/politics/2016-election/fact-checker/)

Other fact-checkers report similar figures. For example, Politifact.org's Truth-O-Meter comparison from November 3, 2016 rated Clinton as having made 72 fully "True" statements compared to Trump's 16; 29 "False" statements compared to Trump's 127; and 7 blatantly deceptive or "Pants on Fire" statements, compared to Trump's 64. The overall percentage of "True" statements for Clinton is 24.5 percent and "Pants on Fire" is 2.3 percent, and for Trump the figures are 4.1 percent "True" and 16.5 percent "Pants on Fire." The number of "Pants on Fire" for Trump is particularly telling, as is the number of Four Pinocchios for Trump compared to Clinton. Trump not only lies more often, but his lies are generally further from the truth than those of other politicians. Before suspecting partisan bias, let's remember that the *Washington Post* Fact Checker column revealed Clinton's lie about landing in Bosnia under sniper fire, and *PolitiFact* labeled Obama's promise that people can keep their plan the biggest lie of the year in 2013.

Trump's lies are not simply a matter of much bigger quantity: they are on a whole different level of *quality*. By contrast to other prominent politicians, when Trump is called out on his deceptive statements by the media, he attacks the credibility of reporters instead of backing down like previous presidents. For instance, on June 13, 2016, he revoked the press credentials of the well-known and highly reputable *Washington Post*, calling the newspaper "phony and dishonest." Trump's statement on revoking the credentials read: "I am no fan of President Obama, but to show you how dishonest the phony *Washington Post* is, they wrote, 'Donald Trump suggests President Obama was involved with Orlando shooting' as their headline. Sad!" Trump referred to the June 12, 2016 shooting in Pulse, a gay Orlando nightclub, an act that combined elements of a terrorist attack and a hate crime, as the shooter's motivations mixed anti-LGBTQ sentiments with Muslim beliefs.

Yet did the *Washington Post* truly get it wrong? Let's examine Trump's response on Fox News after the shooting: "Look, we're led by a man that either is not tough, not smart, or he's got something else in mind. And the something else in mind— you know, people can't believe it." To any reasonable external observer, the "something else in mind" that people "can't believe" is a pretty clear suggestion of then-President Obama's involvement with the shooting, despite any evidence. Such messages appeal well to the conservative-leaning audience of Fox News. Yet when the *Washington Post* called out Trump for his deceptive suggestion, he labeled the newspaper dishonest and revoked its credentials.

Speaking at an August 9, 2016 rally in Wilmington, North Carolina, Trump made a statement about what would happen if Clinton were elected president and chose a Supreme Court nominee whose interpretation of the Second Amendment's "right to bear arms" allowed for tighter gun regulations: "If she gets to pick her judges, nothing you can do, folks. Although the Second Amendment people, maybe there is. I don't know." In response, mainstream media called out Trump for his hinting that gun-rights supporters could shoot Clinton if she got elected to prevent her from appointing judges who would tighten gun laws. For instance, *Esquire* ran a piece by Charles Pierce with the headline "The Moment You Realize Trump Finally Crossed the Line," asking whether Trump's suggestion for Clinton to be shot was the moment when Trump crossed the line that would make him unelectable.

Certainly, Pierce was wrong in Trump being unelectable after that statement, but Pierce's analysis of Trump's statement as suggestive of assassination reflects what any reasonable, objective observer would say. Many other mainstream media outlets had similar interpretations. Yet the Trump campaign sent an email in response to this situation entitled "Trump Campaign Statement on Dishonest Media," which explained Trump's statement as follows: "It's called the power of unification—2nd Amendment people have amazing spirit and are tremendously unified, which gives them great political power. And this year, they will be voting in record numbers, and it won't be for Hillary Clinton, it will be for Donald Trump." Of course, Trump's campaign response did not explain how Second Amendment people voting in record numbers would stop Clinton from picking Supreme Court judges who would tighten gun-control laws if she did get elected—the controversial part of Trump's statement at the rally. Since voting would not stop her from doing so if she was already elected, and since the Second Amendment is about gun rights, the hint of assassination is obvious to any unbiased observer.

Trump is lying when he attacks the media for being dishonest in highlighting this hint.

Another example: When asked by the moderator in his third presidential debate with Clinton whether he would accept the 2016 presidential election results—a question responding to Trump's claims of mainstream voter fraud and election rigging—Trump responded: the "media is so dishonest and so corrupt and the pile-on is so amazing." He went on to say that the election system is rigged as a whole, and singled out the *New York Times* in particular for its reporting on the matter. Trump's statements proved so problematic that the Republican House Speaker Paul Ryan decided he had to step in, and on October 15, 2016 he commented that "Our democracy relies on confidence in election results, and the speaker is fully confident the states will carry out this election with integrity."

After the election, many hoped Trump would abandon his strategy of accusing the media of dishonesty when they called him out on his lies. Not so. As an example, after winning the Electoral College vote and losing the popular vote by nearly 3 million, Trump claimed in a November 17, 2016 tweet: "I won the popular vote if you deduct the millions of people who voted illegally." He was referring to non-mainstream, conservative news sources with a reputation for frequent false statement, which claimed millions of undocumented immigrants voted illegally in the election. However, neither he nor the non-mainstream conservative news offered any evidence. Trump received a great deal of criticism for making such damaging and controversial claims without proof. Evaluating this claim, prominent fact-checkers found that it had no substance: Snopes. com published an article stating that "Zero evidence has been put forth to support the widely parroted claim that 3 million 'illegal aliens' voted in the 2016 presidential election." David Becker, the Executive Director of the Center for Election Innovation & Research, stated that "You're more likely to get eaten by a shark that simultaneously gets hit by lightning than to find a noncitizen voting."

Again, Trump doubled down. He used his presidential powers to convene a task force led by Vice President Mike Pence to investigate this supposed voter fraud, announced on February 5, 2017. Factcheck.org published in response a piece entitled "More Trump Deception on Voter Fraud." Some prominent Republicans came forward again to contradict Trump, for instance Senate Majority Leader Mitch McConnell: "There's no evidence that [voter fraud] occurred in such a significant number that would have changed the presidential election, and I don't think we ought to spend any federal money investigating that." Indeed, President Trump's own legal team filed a complaint in Pennsylvania stating, "There is no evidence—or even an allegation—that any tampering with Pennsylvania's voting systems occurred." Still, Trump kept bashing any media figures or experts who went against his false claims of voter fraud.

In summary, yes, Trump has taken political deception to a whole new level. Analysis of his speeches tends to indicate that he lies 3–6 times more than other politicians, and that these lies are more intense (as seen from the ratings of Four Pinocchios and "Pants on Fire"). Additionally, when caught in a lie by mainstream media with evidence of deception that would be convincing to any reasonable objective observer, Trump doubles down and attacks the media as dishonest and crooked. This combination of quantity and quality makes Trump substantively more deceitful than any modern US president, deserving of the label, "post-truth politician."

Trump's Anti-Media Outbursts: Tactics or Strategy?

Based on the preceding section, we might suppose that Trump is simply using the tactic of slamming the mainstream media to avoid acknowledging his lies. However, evidence suggests that this tactic is part of a broader strategy to undermine the role of the mainstream media in our political system. For example, we can see that Trump does not limit his tactic of disparaging the media to specific instances of vital political significance. When Ben Terris, a well-known reporter for the *Washington Post*, wrote a story about Trump cheating at golf (September 4, 2015), Trump attacked him as a "totally dishonest reporter, a real creep." Trump provided no refutation of the solid facts offered by Terris, who spoke with many credible people who played golf with Trump, such as Mark Mulvoy, former managing editor of *Sports Illustrated*. According to Mulvoy, after a quick break in a golf game with Trump due to rain, they both came out to the green, and a ball appeared 10 feet away from the hole, which Trump claimed was his. Mulvoy stated, "Donald, give me a f—ing break…You've been hacking away in the . . . weeds all day. You do not lie there." Trump responded, "Ahh, the guys I play with cheat all the time…I have to cheat just to keep up with them."

This is far from the only time that Trump responded in such an aggressive and extreme manner to a well-sourced, solidly investigated story that had minor political significance. Indeed, a leading conservative magazine, *National Review*, published a story on August 17, 2016 with the headline "Trump Has Cried Wolf Too Often on Media Bias." The right-leaning author notes that most media figures tend to lean left, and there are some legitimate causes for concern over reporting. Still, he criticizes Trump for going way over the top in claiming media bias, writing that whenever the media called Trump out for "making an offensive remark, he'd dishonestly claim that he was misquoted or taken out of context and that they were just out to get him." The author notes Trump's problematic claims "to have never said something that he was captured on video saying" or insisting "he was taken out of context when the context was clear and reported accurately" or denying "cold, hard facts presented to him by interviewers." As a result of this "overplaying of the media-bias card," it was likely that in the future, "legitimate examples of media malpractice" would be ignored.

Worse still, Trump has attacked the media as a whole without any specific news stories to provoke his ire. For instance, in a February 17, 2017 tweet, Trump stated that NBC, CNN, ABC, CBS, and the *New York Times* — all highly credible news sources — are "the enemy of the American People." He repeated this attack in a speech on February 24, 2017 at the Conservative Political Action Conference (CPAC), stating that much of the press "are the enemy of the people because they have no sources. They just make them up when there are none." As someone who emigrated from the Republic of Moldova, which used to be part of the former Soviet Union before its independence in 1991, this phrase had strong echoes for me. The phrase "enemy of the people" has been a staple of authoritarian dictators for decades, most notably Joseph Stalin, as described in Benedikt Sarnov's 2002 book. The phrase went out of use under Nikita Khrushchev, who denounced it in a 1956 speech to the Soviet Communist Party, where he stated that the "formula 'enemy of the people' was specifically introduced for the purpose of physically annihilating such individuals" (as described in Edward Crankshaw's 2011 *Khrushchev*). While we do not know whether Trump knew the history of this "formula" when he first used it, it's hard to imagine his staff did not alert him to the multitude of news stories that soon emerged about the phrase. The fact that he has used it repeatedly since then raises grave concerns over his intentions toward the media.

The day after the CPAC speech, Trump chose to take the unprecedented step of barring several specific news organizations from an off-camera White House briefing, including CNN, the *New York Times*, *Politico*, *BuzzFeed News*, *The Guardian*, the BBC, and others. The Associated Press and *Time* chose to boycott the briefing despite being invited, due to the exclusion. Commenting on this matter, Dean Baquet, the executive editor of the *New York*

Times, said: "Nothing like this has ever happened at the White House in our long history of covering multiple administrations of different parties."

Trump may go even further. About a year before the CPAC speech, on February 26, 2016, at a rally in Fort Worth, Texas, Trump indicated that when elected he would "open up our libel laws so when...the *New York Times* writes a hit piece, which is a total disgrace, or when the *Washington Post*, which is there for other reasons, writes a hit piece, we can sue them and win money." How could Trump orchestrate a change in libel laws? In February 2019, conservative Supreme Court Justice Clarence Thomas seemed to echo Trump's sentiment, publicly urging the Court to reconsider a landmark 1964 ruling that made it harder for public figures to sue the media for defamation ("Justice Thomas assails landmark U.S. libel ruling that protects media," *Reuters*, February 19, 2019).

Trump and Game Theory: "Working the Refs"

Why does Trump pursue a systematic, strategic approach of destroying the legitimacy of the media in our political system? From the perspective of game theory—the study of conflict and cooperation between rational agents in any given system—politics can be considered a large, multipolar game with many different agents, a perspective explored in James Morrow's 1994 book on this topic. From this game-theory perspective, although the mainstream media have certain biases, overall, they serve the function of the referees. After all, the media themselves cannot "win" the political power game. This game-theory view aligns with the Enlightenment-era conception of the press as the Fourth Estate of our public sphere, serving as a powerful force for mediating between the different political actors in this system.

How does this look in practice? Imagine Democrat Denisha facing off against Republican Rhonda in a race for mayor. Denisha accuses Rhonda of unethical hiring practices at her insurance firm, while Rhonda accuses Denisha—the current mayor—of taking bribes from a contractor in return for hiring him to renovate the town hall. Naturally, both deny the accusations leveled against them. Who is lying—Denisha, Rhonda, or both? I don't know, and neither do you. While I would like to know, as this would help determine my choice of who to vote for, I will not take the time to go to Rhonda's insurance firm and evaluate the hiring practices. Neither will I take the time to look at all the factors involved in the hiring decision for the town hall renovation. You and I have better ways of spending our time.

Instead, we as a society outsource that role to the media. It is the job of investigative reporters to find out who is telling the truth by examining the claims of each politician, and reporting them to us in the form of a newspaper, TV or radio broadcast, or online article. We pay their salaries to get us this information when we buy print newspapers, subscribe to digital newspapers and cable news programs, or in the case of nonprofits, donate to support their work. We also pay for their reporting by paying attention to advertisements, the vehicle that corporations and other entities use to deliver their messages to us. In exchange for these payments, we get an evaluation by a professional journalist of whether Denisha or Rhonda lied, and the circumstances surrounding the deception.

If there were no media, we would not be able to tell who lied. The game would not have referees. Instead, it would be a free-for-all, since we would not know who is telling the truth. From that game-theory perspective, it would not be rational to orient toward the truth if one's goal is to win power through attracting voters. Instead, it would be most effective to make statements that are most likely to appeal to voters and get votes. Truth-telling, as described in Colin Camerer's 2003 book, is an optimal game-theory strategy only when there are specific constraints that provide incentives for truth-telling, or punishments for lying. The media provides these incentives and punishments to tell the truth and avoid lies.

In other words: without a strong media, the best liars win.

Trump's attacks on the media echo those of Richard Nixon. As described in a 2016 article by Christopher Cimaglio and a 2010 book by Mark Feldstein, Nixon had Vice President Spiro Agnew lead a deliberate anti-media campaign. Agnew gave a harshly worded speech criticizing the supposed elite journalists who held a "concentration of power over American public opinion unknown in history." Nixon also attacked individual news sources. He told his staff to give the *Washington Post* "damnable, damnable problems" getting its Federal Communications Commission (FCC) licenses renewed and to damage the newspaper's real estate investments. Nixon tried to make it a felony for reporters to get leaked information and ordered illegal wiretaps of reporters he perceived as unfriendly to him. Nixon clearly knew what he was up to: he termed these strategies "working the refs," as in the referees of the political game. Nixon's deliberate strategies to undermine the media as referees and position himself as the victim of media bias helped fuel the subsequent conservative criticism of the media as inherently liberal and biased against conservatives.

Trump took his anti-media campaign to a whole new level. Like Nixon, he portrays himself as a victim of media bias. Unlike Nixon, Trump challenges the media on simple facts that are clearly true to any reasonable observer, and denies his own statements even when they are caught on video. Trump often does not offer evidence to support his statements, instead relying on his own personal authority and setting himself up as the sole voice of the truth for his supporters. He is pursuing a game-theory strategy aligned with that of a player who is trying to destroy the referees so that he can use lies and deception to win power.

Unfortunately, Trump's tactics proved all too effective in the

2016 US presidential election. Gallup conducts an annual survey about how much Americans trust the mainstream media. The survey asks one question: "How much trust and confidence do you have in the mainstream media when it comes to reporting the news fully, accurately, and fairly—a great deal, a fair amount, not very much, or none at all?" Gallup breaks down the results by party lines, enabling us to evaluate trends in public trust in the media. The poll conducted in early September 2016, and published on Gallup's site with the headline "Americans' Trust in Mass Media Sinks to New Low," describes how overall trust in the media has dropped to 32 percent, from 40 percent in September 2015. More than that, trust among Republicans has fallen by more than half, from 32 percent in September 2015 to 14 percent in September 2016. Gallup's own analysts suggest that this steep decline resulted from "Trump's sharp criticisms of the press," as well as similar criticism by other Republican leaders in the presidential election campaign.

Some may wonder whether other factors besides Trump's broadsides against journalists may be at play in declining

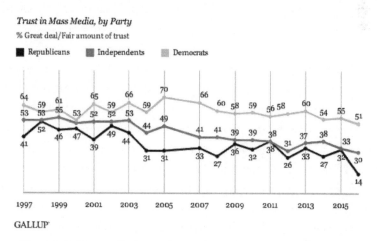

Fig. 4.3 Gallup poll chart of trust in mainstream media broken down by party lines (courtesy of Gallup, http://www.gallup.com/ poll/195542/americans-trust-mainstream-media-sinks-new-low.aspx)

Republican trust in the mainstream media. To address this question, we can compare the trust among Republicans in mainstream media for previous years (see Figure 4.3).

As the chart shows, in September 2013, Republicans expressed trust in the mainstream media at 33 percent, which went down slightly to 27 percent in September 2014 and up again to 32 percent in September 2015. This level has held fairly steady for over a decade, with minor fluctuations. Recent presidential election cycles—such as the highly competitive 2008 one or the less competitive 2012 one—have not resulted in major disturbances in Republican trust in the media. The most likely explanation for the sharp decline of trust in the mainstream media by Republicans from 2015 to 2016 is the effect of Trump's rhetoric.

Right-leaning media have reinforced Trump's anti-media message. According to the *Investor's Daily Business*, "The profound leftward ideological bias of the Big Media is the main reason why America now seems saturated with 'fake news.' Journalists, besotted with their own ideology, are no longer able to recognize their own bias" ("Media Bias: Pretty Much All of Journalism Now Leans Left, Study Shows," November 16, 2018).

Fox News ran a segment entitled "Rushing to Judgement," on February 21, 2019, in which host Sean Hannity declared: "According to the mainstream media, all Trump supporters are racist, sexist, homophobic, xenophobic, Islamophobic—we're all monsters." The segment was about stories the mainstream media had gotten wrong, specifically one about an alleged homophobic, racist hate crime against actor Jussie Smollett. When the story first broke, the media gushed outraged commentary—until police determined it was all a hoax staged by Smollett, and charged him with filing a false report (the charges were later dropped). Hannity, however, used deceptive hyperbole, exaggerating from a few isolated but valid incidents of the media rushing to judgment in order to discredit all mainstream reporting: "Time after time this mob get it wrong. The media and their friends on the left are always happy to besmirch, smear and slander anyone, as long as it fits into their divisive political narrative. Now, this has been the case for decades, but it has never been this bad." In a subsequent commentary he added, "Journalism in this country is dead." The implication of his remark is that mainstream media are so politically motivated that Fox viewers can no longer trust them as a source of objective news.

"Working the Refs" Around the Globe

Trump's actions bear a number of similarities to those pursued by another post-truth political leader, Vladimir Putin, in his early years in office (see Jonathan Becker's 2004 peer-reviewed article, "Lessons from Russia: a neo-authoritarian media system"). After achieving power first as Prime Minister in 1999 and then President in 2000, Putin quickly moved to attack the media. An article published in 2000 in the opposition newspaper *Kommersant* prior to Putin's election, entitled "The Reform of the Administration of the President of the Russian Federation," included apparent leaks of Putin's media plans. He wanted to impose central government control over the mass media with the goal of suppressing criticism of the government and painting Putin and his administration in a favorable light, while denigrating the opposition.

Putin's methods included not simply spin and lying, but also imposing financial pressure on the media for criticizing the government, a sentiment echoed by Trump's suggestion of libel laws. Putin's administration acted on these plans quickly, with the government in 2000–2001 taking control over the three federal TV channels through buyouts, while closing others through imposing fines. Similar actions occurred for major newspapers. Moreover, the plans called for surveillance of journalists perceived as critical of Putin. The government implemented these plans with increasing harassment, violence, and murder of reporters. In March 2019, the Russian parliament passed a new law allowing courts to jail people for online "disrespect" of government or state officials, including Putin. No wonder freedom of the press in Russia, as rated by Freedom House, steadily grew worse. It went from a score of 60 (0 best, 100 worst) in 2002, the first year for which a rating is available, to 66 in 2003, 67 in 2004, 72 in 2006, and 83 in 2016. By comparison, the United States is at 21, while Afghanistan is at 62, Libya is at 76, and Iraq is at 71—all better than Russia.

We see similar developments at an earlier stage in Turkey, under the leadership of Recep Tayyip Erdogan. Freedom House scores for media freedom in Turkey fell rapidly as Erdogan consolidated power in this formerly democratic country, from 54 in 2010, to 62 in 2013, to 71 in 2016. Erdogan's administration uses anti-terrorism laws to arrest journalists and censor and close down media outlets. Turkey had more journalists imprisoned than in any other country in the world in 2012 according to Freedom House and the Committee to Protect Journalists (CPJ). The government pressured media outlets to fire journalists who covered anti-government protests in Gezi Park in Istanbul in May 2013. The year after that, Erdogan combined continued harsh criticism of journalists, in the style of Trump, with passing new laws that enabled the government to block more websites and also surveil journalists. In 2015, the government took over the prominent media company Koza Ipek Holding, and imposed more bureaucratic burdens for journalistic accreditation to place journalists under further state authority. These transformations paved the way for Erdogan to seize more political power, transforming the country from a democratic nation to one characterized by growing authoritarianism. On April 16, 2017, Erdogan's administration pushed through a referendum by popular vote to transform the country's parliamentary system into one with an extremely powerful executive presidency. Many experts on Turkey call it the ending of Turkish democracy. The referendum has been widely marred by reports of vote rigging, physical assaults on opposition figures, and other forms of election fraud. However, with the state's increased control over the media, these facts are not known to many Turkish citizens. In an interview with CNN released on April 18, 2017, under the title "Erdogan insists Turkey reforms don't make him a dictator," he stated—in a clear example of post-truth rhetoric—that the referendum did not represent "a step towards dictatorship." Many democratic countries condemned the referendum and the electoral fraud accompanying it, as well as Turkey's broader slide into authoritarianism. The US State Department issued a statement criticizing the referendum, highlighting the many voting irregularities.

However, in an unfortunate case of mixed messages, Trump called Erdogan to congratulate him on his victory, without mentioning any of the electoral problems or the slide toward dictatorship. Trump also expressed supporting words toward Putin, for instance praising Putin's "strong control over a country" in a televised forum with the *Today Show*'s Matt Lauer. Additionally, when asked by former GOP congressman and MSNBC host Joe Scarborough what he thought of Putin killing journalists who don't agree with him, Trump sidestepped the question, saying, "I think that our country does plenty of killing, too, Joe."

Given Trump's praise and support for Erdogan and Putin, and the similarity of their post-truth tactics and media attacks, we should have grave concerns for the future of the US. I am not saying Trump will definitely take this path. He may change his stripes. He may stop calling the media "enemies of the people." Still, Trump's actions to date are similar to those of other leaders who put their nations on the path to authoritarianism.

The Media Deserve Some Blame

Let me be clear: the US media is far from innocent in its own decline. Even before Trump, Gallup showed a clear decrease in American trust in the media. Starting in the low 50s in the late 1990s, trust in the media gradually fell through the 2000s to end in the low 40s in the mid-2010s, before Trump's intervention (see Fig. 4.3, above). According to Jonathan Ladd's 2011 book *Why Americans Hate the Media and How It Matters*, trust in the media was higher in the 1950s. The 1956 American National Election Study (ANES) found that only 27 percent of Americans believed newspapers were "unfair," and 66 believed them to be "fair," with 64 percent of Democrats and 78 percent of Republicans perceiving newspapers as "fair." What explains the other elements of declining mass media influence besides criticism from Trump?

Beginning with Nixon, the Republican Party has a history of launching anti-media attacks. This is fundamental to understanding the disparity in trust in the media between Republicans and Democrats. For instance, in 1997, 64 percent of Democrats had trust in the media and only 41 percent of Republicans trusted the media, with Independents slightly closer to Democrats at 53 percent. This gap of around 25 percent, while fluctuating over the two decades to 2016, remained relatively steady before Trump. Then in 2016 the gap of trust widened by over 50 percent, with Democrats at 51 percent and Republicans at 14 percent. Nonetheless, despite these political differences, we see trust among Democrats and Republicans alike decreasing in the media throughout this period. So, we need to consider six other factors besides Republican criticism of the media, factors internal to the media industry itself.

Declining Revenues Led to Lower Budgets for Investigative Journalism

One of the biggest problems comes from the budget cuts in mainstream media's investigative journalism in recent decades. To a large extent this has been driven by the rise of digital media. For example, a paper presented by James Hamilton at the Duke Conference on Nonprofit Media in 2009 reported that 2008 witnessed the disappearance of at least 15,970 newspaper jobs. Hamilton described how the cuts targeted investigative reporting most of all because of the expense associated with this area of reporting. He found that the number of full-time newspaper reporters covering state capitals decreased by 32 percent from 2003 to 2009. Over this same period, the membership rosters of Investigative Reporters and Editors fell from 5,391 to 3,695—more than 30 percent, according to a 2010 article by Mary Walton in the *American Journalism Review*. Walton's article describes a former investigative reporter at the *Palm Beach Post* whose coverage of corruption on a local level put three county commissioners and others in jail, but who left due to a staff reduction in 2008 from 300 to 170, as he was on the verge of investigating a fourth commissioner. When asked by Walton what happens when people like him vanish, the reporter said, "The bad guys get away with stuff." This research underscores how the deterioration in investigative reporting undermines trust in the mainstream media.

Concentration of Ownership

Another problem stems from media consolidation, well described in the 2009 *Media Ownership and Concentration in America* by Eli Noam. Already on the rise before the appearance of digital media, the Internet vastly accelerated media buyouts, along with the passage of the Telecommunications Act of 1996, which facilitated media cross-ownership. Due to this act and the financial pressure of online media, the number of major media-holding companies decreased from 10 in 1996 to 6 in 2005, as described in Ben Bagdikian's 2014 book. The number of radio station owners also decreased drastically, and their content has become much more standardized, as Anastasia Bednarski finds in a 2002 article. A piece by Dell Champlin and Janet Knoedler in the *Journal of Economic Issues* demonstrates that, as a result of media consolidation, news coverage has gone down both in quantity and quality, with the latter meaning that the reporting shifted more into the arena of "infotainment" and away from serious journalism. All of these factors undercut trust in the mainstream media.

Blurring the Boundary Between News Reporting and Opinion
More recently, the rise to prominence of opinion-driven reporting in certain mainstream media outlets has undermined the credibility of the journalistic profession. The code of ethics of the Society of Professional Journalists includes phrases such as: "Ethical journalism should be accurate and fair"; "Journalists should be honest and courageous"; "Take special care not to misrepresent or oversimplify"; "Never deliberately distort facts or context, including visual information"; "Label advocacy and commentary" and so on. These worthwhile values have been compromised by the recent rise of "an opinion-driven free-for-all news culture stripped of traditional editorial values of accuracy and fairness," according to Steven Barnett's 2012 article. Barnett goes on to state that "the news channel that has most exploited American television's freedom to be overtly partisan—Rupert Murdoch's Fox News Channel—has become renowned for undermining traditional tenets of truth-seeking in broadcast journalism."

While Fox has led the way, other channels have followed. In a *USA Today* article on November 3, 2006, "Cable rantings boost ratings," the author describes how such strategies, while first adopted by Fox, have since appeared elsewhere, for instance on MSNBC. Such opinion-driven reporting may boost ratings, as the *USA Today* article noted, but it takes away from the perception of journalists as referees, instead placing them as players in the political spin game.
False Equivalence

False equivalence is a mental error in which two completely opposing arguments appear to be logically equivalent when in fact they are not. Some reporters misinterpret "fair reporting" as if it means simply stating what different sources say about the issue, with no factual context. In cases where only one side of the story is actually correct, this practice undermines fairness, honesty, and accuracy. In short, it misleads. For instance, some reporters "balance" the views of climate scientists—whose findings clearly show human-caused climate change—with those of climate-change deniers, mostly funded by fossil fuel companies. Such false equivalence deceives readers by failing to highlight the fact that the scientific consensus for climate change is a remarkable 97 percent. Comedian John Oliver parodied such reporting on his show *Last Week Tonight*, in a mock debate pitting 3 climate deniers against 97 climate scientists crammed into a room. Herbert Gans's 2014 article in the *International Journal of Communication* describes how such false equivalence functions in the political arena, where journalists report on claims made by different politicians as though they are equally valid. This approach conveys a false impression to readers when one politician is less radical and another is more radical, as when comparing the claims of a Tea Party Republican and those of a moderate Democrat.

False equivalence grew especially problematic with Trump, as related by Victor Pickard in his 2017 piece, "Media failures in the Age of Trump." Many media venues, when covering Trump's exaggerated claims and outright lies, also spent a similar amount of time covering Clinton's lies, regardless of the evidence from reputable fact-checking websites that Clinton lied much less often and intensely than Trump. The audiences of these venues garnered the false impression that Clinton and Trump both lied very extensively, despite the reality of Clinton's deception being about average among politicians.

Deceptive Headlines

Writing misleading headlines is an unethical practice, according to the Society of Professional Journalists' code of ethics. Yet a 2009 study of headlines on health issues by Nikki Turner et al. analyzed 51 articles and found that 26 of them had inaccurate headlines and 6 were at least misleading when compared with the content of the article. That makes 61 percent deceptive headlines from the study. Deceptive headlines tend to be attention-grabbing and sensationalist, according to Ladd's 2011 book. They are designed to get people to buy the newspaper or click on an article. Why does this happen? In most newsrooms, the editor who writes the headline is a different person than the journalist who writes the story. Often that person has a lot of headlines to write, so they themselves don't read the whole articles, but just skim to find what they think is the main thrust, and then search for something attention grabbing. Two examples:

- "Woman Jailed for Baptizing Her Daughter in Violation of Court Order" (*Time Magazine*, February 17, 2018). The headline implies the court jailed a woman for her religious convictions. That's not what happened. In the midst of a custody battle, the mother had the baby christened without her Catholic ex-husband present, depriving him of the experience. The judge had specifically ordered her not to do this spiteful act, and punished her for defying the court order.
- "Cell phones ARE linked to cancer, landmark study finds: Results show 'clear evidence' of tumor growth after repeated exposure to radiation" (*Daily Mail* (UK), November 1, 2018). The article says the tests were done on rodents, at levels much higher than humans are exposed to.

A 2014 survey by the American Press Institute reported that only 41 percent of Americans go beyond simply skimming the headline. *That's six out of ten who only look at the headline.* Given this situation, we can see that most Americans would get the wrong impression from their exposure to news. Additionally, those who do read deeper and notice the headline is a distortion may feel less inclined to trust media reporting over all.

Here's a case in which sensational headlines seriously misled the public: Regardless of their political affiliation, most who follow politics in any depth easily dismissed Trump's series of Twitter accusations on March 4, 2017 that Barack Obama had ordered Trump Tower wiretapped before the 2016 election. Trump offered no evidence, but instead used inflammatory language such as calling Obama "sick" and "bad," and requested that Congress conduct an investigation into the Obama administration. A deluge of articles from AP News and many other media outlets covered the story, with headlines describing Trump's "startling allegation of abuse of power." The articles themselves reported the lack of evidence, and an analysis that the claims were highly improbable. The impact? Four days after the first tweet, a March 8, 2017 Rasmussen Reports poll showed 44 percent of respondents considered it likely the allegation was true. Even after multiple denials by the FBI and other federal agencies, and debunking by reputable fact-checkers such as Factcheck.org and *PolitiFact*, a CBS News poll on March 29, 2017 found that 47 percent of respondents thought that the US government had deliberately surveilled Trump Tower in the campaign.

Hyper-Focus on Extreme Emotion and Outrage

"If it bleeds it leads." A journalist I know at an international radio station told me this was the credo of every newsroom. The media relentlessly covers high-emotion stories: war, disaster, scandal, outrage. Why? Human nature. Bad news sells. We can't help but slow down and rubberneck when we pass an accident on the highway. Evolution has fine-tuned us to pay attention when bad things happen, whether the destruction is due to a tornado, a shark, or the self-inflicted wound of a philandering politician. The move to the 24-hour news cycle (a feature of the digital age) has supercharged this tendency, priming journalists to report on sensational bad news as quickly as possible, and thus putting pressure on them to rush their fact-checking of sources. This leaves the media especially vulnerable to politicians who take advantage of this tendency. They can make headlines easily by declaring a threat where there is none, by slandering an opponent without basis, or by making any false claim. So long as it is outrageous enough to trigger fear, anger, or disgust, the media will report it. They simply can't help themselves. They are like sharks that smell blood in the water and go into a feeding frenzy. The blood—the high emotion—seems to impair their judgment as they rush to get the story into print. Twitter has enabled politicians like Donald Trump to virtually hijack the nervous system of the mainstream media, feeding it regular jolts of outrage like a drug pusher dealing crack. Even when journalists know that the latest tweet is baseless, they are compelled to report it, and then pundits debate each false claim endlessly on cable TV. Even if baseless claims are corrected later in the article, as the illusory truth effect kicks in, the public more likely remembers the charge, while the correcting information fades.

This process feeds the powerful *availability heuristic*, which deceives people into thinking "what you see is all there is." For example, in January 2019, Trump's shutdown of the government over funding for his Mexico border wall dominated the media. Almost every outlet reported false claims he made about criminals crossing the border, a "humanitarian crisis" of trafficking, and blatant lies about the numbers of illegal crossings increasing, while in fact, according to the government's statistics, illegal crossings were at historically low levels. The high drama of the whole situation kept the media hyper-focused on this issue.

Meanwhile, Trump ended a nuclear non-proliferation treaty with Russia and announced troop withdrawals in Syria, just to name two events underreported by the media in that period that are clearly of far greater importance than a spat over the wall. Even though Trump lost the congressional battle for his wall in early 2019, he deftly manipulated the news cycle, keeping the nation's attention focused where he wanted it—and away from more important and alarming issues that deserved the media's attention, and ours.

The Media Can Evolve Toward Pro-Truth Reporting, and You Can Help

Fortunately, honest and ethical journalists can change their reporting style. Trump keeps making claims with no evidence, and will keep doing so, because he gets exactly what he wants: millions of people believing his baseless allegations. Reframing the media coverage of Trump's claims, and using techniques informed by behavioral science, would disincentivize Trump from making baseless statements instead of rewarding him. Rather than focusing on relating the details of the specific claims made by Trump, reporters should use news headlines and introductory paragraphs to foreground the pattern of our president systematically making claims lacking evidence. For instance, in the falsehoods about wiretapping, AP News could have run the headline "Trump Delivers Another Accusation Without Evidence, This Time Against Obama." CNN could have introduced the story by focusing on Trump's pattern of making serial allegations of immoral and illegal actions by his political opponents without any evidence, this time accusing his predecessor. Then, deeper in the article where the shallow skimmers do not reach, the story could have detailed the allegations made by Trump, backed up by facts.

The same approaches can be used by the media to address the problem of false equivalence and opinion-driven reporting.

However, to do so, the media have to place their ethics code (reporting events fairly and accurately) above ratings. We have to recognize that's not easy for media outlets that depend on click-based revenues to survive.

The media can do better. But they only *will* do better when the incentive for their survival changes. The media can evolve. They can become more aware of political attempts to manipulate their coverage and resist them. They can keep the public's attention on the issues that actually have the greatest consequences for citizens—such as embarking on a new arms race, or creating a vacuum for terrorists in Syria.

You as a media consumer can make a difference. First, though, let's redefine that relationship. The media in the United States are considered the Fourth Estate, after the executive, legislative, and judiciary branches of government. Although for the most part not funded by taxpayers, a free and ethical press is a foundation of any democracy. Why? Because without accurate and unbiased information, citizens can't wisely evaluate the best policies, nor elect the best candidates. Around the world, authoritarian regimes persecute, imprison, and murder journalists who strive to tell the truth. In democratic, free nations, we should never take our media for granted, and *never* tolerate lax standards for reporting the truth.

What you can do:

1. *Pay for the media.* Your taxes pay for the first three estates of your democracy. It's up to you to pay for the fourth. Online subscriptions for newspapers are ludicrously inexpensive, about the equivalent of a few slices of pizza. Consider devoting the cost of a pizza each month to three or four media sources you trust. Incidentally, being a subscriber gives you much greater leverage when you write to the editors. Remembering myself as a college student surviving on ramen noodles, you might genuinely

be unable to afford giving up those slices of pizza. In that case, at least make sure to unblock your ad blocker when you visit news sites where they get paid by the click, and encourage those around you who are eating sushi instead of ramen noodles to pay for quality journalism.

2. *Promote truth to the media.* These days most news stories give you the option of adding a comment or emailing the journalist. Use this option to thank journalists who are vigilant about truth, as well as criticizing them when they fall short. As Tim, my co-author and a former journalist attests, feedback from readers has a huge impact. Let them know you value truth-first reporting. Along this line, you can encourage reporters and editors to take the Pro-Truth Pledge (see Chapter 7), to shift the incentives for them to orient toward truthful and accurate reporting.

3. *Police the media.* When media venues feature misleading headlines, opinion-driven reporting, false equivalence, and hyper-focus on high emotion, write letters to the editor encouraging them to reframe their reporting so that the truth comes first—not the emotion. By doing so, you will help address the distrust in the referees of our political system, as well as create appropriate incentives for politicians to avoid false claims. You can assure media channels that they will get your loyalty if they put truth first. Broadcast media are even more responsive to their sponsors, so write to them if a broadcast journalist is particularly pernicious. Both Fox News and MSNBC have fired on-air talent when their shows have been called out for bad behavior, and advertisers have dropped them.

Pro-Truth Reporting for Journalists

If you are a journalist reading this book, thank you for your commitment to the truth. Too often, the odds seem stacked against you. You are rewarded for speed and sensationalism, not meticulously grinding through the lies, the spin, the conflicting evidence. You work on a deadline, yet the truth takes so much *time*. It's important nonetheless to recognize that the media is undergoing a crisis of credibility. The President of the United States has attacked you as purveyors of "fake news" and the "enemy of the people." At the same time, to his critics he has made abundantly clear how easily you can be manipulated. You cannot cling to today's practices and hope to survive. As the current social media meme aptly puts it, "Evolve or die." It's no metaphor. On the African savannah, antelopes evolve to become faster and warier than their predators; lions evolve to become more stealthy and faster than antelopes. The dull and the slow get eaten.

Trump's arrival has been like that of a super-predator at the waterhole. The old strategies for survival not only don't work, they have been turned against you. Evolution has programmed you to cover crisis and outrage. Trump uses your impulse as a decoy to get you to focus all your attention where he wants it. In the past, uncovering outrageous lies of politicians used to kill the beast through contrition and perhaps resignation. Trump simply moves along, unscathed, from the carcass of one crisis and outrage to another. His blizzards of disinformation not only overwhelm your fact-checkers, they dull the senses of your readers and viewers. Also, his direct attacks on the media have not only startled you, they have revealed that you are ill-prepared to deal with an assault on your institutional credibility.

The good news is you have realized the game has changed. Media outlets have made several smart adaptations since the 2016 election:

- *Leading with the truth.* Headline writers are getting better at leading with the truth, not the sensational lie; for example, "Trump Again Makes False Claims about Border Crisis." This is better than repeating the false claim. Readers tend to remember the claim itself, especially if it contains high emotion, and forget the denial.

- *Fact-checking in real time.* It is no longer acceptable to report what the president (or his spokesperson) says, and then later fact-check for accuracy. So much disinformation has been pushed by the Trump administration, new outlets have made the right decision to fact-check during the first reporting of events, rather than later, when much of the public is not paying attention.

- *Covering actions, not advertisements.* Broadcast media has grown more suspicious of Trump's declarations that he is going to make an announcement worthy of prime-time live TV coverage. Unless a clear action is going to be announced, probabilities are now weighted toward the coverage being used to promote a political agenda, not deliver hard news.

To these laudable evolutions, here are four Rs for journalists, editors and producers to consider in implementing a pro-truth agenda:

1. *Resist reporting outrage.* The media's reflex is to report an outrageous tweet. Learn to perceive manipulative tweets and announcements as attempts to hijack your outlet. Otherwise, you are doing more harm than good. It's not really sufficient to report that Trump made a false claim. Journalists need to learn *not to cover* a tweet that makes a false claim. This is hard, because the public is addicted to the outrage, and the story is easy to write. But too often you feed the addiction. Consider the actual news value of a tweet: if it spreads a conspiracy theory, smears a political rival, or arouses hatred for no reason—resist the temptation. Let the tweet die in obscurity.

2. *Redefine the concept of balance quantitatively so as to avoid false*

equivalence. Refuse to accept that "balanced reporting" is achieved by including *any* opposing point of view, no matter how much of an outlier. To help with this mental shift, don't use the metaphor of the scales for balance. If you were reporting on the first manned flight orbiting the earth, would you have felt impelled, for the sake of balance, to include a quote from the Flat Earth Society? Instead, think of balance quantitatively, on a numeric scale. How many different voices are there on the issue you are reporting? If 97 percent of scientists agree that global warming is going to hit us in the next decade, and you only have room for quotes from three experts, the quantitative balance would not include a quote from a climate denier. Perhaps nuanced views from three climate scientists would give a more accurate spectrum of expert opinion. Think of it this way: You would have to quote 33 experts in your story in order to quantitatively justify quoting a single climate denier.

3. *Rush NOT to judgment.* Mainstream journalists must become more aware that their biases expose them to the *narrative fallacy* — our tendency to want to fit whatever information we have available into a story that makes intuitive sense to us. Especially when a story breaks that seems to neatly fit those "hot-button" political issues. Failure to determine the relevant facts before publishing is no longer just an individual lapse: It feeds the Trumpian narrative that you are all "fake news." Take the lesson of the Jussie Smollett hoax to heart, and treat every tempting narrative as a potential hoax. Resist the rush, and remember it is journalism itself that will be judged if you get the story wrong.

4. *Re-label opinion and news stories more distinctly.* Ethical journalists know the difference between news and commentary and strive to keep their news stories objective.

But their audiences often don't make this distinction. This inadvertently feeds Trump's narrative that the mainstream media is out to get him. As a Republican friend of my co-author recently told him: "There were six stories bashing Trump in the *NYT* today, and only *one* factual story about him. I can't believe how unfair the liberal media is!" The friend had tallied the headlines, unaware that these were mostly opinion pieces, not news reports. Part of the problem is that most people no longer read their news in a paper newspaper. On social media, there's no easy way to tell news stories from opinion pieces. A story shows up on one's feed simply as from the *New York Times*. If you click the link, you might find "Opinion" in tiny print next to the headline. The fix here is pretty simple: Use prominent labels. Similarly, broadcast media needs a much clearer distinction between news shows and commentary segments. Something on the screen at all times would help prevent viewers from making this mistake.

Important Terms Referenced in This Chapter

Confirmation bias: the tendency to look for and interpret new information in a way that conforms to our existing beliefs, and ignore or reject new information that goes against our current beliefs.

Illusory truth effect: a mental error that causes us to perceive something to be true when we hear it repeated frequently and persistently, regardless of whether it is objectively true, or whether or not we are presented with evidence supporting it.

False equivalence: the intention to evaluate all sides of an issue as equal; this undermines fairness, honesty, and accuracy in cases where one perspective on the story is actually correct while the others are false.

Narrative fallacy: our tendency to want to fit whatever information we have available into a story that makes intuitive sense to us.

Availability bias: only considering significant what is in front of us; this bias deceives people into falsely thinking "what you see is all there is."

Chapter 5

The Rise of Online and Social Media—and Viral Deception

Imagine you are African American and you are checking out Facebook one evening in mid-2016. Suddenly, a video advertisement pops up. It's a *South Park*-style animation of Hillary Clinton saying that there are African American kids who are super-predators, with "no conscience, no empathy," who commit crimes and must be "brought to heel." The video uses Clinton's own voice, which you recognize from her numerous ads on television. A cartoon text pops up around her image saying "Hillary Thinks African Americans are Super-Predators."

How would this animation make you feel? Would it make you less likely to go out and vote for Clinton? That's what Donald Trump's team hoped with its voter suppression efforts, described in a series of interviews with the digital marketing team of the Trump campaign, in an October 27, 2016 *Bloomberg Businessweek* article, "Inside the Trump Bunker, with Days to Go." Brad Pascale, the head of Trump's digital team, described how the Trump team relied on Facebook digital marketing tools such as "dark posts," meaning non-public posts seen only by people that the Trump campaign was targeting in key swing states. As Pascale stated: "only the people we want to see it, see it."

This targeting of African American voters in the US represented only one aspect of Trump's voter suppression efforts. Let me be clear—I am not using the term "voter suppression" lightly. I am quoting a senior Trump official, who stated in that *Bloomberg Businessweek* story: "we have three major voter suppression operations under way." Besides the targeting of African Americans, the voter suppression aimed to turn off

idealistic white liberals who supported Bernie Sanders as well
as separately young women. Regarding the former, the Trump
campaign used messaging focused on Clinton's WikiLeaks
emails and her endorsement of the Trans-Pacific Partnership.
For the latter, the campaign highlighted women who claimed
that Bill Clinton had sexually assaulted them. In that article, the
Trump campaign staff described how they thought that their
efforts would be effective because "we've modeled this…it will
dramatically affect her ability to turn these people out."

Other voter suppression efforts popped up after *Bloomberg
Businessweek* published that article. For example, a November 3,
2016 article in the *Washington Post* described fake ads on Twitter
that targeted African Americans and conveyed the false message
that you can vote from home by text. The ad looked realistic, as
you can see in Figure 5.1, with a message at the bottom saying
"Paid for by Hillary for President 2016," and using hashtags (the
"#" sign) common to Twitter supporters of Clinton.

**Fig. 5.1 Image from the *Washington Post* story about voter
suppression tactics (courtesy of the *Washington Post*)**

Such ads are not illegal, even though they convey false information. In fact, Twitter at first refused to remove the ads even after they were reported, as they did not constitute a violation of its Terms of Service. But eventually Twitter CEO Jack Dorsey gave in to public pressure and had such ads removed. While the source of such ads is uncertain, it certainly fits well the voter suppression efforts pursued by the Trump campaign.

While we can't directly parse out the role played by the Trump digital marketing team's voter suppression efforts from other dynamics in the campaign, we can estimate that they played at least some role in Trump's victory, given that he won by only about 60,000 votes in several key swing states. There's a reason Trump spent $70 million a month on his digital operations in the late stage of his campaign, with the large majority of this money going to Facebook advertisements to motivate Trump supporters and demotivate Clinton supporters, according to the *Bloomberg Businessweek* story.

Given Trump's surprise victory, which went against public polls, we need to take seriously his pre-election claims, in late October and early November 2016, that he possessed hidden strategies and strengths that would come to fruition in the vote itself. For instance, Trump made a number of statements at late-October 2016 rallies in North Carolina and Pennsylvania that the 2016 presidential election would be "beyond Brexit" and "Brexit times five," by which he meant that polls showing Trump losing were just as inaccurate as those showing that the "Remain" side of the Brexit campaign would win, and the result just as shocking in breaking expectations. Indeed, the London firm Cambridge Analytica, which provided extensive social media and other data analysis services for the "Leave" side of Brexit, worked for the Trump campaign in targeting what Cambridge Analytica "identified as a small, fluctuating group of people who are reluctant to admit their support for Trump and may be throwing off public polls" in the words of *Bloomberg Businessweek*.

Contrary to many commentators' opinions, Trump's rhetoric was not empty bluster, even if his hidden strengths involved suppressing his opponent's base.

To understand Trump's victory, and post-truth politics more broadly, we need to consider the role of digital media in shaping the public sphere. By digital media I mean both online news sources and social media networks, but I'll discuss the two separately, starting with the latter.

The Brain Science of Social Media

Whether or not you post or tweet, no one should underestimate the influence of social media. A 2016 study by Pew Research Center shows that 62 percent of all adults get at least some news on social media, a number that increased from 49 percent in 2012. Facebook remained the most popular social media network in 2016, with 67 percent of all adults using it, and 66 percent of Facebook users getting news from the site. As for Twitter, about 16 percent of Americans used it that year, and 59 percent of those who use Twitter get news there. Furthermore, the study revealed that those who get news from social media are less likely to turn to mainstream media, making them more reliant on social media and online websites as the source of their news ("News Use Across Social Media Platforms," Pew Research Center, May 26, 2016).

The fact that social media news consumers rely less on mass media sources of news contributes to a problematic phenomenon known as the *filter bubble*. While the mass media reports on the main news of the day, whether we like this news or not, social media functions differently. For instance, Facebook—the main provider of news on social media—specifically creates algorithms that show us news that fits our preferences based on the kind of articles we have clicked "like" on in the past. Likewise, the people and organizations we follow on Twitter, those we "friend" and the organizations whose pages we "like" on Facebook are quite likely to reflect our own perspectives, rather than the diversity of viewpoints within our society.

Even deliberate efforts to "friend" people on Facebook and other social media may not solve this problem. As an example, at a 2011 Technology, Entertainment, and Design (TED) talk entitled "Beware Online 'Filter Bubbles,'" the former director of the liberal organization MoveOn.org, Eli Pariser, discussed how he made efforts to have both conservative and liberal Facebook friends. Yet over time posts from conservative friends decreased more and more, because Pariser engaged more with liberal friends, and Facebook's algorithm "edited out" the conservative ones. This is not a problem for social media only: online news apps enable us to select the kind of news we prefer, and search engines deliver search results customized to our perspectives based on our previous search engine use. Researchers such as Paul Resnick (and others in papers presented at a 2013 conference) have shown that such selective exposure to information through social media and other forms of digital media results in people forming inaccurate impressions of reality.

Self-created filters plus the filters imposed on us by complex algorithms distort reality for users of social media. In other words, most of us. Getting such one-sided perspectives supercharges a cognitive bias called the *false consensus effect*, the tendency to overestimate the degree to which other people believe the same things that we do. A study by Magdalena Wojcieszak (published in *Public Opinion Quarterly* in 2008) evaluated two online venues characterized by ideological homogeneity, one on the far right and another on the far left. Both groups exaggerated the extent to which the broader public supported their ideological perspectives, despite the existence of clear evidence in the form of polls and other data about the actual support of the public for both far-right and far-left positions. Another study by Kathleen Bauman and Glenn Geher published in 2002 showed that presenting a diversity of perspectives to study participants served to reduce the false consensus effect. However, the filter bubble of social media makes it less likely that those who consume their news that way will ever get that diversity of perspectives.

This false consensus effect starts with our basic human trust in friends and family, which forms the basis for the connections on social media. Having surveyed people in 60 countries, the 2015 Nielsen Global Trust in Advertising Report found that a whopping 83 percent say they trust recommendations made by friends and family. A classic 1977 article by Richard Nisbett and Timothy Wilson shows how our brains experience the *halo effect*, a cognitive bias in which if we like one aspect of a whole, we have an excessively positive evaluation of all aspects of that whole.

So, if we trust our friends and those friends are connected with us on social media, research on the halo effect suggests we are likely to trust the recommendations they make about what articles we should read. Indeed, more recent research by Abhishek Borah and Gerard Tellis in 2016—conducted on products rather than news—demonstrates that halo effects through social media have powerful impacts on sales. A 2016 joint study by Twitter and the analytics firm Annalect supports the spreading of trust from friends to others on social media: while 56 percent of Twitter users report using recommendations from friends to purchase products, 49 percent rely on influencers, whether public notables or organizations. The gap between friends and influencers is surprisingly small. Even more telling, the American Press Institute conducted a survey in 2016 to evaluate trust in social media and other online media. When asked whether they trust news on any given social media network "a great deal," "a lot," "somewhat," "a little," or "not at all," a whopping 60 percent of Facebook users and 61 percent of Twitter users who get news on these social media expressed "somewhat" or more trust in the news they get there. Finally, and most relevant to the 2016 US presidential election, a 2017 study (by Hunt Allcott and Matthew Gentzkow, published by the National Bureau of Economic Research) of social media in the election found that 14 percent of all Americans called social media their "most important" source of news about the election process.

So now we know that consumers of news on social media are more likely to form inaccurate beliefs about reality than do consumers of mass media, due to the filtering effect of social media, the false consensus effect, and trust in news information there. Yet what do these findings tell us about how political advertisements on Twitter and Facebook, such as those spread by the Trump team and his allies, impact consumers of news on social media? After all, Facebook and Twitter advertisements come clearly marked with "sponsored content" headings, making it clear that this post is not a real news story. Here's some more bad news: Research casts doubt on the ability of people to differentiate between real news stories and advertisements online.

In a 2016 study from Stanford University, "Evaluating Information: The Cornerstone of Civic Online Reasoning," researchers asked students from middle and high school, as well as college undergraduates—thus people well versed in social media—to perform a variety of tasks associated with evaluating posts for credibility. Unfortunately, when asked to evaluate online content that looked like a real news story except for the words "sponsored content," a shockingly high number—over 80 percent—thought this was a real news story! For those not well versed in social media, such as older adults—who tend to vote at a higher proportion than students—the numbers would likely be higher. Some study participants apparently noticed the term "sponsored content" but still thought that it was a genuine news article, which the researchers suggest indicates that the students did not understand what "sponsored content" means. Good news for advertisers, whether commercial or political, but bad news for democracy.

Another aspect of the study showed a photo on the popular photo-sharing site Imgur of flowers that had apparent birth defects (see Figure 5.2). The post claimed these came from the Fukushima nuclear reactor and provided evidence of birth defects resulting from Japan's Fukushima Daiichi nuclear disaster.

Fig. 5.2 Photo of flowers from study "Evaluating Information: The Cornerstone of Civic Online Reasoning" (courtesy of Stanford University History Group, November 22, 2016)

Study participants "were captivated by the photograph and relied on it to evaluate the trustworthiness of the post," as page 17 of the study reports. Less than 20 percent of all students questioned either the source of the post or the source of the photo. Nearly 40 percent argued that the post represented strong evidence, while 25 percent argued it did not provide strong evidence because it showed only flowers as opposed to other living beings.

The study evaluated the capacity of participants to evaluate the quality of sources on social media. For instance, it asked students to evaluate two Facebook posts announcing Trump's run for the presidency. One came from a verified account by Fox

News, with a blue checkmark, and another came from another account that masqueraded as Fox News and did not have a blue checkmark. However, only a quarter of study participants recognized the blue checkmark as indicating credibility on Facebook. Over 30 percent instead considered the fake account more credible because it had a larger photo, thus playing into the visual appeal element that also characterized the flower image.

Twitter also fooled many. The study asked participants to evaluate a tweet from a liberal organization, MoveOn.org, saying: "New polling shows the @NRA is out of touch with gun owners and their own members." A graphic in the tweet claimed: "Two out of three gun owners say they would be more likely to vote for a candidate who supported background checks." The tweet included a link by the sponsor of the poll, the Center for American Progress, a liberal organization just like MoveOn. org, with a description of the survey conducted by Public Policy Polling, a professional polling firm known as somewhat liberal-leaning but overall high-quality. Participants in the study, asked to evaluate the quality of the information provided by the tweet, did not fare well. Less than a third could explain how the political agendas of Center for American Progress and MoveOn.org might shape the tweet. Shockingly, despite being asked to assess the tweet, over half the students did not click on the link within the tweet. The study concluded with the researchers expressing grave concerns over how the lack of education in evaluating information on social media impacts our political environment.

Further bad news comes from a study by Sander van der Linden et al. (published in 2017 in *Global Challenges*) researching the impact of misinformation presented in an online format about climate change. Researchers first evaluated all study participants on whether they believed in human-caused climate change, on a 0–100 scale. They then exposed one group of study participants to accurate information about climate change, namely "97% of climate scientists have concluded that human-caused climate change is happening." This resulted in a large increase of an average of +19.72 points in whether study participants believed in human-caused climate change. Then, they exposed another group—not the same as the first—to the false statement that "there is no consensus on human-caused climate change." The consequence? A substantial though smaller decrease in belief in climate change caused by humans, -8.99 points on the scale. The most depressing aspect of the study was yet another experiment, where participants first got the true statement, then the false statement. This combination resulted in no statistically significant change, with a +.51-average increase. In essence, the study showed that regardless of the truth about climate change, lies can fully counter the effect of people hearing the truth. It all comes down to who has a larger megaphone, truth or lies. The more lies are spread, the more people will believe them.

What Happened with Social Media in the 2016 Election?

Given this evidence of how easy it is to fool people on social media, it is no wonder that the Trump campaign staff used dark posts and targeted advertising to convey false information—whether Facebook ads misrepresenting Clinton's views of African Americans, or tweets on Twitter telling Clinton voters they could vote by text. Simply put, these types of tactics work due to how our brains are wired, along with a lack of appropriate education in critically evaluating social media.

"Viral Deception" Is More Accurate Than "Fake News"

Such deceptive tactics fed into the broader maelstrom of political misinformation on social media. Originally called "fake news," this tide of falsehood has more recently been termed "viral deception" by Kathleen Hall Jamieson, director of the Annenberg Public Policy Center. In an appearance on CNN's *Reliable Sources* on March 5, 2017, she pointed out that if you term this misinformation "fake news," you get into a debate about what is "real news." By contrast, calling a piece of content "viral deception" much more clearly conveys the two essential problems of lies on social media: the "deception" part speaks to the falsehood of the content, while the "viral" describes the problem of this content spreading via people sharing it on social media. Likewise, while "fake news" only applies to false news articles, "viral deception" can apply to anything: false quotes, misleading infographics, deceptive statistics, altered images, and so on.

An Epidemic of Viral Deception

The 2016 election cycle witnessed an epidemic of viral deception. *BuzzFeed News* conducted an analysis focused on deceptive news articles on Facebook in the final few months of the US presidential campaign. It was published on November 16, 2016 with the title "This Analysis Shows How Viral Fake Election News Stories Outperformed Real News on Facebook." Its analysis focused on comparing Facebook engagements—shares, reactions, and comments—on the top 20 false news stories from non-reputable sources and the top 20 credible news articles (see Figure 5.3). The latter came from 19 major reputable websites, such as *The Wall Street Journal, The New York Times, The Washington Post, New York Daily News, FOX News, New York Post, CNN, USA Today,* and others. In the six months between February and July 2016, the top 20 false stories received a hair-raising 6 million engagements. We can be thankful that the credible news stories received more engagements, around 21 million, outperforming fake news by over 3 to 1.

The situation grew much worse closer to election day. In the last three months, from August through early November, the top 20 deceptive news stories received 8,711,000 engagements, while the top 20 true stories had only 7,367,000. It's hard to tell whether the hoax websites stepped up their game in producing articles better designed to appeal to Facebook users, or whether the hyper-partisan mood of the last few months bred a greater willingness to share misleading news stories, but the outcome remains: viral deception won in this instance.

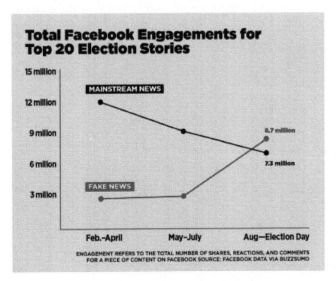

Fig. 5.3 Chart from *BuzzFeed News* analysis comparing Facebook engagement for top 20 false vs. true news articles (courtesy of *BuzzFeed News*)

The 2017 study by Allcott and Gentzkow mentioned above enables us to dive deeper into the data on sharing false news articles on Facebook. The authors worked with an archive of 156 election-related news stories that leading fact-checking websites categorized as false in the three months prior to the election. Focused on re-shares of articles on Facebook, rather than the total extent of engagement with each piece, the authors found that these 156 misleading news stories got just under 38 million shares. Using previously available data for how many people click on news links shared on social media, the study suggests that this number of re-shares resulted in Facebook users reading fake news articles just over *three-quarters of a billion times*.

Given that there are approximately 325 million Americans (according to US census results), and the Pew Center's study that 67 percent of Americans use Facebook, and that about 66 percent of them get news from it, we get approximately just under 150 million Americans using Facebook. If we assume that the large majority of false news articles were read by Americans—it was the US election, after all—then each American Facebook user on average read 5 false news articles. Of course, it is likely that there are many people who read no false news articles and many who read more than 10, yet the numbers are still very concerning.

Fortunately, Allcott and Gentzkow avoided the fallacious approach of *false equivalence* (a mental error in which two completely opposing arguments are treated as logically equivalent when in fact they are not), and chose to rate the misleading news stories as either favorable to Trump or Clinton. Of the total 156 misleading stories, they found that false news stories favoring Trump (including anti-Clinton) were shared a total of 30.3 million times. By contrast, Facebook users shared deceptive news stories critical of Trump or supportive of Clinton 7.6 million times. According to the study's findings, just over half of those who saw the false articles believed in their content. The more people consumed news on social media, the more likely they were to believe in misleading articles. Additionally, those who had more Facebook friends who shared their ideological perspectives tended to have a greater likelihood of believing in headlines that aligned with their ideology, whether the headline conveyed accurate or inaccurate information. By contrast, those with more education tended to have less belief in false news stories.

Anecdotal evidence from producers of viral deceptions supports the results of the studies showing that Republicans both shared more fake news and believed in fake news to a greater extent than Democrats. In an interview published in the *Washington Post* on November 17, 2016, entitled "Facebook fake news writer: 'I think Donald Trump is in the White House because of me,'" a prominent purveyor of viral deception on Facebook describes how Trump's "followers don't fact-check anything—they'll post everything, believe anything." By contrast, another creator of viral deception, in an interview with National Public Radio (NPR) on November 23, 2016, published as "We Tracked Down a Fake-News Creator in the Suburbs. Here's What We Learned," described how he "tried to write fake news for liberals—but they just never take the bait" due to liberals more likely fact-checking and debunking.

The Source of Viral Deception: Online Media

Mass media convey a diversity of perspectives in news reporting, with an eye toward being "accurate, fair, and thorough" and acting "with integrity," according to the code of ethics of the Society of Professional Journalists (SPJ), the main association for journalists. Now, journalists are far from always held accountable for ethical lapses. However, in many cases journalists have been disciplined and fired for violating this code, especially if they transgress more than once, as seen in a 2007 report compiled by The First Amendment Center—Ethics in Journalism. Perhaps the most prominent example in recent US history comes in February 2015, when Brian Williams, anchorman for *NBC Nightly News*, and the most-watched anchor on television, was fired for lying. He claimed that in 2003, he was flying in a helicopter on a reporting trip for NBC News when that helicopter went down under enemy fire. It turned out that Williams actually took a different helicopter that did not suffer enemy fire. Whether Williams engaged in confabulation—non-deliberate deception due to faulty memory—or blatant lying, his false statements cost him his job.

Unfortunately, many new online media sites do not follow this code of ethics and freely report whatever they wish, regardless of the truth. In doing so, they resemble supermarket tabloids, such as the *National Enquirer* in the US or the *Daily Mail* in the UK. Consumers of news have learned from long exposure and cultural norms that supermarket tabloids do not deserve trust as credible sources of information. Yet since online media has arisen so recently, there are few clear markers of credibility. Lacking education in how to distinguish reputable news sources from misleading ones, many online readers lack the capacity to separate the wheat from the chaff. Research by Matthew Baum and Tim Groeling, in an article entitled "New media and the polarization of American political discourse," showed that such new media is much more polarized and polarizing than traditional mass media.

To be clear, there are many high-quality sources of news online. For example, Reason.com is a reputable source on the right, *Vox* is a good source on the left, and *The Hill* is centrist. Reporters there hold to the SPJ code of ethics. Unfortunately, there are many more news sources that do not deserve trust and peddle viral deception. Too numerous to list here, some of the more prominent supermarket tabloid-style online news sources include OccupyDemocrats.com and AddictingInfo.org on the left, and Breitbart.com and InfoWars.com on the right. While not all articles on these sites convey false information, many do, and these sites unabashedly promote a biased, partisan agenda.

Far from all online sites promote false news stories from a partisan desire to influence public opinion: Some are simply motivated by profit. The viral deception entrepreneur who spoke with NPR in the interview cited above—Jestin Coler—makes good money from his deceptive articles. Here's how his business model works: Coler has between 20 and 25 people working for him, writing false news stories that they then post on a website owned by Coler's company, Disinfomedia. Designed to look realistic at first glance, each website has a lot of advertising around the deceptive news stories. Coler's staffers then post the articles in Facebook groups likely to spread viral deception, and their articles often go viral. Masses of people visit the website, some of them click on advertising, and as a result, Coler earns anywhere between $10,000 and $30,000 a month.

For example, over 1.6 million people visited a news site over ten days with the false news story: "FBI Agent Suspected in Hillary Email Leaks Found Dead in Apparent Murder-Suicide." This article appeared on a website, Denverguardian.com, that had the appearance of a local newspaper, including local weather. Someone going to this article from Facebook and taking a casual glance at this website would be easily fooled into thinking it actually is a local newspaper. However, the only news story on the website was the false one. This article represented the kind of stories produced by Coler's company, ones that fit into existing right-wing narratives. Coler describes how he—as a registered Democrat—did not seek to influence the election. Instead, he had his writers try to write fake news stories for liberals, but they proved much less likely to share such stories, thus providing a much less lucrative market.

Viral deception entrepreneurs in the US are not the only ones making money from the credulity of voters. A December 5, 2016 story from the BBC, "The city getting rich from fake news," describes how many of the most prominent sources of viral deception in the US presidential election campaign and afterward stemmed from Veles, Macedonia, created by tech-savvy teenagers. The reporter talked to one who described how he copy-pasted right-wing news stories, put click-baity new titles on them, and promoted them on Facebook to conservative Americans. Working only on this area for a month, he earned nearly $2000, but his friends who worked on this for a while earned thousands a day. When asked whether he worried about the influence of these right-wing news stories on the US election, he said: "Teenagers in our city don't care how Americans vote… They are only satisfied that they make money and can buy expensive clothes and drinks!...The Americans loved our stories and we make money from them...Who cares if they are true or false?"

While plenty of misleading news stories stemmed from viral deception entrepreneurs desiring to make money, and spreading conservative-themed stories because Republicans are less trusting of mass media and more willing to click on and share false but appealing news stories, many other pieces of viral content came from deliberate efforts to shape American public opinion. Russia's government was one major culprit. A Reuters article on April 21, 2017, entitled "Putin-linked think tank drew up plan to sway 2016 US election—documents," described a strategy drawn up by the Russian Institute for Strategic Studies in Moscow to help get Trump elected and undermine faith in the US electoral system. Directed by retired Russian foreign intelligence officials appointed by Putin's office, the Institute report recommended a propaganda campaign via social media and Russian government-financed news outlets. These documents helped shape the conclusion of US intelligence agencies that Russia had launched a viral deception initiative against the Democratic Party and Clinton in particular.

This effort involved not only hacking the Clinton campaign's emails and the Democratic National Committee and releasing the information to WikiLeaks, but also pumping out a steady stream of viral deception. An April 3, 2017 article by NPR called "How Russian Twitter Bots Pumped Out Fake News During the 2016 Election" described the testimony of Clint Watts, a former FBI agent and current senior fellow at the Foreign Policy Research Institute. Watts spoke to the Senate Intelligence Committee, which is investigating Russia's interference in the election, about how Russian government officials used a host of Twitter bots to spread false news articles through accounts that pretended to be those of Midwestern swing-voter Republicans. According to Watts, "that way whenever you're trying to socially engineer them and convince them that the information is true, it's much more simple because you see somebody and they look exactly like you, even down to the pictures."

These efforts continued after the election. For example, Watts related that "if you went online today, you could see these accounts—either bots or actual personas somewhere—that are trying to connect with the administration. They might broadcast stories and then follow up with another tweet that tries to gain the president's attention, or they'll try and answer the tweets that the president puts out." As an example, when Trump tweeted false claims about Barack Obama ordering Trump Tower wiretapped during the 2016 election campaign, the Russian government-controlled tweets "respond[ed] to the wiretapping claim with further conspiracy theories about that claim and that just amplifies the message in the ecosystem." A

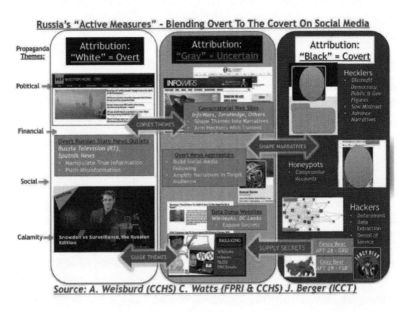

Fig. 5.4 Infographic depicting Russian propaganda campaign from November 6, 2016 article in *War on the Rocks*, called "Trolling for Trump: How Russia Is Trying to Destroy Our Democracy" (courtesy of warontherocks.com, November 2016)

November 6, 2016 article in *War on the Rocks*, called "Trolling for Trump: How Russia Is Trying to Destroy Our Democracy," presents an insightful infographic that clarifies the various ways that the Russian propaganda campaign tries to shape American public opinion (see Figure 5.4).

Russia's government first developed these techniques of hiring people to create fake accounts and spread lies in managing its own domestic public opinion and then its near abroad, as related in a June 2, 2015 article, "The Agency," in the *New York Times*. The Kremlin then began to use perfected versions of these techniques to sway elections and public opinion more broadly outside of its immediate zone of influence, such as in the US and western Europe. As related by *The Telegraph* in a January 24, 2017 article, "Russia is targeting French, Dutch and German elections with fake news, EU task force warns," the European Union set up a task force dedicated to countering this threat, which became clearly visible after the success of Russia in influencing the US election.

Of course, it's not simply Russia; it's also Trump and his allies, as the viral deception spread by Trump's campaign to suppress Clinton's voters shows. Trump himself is directly implicated in a whole host of viral deceptions, both creating his own, such as false claims that Obama had Trump Tower wiretapped, and boosting the signal for other false stories. As an example, Trump on May 3, 2016 on *Fox and Friends* made the deceptive statement that Senator Ted Cruz's father had associated with Lee Harvey Oswald just a short period before the latter assassinated President John F. Kennedy. These remarks followed a piece in the *National Enquirer* claiming it had photographic proof that Mr. Cruz's father, Rafael Cruz, spent time "palling around" with Mr. Oswald. *PolitiFact* rated Trump's claim "Pants on Fire." The *New York Times* published an article on January 18, 2017 called "10 Times Trump Spread Fake News."

Trump's associates spread viral deception as well; for example, his former National Security Adviser Mike Flynn. A December 5, 2016 article entitled "Flynn under fire for fake news" in *Politico* described how Flynn retweeted false claims about Clinton being associated with child sex trafficking and Obama being a "jihadi" who supported Muslim terrorists financially. Another close Trump ally, conservative radio host Laura Ingraham, put out many pieces of viral deception. As described in an article on *The Intercept*, published on November 26, 2016 under the title "Some Fake News Publishers Just Happen to Be Donald Trump's Cronies," Ingraham owns several websites such as *LifeZette*. A video produced by *LifeZette* in the summer of 2016, entitled "Clinton Body Count," advanced the baseless conspiracy theory that the Clinton family had a role in the deaths of various friends and Democrats, including the plane crash of John F. Kennedy, Jr. *LifeZette's* video, released on Facebook from the verified account of *LifeZette*, ended up getting more than 400,000 shares and 14 million views.

An additional problem for the credibility of online media comes from how easy it is to manipulate it, and conservatives have invested a lot of resources into doing so. A February 26, 2017 article in *The Guardian*, one of the top UK newspapers, entitled "Robert Mercer: the big data billionaire waging war on mainstream media," describes how this takes place. The story, published shortly after a news conference where Trump accused the mass media of being liars, started off with describing how the reporter typed in "mainstream media is..." into Google. The first link on the Google search—the one most likely to be clicked by searchers—did not lead to a reputable news organization such as CNN, ABC, the *New York Times*, or the *Wall Street Journal*, but instead to a website called CNSnews.com and an article entitled "The Mainstream Media Are Dead."

CNSnews is owned by Media Research Center, which is devoted to "unwavering commitment to neutralizing left-wing bias in the news media and popular culture." A large portion of its funding came from Robert Mercer, a hedge fund billionaire who made his money in IT and provided a great deal of funding for Trump's election campaign. He also provided the funding to start *Breitbart*, the far-right news site that has 2 billion pageviews a year, formerly led by Steve Bannon, a former Trump adviser. *Breitbart* rates as the 29th most popular site in America, bigger than *Huffington Post*, and has the largest political site social media following on Facebook and Twitter.

Cambridge Analytica: Data Mining and Manipulation

Mercer had a large stake in Cambridge Analytica, where Bannon served as Vice-President. This data analytics company worked for a number of Republican candidates in the US—no Democrats—and also supported the UK "Leave" campaign in Brexit, as well as a number of campaigns in developing countries. On its website, Cambridge Analytica promised to "find your voters and move them to action" through using data analytics to learn about voters and shape their behavior. The website describes how it participated in the 2016 US presidential election, where it worked for Trump's campaign to "locate the key voters that could swing the election and establish creative ways to reach and interact with this audience to move them to action." Its website boasted that by using "vast troves of existing data on individual voters, constructing highly advanced data models, and prioritizing voters by their likelihood to vote and feelings of favorability towards each candidate," Cambridge Analytica focused "efforts and funding on the truly undecided voters in key regions of the electoral map that would ultimately decide the race." Much of its efforts took place through social media, where "accounts on Twitter, Facebook, and YouTube were started from scratch and maintained to create an organic presence," overall "reaching 50 million Facebook users, creating 1.5 million impressions on Twitter, 3.3 million on Snapchat, [and] accruing over 28 million views on their digital videos."

The *Guardian* article described how the company perfected its methods in developing countries by practicing what the military calls "psyops," psychological operations, or in more colloquial terms, propaganda that mainly targets emotions. To go back to the Google search, another article in *The Guardian*, on December 4, 2016, entitled "Google, democracy and the truth about internet search," describes how Cambridge Analytica is enmeshed in a right-wing news ecosystem that dominates Google's search results around certain topics. These topics include not only "mainstream media is...," but also depictions of Jews, Muslims, and women as evil, and Adolf Hitler and the Nazis as good.

The Guardian clarifies that these right-wing sites hack Google's search algorithm through interlinking and other strategies to move themselves to the top of the search page. These findings come from the research of Jonathan Albright, an assistant professor of communications at Elon University in North Carolina, who published on his *Medium* blog preliminary results of a study of these sites, in a November 18, 2016 post entitled "The #Election2016 Micro-Propaganda Machine." His analysis showed how right-wing news sites that produce viral deception use hyperlinking to surround prominent news and search engine sites. This is how CNSnews came to be listed before credible sites.

The Guardian wrote about how Cambridge Analytica collected the data on people who visited the right-wing viral deception sites, building up the trove of data that it boasted about on its website. The company combined this knowledge of people's behavior with research stemming from personality models created by scientists at Cambridge University's Psychometric Centre. This allowed them to build very accurate profiles of people's personalities based simply on Facebook "likes." According to the leading scientist at the Psychometric Centre, just by learning about 150 Facebook "likes," their model predicted someone's personality better than that person's spouse. All these resources enabled Cambridge Analytica to trace individuals around the web and target them with personalized political messages meant to change their behavior. Under investigation by the British High Court, Cambridge Analytica filed for insolvency and ceased operations in May 2018.

So how did Clinton fare among these demographics targeted by the Trump digital marketing team, which hired Cambridge Analytica to provide it with targeting data and messaging for key demographics in swing states? A CNN story on November 9, 2016, "How Hillary Clinton Lost," and another one by Pew Research on the same day, "Behind Trump's Victory: Divisions by Race, Gender, Education," as well as a more thorough CNN story "Exit Polls" on November 23, 2016, describes Clinton underperforming compared to Barack Obama in all the demographics targeted by Trump's digital marketing team. Only 88 percent of African Americans voted for Clinton, while 93 percent voted for Obama, despite Trump's widely condemned remarks about black communities in the US, such as claiming that black people live in poverty and have no jobs. Moreover, the number of African Americans who voted dropped substantially, with only 60 percent turning out at the polls compared to 67 percent in 2012.

What about white liberals? Clinton won 37 percent of all white voters, compared to 39 percent for Obama. Similarly, Clinton claimed only 55 percent of young voters, both men and women, compared to 60 percent for Obama. And, despite the obvious gender identity affiliation of women with Clinton, and Trump's crude and sexist remarks about them, Clinton only won 54 percent of all women voters, compared to 55 percent for Obama.

Selective targeting with advertising that heavily featured viral deception, such as the voter suppression efforts described in the early part of this chapter, helps explain Trump's surprising victory. Traditional polling did not account for this type of advertising and targeting, which helps explain why the polls were several points off. Not coincidentally, Cambridge Analytica and associated companies—such as SCL Group and AggregateIQ—contributed greatly to the targeted advertising and viral deception in the Brexit "Leave" campaign, which also won to the surprise of pollsters, since traditional polling indicated that the "Remain" campaign would win. *The Guardian* describes these ties in a May 7, 2017 article entitled "The great British Brexit robbery: how our democracy was hijacked," detailing the close ties between Cambridge Analytica and AggregateIQ, a company in Canada where "Vote Leave," the central organization of the "Leave" campaign, spent more than half of its official budget.

One reason it spent this money in Canada, according to the article, stemmed from a desire to circumvent UK election laws. The article described ties between Mercer's activities and those of Peter Thiel, another software billionaire who is a well-known Trump supporter. Thiel also owns the data-mining company Palantir, which according to *The Guardian* had some associations with Cambridge Analytica. All of this evidence raises serious questions about the use of digital media to manipulate the US and UK election process, whether by wealthy individuals such as Mercer or foreign governments such as Russia.

The series of high-quality investigative articles by *The Guardian* triggered investigations by the UK Information Commissioner's Office on whether data was used illegally in the elections, and another by the UK Electoral Commission "focused on whether one or more donations—including services—accepted by Leave. EU was 'impermissible.'" However, the vote—both in the UK and the US—has already occurred, and the outcome would not be changed by these investigations. Another article in *The Guardian*, on April 1, 2017, entitled "'Dark money' is threat to integrity of UK elections, say leading academics," describes how the existing electoral laws simply are insufficient to deal with the problems posed by data analytics, digital media, and global interconnections. The article cites an interview with Arron Banks, the founder of the Leave.EU campaign, who said things such as "We were just cleverer than the regulators and the politicians," and when the reporter asked him if he had concerns about the Electoral Commission's investigation into Leave.EU, replied: "I don't give a monkey's <bleep> about the Electoral Commission."

In sum, Mercer follows in the footsteps of other wealthy billionaires such as Rupert Murdoch with Fox News in the US and Sky Television in the UK, who desire to influence public opinion into a more right-wing perspective. Mercer simply has adapted these strategies to the new digital media world, combining data analytics with manipulation of social media and online news sources. He found willing allies in Trump and his associates in the US, and the "Leave" campaign in the UK, and helped both of them win through targeted reshaping of public opinion. Such reshaping was enabled in large part due to the credulity of voters, many of whom lack the knowledge needed to spot advertising targeted at them to sway their opinion via viral deception and fake news stories. In large part, this lack stems from social media being a new source of information that people trust excessively, due to associations of social media with friendship networks. Likewise, both social and online media offer people a chance to be in the safe space of a filter bubble. With their sources unchallenged by credible information, they fall into the false consensus effect. The problem is particularly large for conservatives, as seen from the much more extensive sharing of viral deception among conservatives than liberals, by a factor of 3–4 according to Facebook shares.

Perhaps inspired by the success of Cambridge Analytica, other political consultancy companies have increasingly relied on digital misinformation tactics, not only in the US and UK, but also around the world. An April 24, 2019 article in *Foreign Policy* entitled "Disinformation Is Drowning Democracy" describes how companies such as SCL Group and Targeted

Victory support political leaders in India, Indonesia, and Brazil using misinformation tactics to sway the electorate there. The Bharatiya Janata Party (BJP) in India, the Great Indonesia Movement Party in Indonesia, and Jair Bolsonaro's campaign in Brazil used such consultancy groups to produce false digital content spread via YouTube, WhatsApp, and other social media venues to accomplish partisan goals in local election campaigns.

How Can We Protect Ourselves Against Viral Deceptions?

Our brains are not wired for social media. Our natural intuition leads us to form false beliefs and share misinformation online. To protect ourselves from viral deception, we need deliberate education in how to filter and process online information. Schools must integrate this kind of education into their curricula for future generations. Indeed, this is happening already. Responding to the avalanche of misinformation in social media in the 2016 election, in 2017 several states passed laws promoting digital literacy. For example, a bipartisan effort in the Washington state legislature encouraged schools to teach topics such as media literacy, Internet safety, and digital citizenship, calling for a mix of sources and perspectives while doing so. The same year, legislation advocating the teaching of media and digital citizenship passed in Connecticut, Rhode Island, and New Mexico.

However, better schooling does not address the problem for adults of all ages being fooled into texting their vote or being more prone to believing and spreading lies. Getting adults to change their behavior requires two things: 1) getting them emotionally invested into caring about the truth, and 2) providing them with the tools to parse truth from falsehood. Emotional investment needs to come before tools. We know that tools such as fact-checkers are available. But as we have seen, the large majority of conservatives and a substantial portion of liberals do not engage in fact-checking, as evidenced both by polls and widespread sharing of viral deception.

Individuals who sign the Pro-Truth Pledge have already made the emotional investment. If you have read this far, you know about the pledge and are likely aware of the behaviors it encourages you to adopt. I hope you have already signed it! What else can you do to encourage others in your social circles— especially online—to adopt behaviors that can protect them from contracting and spreading viral deceptions? Changing social behavior is difficult, but not impossible. In fact, the metaphor of "viruses" we have been using in this chapter offers clues to some effective strategies. Think, for example, of some recent behavior changes in the wake of some communicable disease crises:

- Sneezing into the inside of your elbow, not your hand, so that your handshake won't pass on germs
- Wiping your hands with antibacterial lotions
- Getting a flu shot
- Wearing a condom

How did these new behaviors get adopted? First, people became emotionally invested in not contracting the specific diseases. Good public communications are important here, using signs, public service announcements (PSAs), even celebrity endorsements. Remember Madonna's catchy PSA during the AIDS crisis: "Don't be silly, put a condom on your willy!" Second, people became empathetically invested in not passing the disease on to others. Third, the new behaviors spread as others observed them in social situations and then learned about the reasons for the new behaviors. Fourth, governments, businesses and civil organizations made the right tools readily available: antibacterial lotions in malls, flu shots in drug stores, condoms, well, wherever they are likely to be used.

How might these strategies translate into a campaign against viral deception—and how can you do your part?

1. *Become invested in not contracting viral deceptions.* Develop a healthy skepticism of everything you encounter online. This takes more than just honoring the Pro-Truth Pledge. Remember, the filters of online algorithms are designed to keep you in your bubble. Acknowledge the online world is full of viruses. The false consensus and halo effects make you vulnerable to what you read online, compounded by your own confirmation and availability biases, plus the illusory truth effect, inclining you to believe something just because you see it a lot. Be careful you don't add to this the *illusion of superiority*, a bias that causes a person to overestimate their own qualities and abilities in relation to the same qualities and abilities of other persons. (This is like the person who thinks they will never catch the flu because they have a strong immune system, or the person who has unprotected sex because they believe they are a good judge of potential sexual partners.) Basically, carry your skepticism with you like a mental condom. Stay vigilant. Fact-check new information. Make this part of your online health. Search out credible news sources with different perspectives that aren't being fed to you by algorithms. Will this reduce the fun and pleasure of your online activities? It will certainly make you less passive about what you believe. Remember Madonna's warning, and don't be silly.

2. *Become invested in telling others about viral deception.* Share your fact-checking online. Correct misinformation with links to reliable sources and fact-checking websites. Of course, you have to be careful not to do this too aggressively, but rather encouragingly and respectfully. My co-author Tim's 90-year-old father, for example, sometimes passes along viral deceptions with links in

mass emails to his friends and family. Tim sends gentle corrections with links to his father, encouraging him to share the correction with his friends—rather than aggressively copying them all. Particularly if you have an independent or liberal-leaning mind, you can cultivate online friendships with conservatives—those statistically less likely to fact-check. Here, the techniques for *rational communication* (see Chapter 8) are most important, so you don't end up doing more harm than good. In responding to friends who don't fact-check, you can not only correct and debunk their viral deceptions, you can also confirm facts in their feed that check out as true. Try something like: "Hey Charlie, I fact-checked this Fox News post and confirmed the information was true. I had never heard this before, and it has given me something to think about, thanks!"

3. *Post signage and tools for reliable sources and fact-checking.* Chapter 7 on the Pro-Truth Pledge suggests you add the fact you have signed to your social media profile pages. But why not also add the websites you use for fact-checking? If people on social media shared this information as a regular part of the information about them, it would subtly reinforce fact-checking as a social norm. You can also refer to fact-checking in any articles you share online. State that you have fact-checked whatever the key information is, and give the sites that you used. If the information is new, but seems credible, you can cite other news sources you checked to verify before you share. If you have a blog, website or social media business page, look for where you could post something about your favored fact-check engines.

4. *Warn others about websites that are lax about viral deceptions.* It's becoming a social norm to complain to social media providers if they promote "fake news," and sites such

as Facebook have easy ways you can report troublesome content. Use that option whenever you encounter viral deceptions. You can also send complaints to media sites that let viral deceptions fall through the cracks. When you discover such sites, warn your friends. Just like you would tell your friends not to frequent a restaurant where you got food poisoning, tell others to beware of sites that allow viral deception to thrive.

Verified International Fact-Checkers

You will find a list of reliable fact-checkers, and their code of principles, at the Poynter Institutes' website. The website states: "This code of principles is for organizations that regularly publish nonpartisan reports on the accuracy of statements by public figures, major institutions, and other widely circulated claims of interest to society. It is the result of consultations among fact-checkers from around the world and offers conscientious practitioners principles to aspire to in their everyday work." https://ifcncodeofprinciples.poynter.org/signatories

Important Terms Referenced in This Chapter

False consensus effect: the tendency to overestimate the degree to which other people believe the same things that we do.

False equivalence: a mental error in which two completely opposing arguments are treated as logically equivalent when in fact they are not; in news reporting this undermines fairness, honesty, and accuracy in cases where one side of the story is actually correct and the others are false.

Halo effect: when we positively evaluate one thing about a person (or ethnicity, political party, or nation), we tend to make positive evaluations about other unrelated characteristics of the person (or ethnicity, political party, or nation).

Filter bubble: the way social media algorithms distort reality by showing us news that fits our preferences and feeding us more posts from the people and organizations we "follow," "friend," and "like," rather than the diversity of viewpoints within our society.

Illusion of superiority: a bias that causes a person to overestimate their own qualities and abilities in relation to the same qualities and abilities of other persons.

Chapter 6

Truth and the Tragedy of the Commons

Trump the Hacker

On December 26, 2016, the day after Christmas, Donald Trump sent two tweets:

Fig. 6.1 Screenshot of Donald Trump tweet (courtesy of Twitter)

Fig. 6.2 Screenshot of Donald Trump tweet (courtesy of Twitter)

These tweets were part of Trump's broader efforts to portray himself as a generous philanthropist during the 2016 election, because we tend to perceive charitable people as more trustworthy (according to research by Pat Barclay in 2004 and Sebastian Fehrler and Wojtek Przepiorka in 2013, both in *Evolution and Human Behavior*). However, a reputation for charitable giving may stem from either actual charitable intentions or from putting on a false front of charitable behavior without actually engaging in charitable acts. The *Washington Post*'s journalists conducted an intensive search and found that between 2010 and the spring of 2016, Trump did not make any personal charitable donations. The *Post* concluded Trump "spent years constructing an image as a philanthropist by appearing at charity events and by making very public—even nationally televised—promises to give his own money away. It was, in large part, a facade." As various other news reports revealed:

- Trump used his charity to settle legal problems. For example, Trump's Mar-a-Lago Club was involved in a legal dispute in 2007 over $120,000 in unpaid fines to the town of Palm Beach, Florida. Trump had his foundation write a check to cover the fine, instead of his business.
- Trump used his charity to "self-deal." For example, in 2014 he had the foundation buy a portrait of himself at a charity fundraiser for $10,000. It was later found hanging in Trump National Doral Miami golf resort. Tax law, according to experts quoted in the *Post's* stories, prohibits nonprofit leaders from spending charity money to buy things for themselves.
- Trump used his charity to make political gifts (which is also against the law). The foundation donated $25,000 to a group supporting the campaign of Florida Attorney General Pam Bondi (R) in 2014 at the same time that Bondi's office was considering an investigation of Trump University for fraud. Bondi, after receiving the gift, chose not to investigate.

After the *Post's* report, the New York Attorney General investigated, discovering what the judge called a "shocking pattern of illegality." The court ordered the foundation shut on December 18, 2018.

A similar tale of deception played out with Trump University. This for-profit education company, owned and run by the Trump

Organization, offered a training program in real estate from 2005 to 2010. As detailed in a *Vanity Fair* piece from January 2014 ("Big Hair on Campus: Did Donald Trump Defraud Thousands of Real-Estate Students?"), the office of New York Attorney General Eric Schneiderman filed a lawsuit in August 2013 for $40 million. The office claimed:

- Trump and his associates intentionally misled "over 5,000 individuals nationwide" who paid to "participate in live seminars and mentorship programs with the promise of learning Trump's real estate investing techniques." In reality, "Trump never participated in developing the curriculum."
- Trump University violated the law by calling itself a "university" without any license from New York state.
- Advertisements, website, and marketing materials lied blatantly about the contents of the course.

According to Schneiderman, Trump personally got about $5 million from the university, and although Trump said he intended to donate profits to charity, he never did so. In addition to the lawsuit from Schneiderman's office, Trump faced two additional class-action lawsuits from students claiming to have been defrauded by Trump University. Trump settled rather than go to court (see *USA Today*, November 18, 2016, "Trump settles fraud case against Trump University for $25M").

Trump's dishonest practices also took place in his real estate development business. A *USA Today* article on June 9, 2016, "Hundreds allege Donald Trump doesn't pay his bills," described how Trump ripped off people who worked for him:

- Edward J. Friel Co. received a $400,000 contract for wooden installations at Harrah's at Trump Plaza in Atlantic City. Trump claimed that the work of Friel's company was inferior, and refused to pay the final $83,600 invoice. Hundreds of other contractors had similar experiences of the "Trumps paying late or renegotiating deals for dimes on the dollar."

- Professionals who worked for Trump were also defrauded. Real estate broker Rana Williams, who worked for Trump for two decades, sued in 2013, claiming Trump refused to pay her $735,212 in commissions "based on nothing more than whimsy."

- His own lawyers sued him. In 2012, the law firm Cook, Heyward, Lee, Hopper & Feehan sued the Trump Organization for $94,511 for failing to pay legal fees and costs, and Trump's senior deputies attacked the quality of work of this firm in the media, with the firm making a claim of defamation.

Many of those whom Trump refused to pay chose not to sue because of Trump's record of trying to drag cases out in court to maximize legal bills for small contractors, making the legal fees more than they could expect to recover. Likewise, Trump spread negative rumors about those who refused to settle. Plenty of these smaller companies closed down because Trump stiffed them. For anyone interested in a much fuller list of Trump's problematic behavior, *The Atlantic* published "The Many Scandals of Donald Trump: A Cheat Sheet," on January 23, 2017. The article lists, among other issues: real estate fraud, hiring undocumented immigrants, unsafe working conditions, sexual abuse, casino fraud and Mafia ties.

What ties all of these together is Trump engaging in a systematic approach of winning and getting what he wanted through lying and destroying trust, then having other people pay his costs. For example, by ripping off his contractors, he also diminished trust in the labor contract system, where those doing the work trust those who hire them to pay them their fair wages. Through exploiting students and besmirching the term "university" he diminished trust in higher education institutions. Similarly, Trump's foundation scandals diminished trust in charities, making potential givers suspicious and less likely to donate for fear of their money being misused.

Regardless of your personal judgment of Trump's behavior, it is consistent, and it is predictable. Trump pursues a zero-sum game: He wins, you lose. The record shows he exploits social systems of trust for personal advantage. Trump may be seen as a hacker, someone who looks for systemic security vulnerabilities that depend on trust and honesty, and then uses these vulnerabilities to achieve his goals. Since 2017, he has brought this mindset to the Oval Office and the heart of the US government's executive branch.

Trump and the Tragedy of the Commons

Trump's zero-sum behavior at the expense of social trust is an example of the "tragedy of the commons." This famous term was coined in a 1968 article in *Science* by Garret Hardin. Hardin demonstrated that in areas where a group of people share a common resource—the commons—without any controls on the use of this resource, individual self-interest may lead to disaster for all involved. For example, communities of livestock herders often share a common pastureland. Each herder has an individual incentive to increase his or her personal herd, prospering at the expense of the other herders: if their animals eat more grass, that leaves less for the others' herds. But each herder might fear the others are already acting selfishly, and so it seems to their advantage to expand their own herds, too. When too many herders follow this zero-sum strategy, they accelerate overgrazing, deplete the commons, and potentially destroy the pasture's ability to regenerate—turning the very source of their livelihood into a wasteland. The tragedy of the commons has occurred the world over; for example, after 500 years of a thriving cod fishery off Canada's east coast, in the 1980s, overfishing pushed the stocks to collapse. Despite a moratorium in 1992, attempts to bring the cod back to a level supporting sustainable fisheries so far have failed (see Wikipedia's "Collapse of the Atlantic Northwest Cod Fishery"). A similar story can be told around the world about polluted rivers and skies, as individual companies cut costs by contaminating the water and air. The community as a whole must bear the health costs and environmental degradation. In such cases, the commons are destroyed not by something valuable taken out, but by something toxic added in.

What prevents this tragedy of the commons from happening everywhere? Privatization is one strategy — dividing the commons up so that each member has their individual plot or quota. But while that might work for herders, there are many kinds of commons that can't be neatly divided and privatized, such as fish in the sea or clean air. According to Hardin, maintaining these types of commons depends on "mutual coercion, mutually agreed upon by the majority of the people affected," so as to prevent these harmful outcomes, where a few profit at the cost of everyone else. Hardin does not mean simply physical force, but also various forms of payments, such as installing parking meters with time limits to manage the commons of empty parking spaces. Additional solutions may involve softer, more informal mechanisms of coercion, such as the use of social norms and customs, which help prevent overgrazing among Turkana pastoralists in Kenya (as reported by Terrence McCabe in a 1990 article in *Human Ecology*), or customary, unwritten regulations in community-based fisheries in Japan (described in a 1985 piece by Fikret Berkes in *Environmental Conservation*). However, such informal mechanisms of coercion require community buy-in for coordination and enforcement. Otherwise some other agent, such as the government or an organized group of non-governmental organizations and activists, needs to provide coordination of coercive mechanisms that solve the tragedy of the commons.

A 2003 volume edited by Valerie Braithwaite and Margaret Levi, *Trust and Governance*, elaborates on the importance of trust in government. The editors describe how governments, especially democracies, depend on the confidence of citizens in their governing bodies. Such confidence leads to cooperation of citizens with their government: timely tax payments that do not require burdensome collection efforts by the state, compliance with laws and judicial rulings, support of various social service efforts, and much more. At the same time, citizens expect officials to show trustworthiness and honesty; otherwise, that trust gets destroyed. Kenneth Newton in a 2001 empirical study, published in *International Political Science Review*, used survey data to confirm the importance of trust within any given country to ensure a strong civil society and democratic politics. Basically, when trust erodes, society deteriorates. If a contractor can't count on being paid, she will be less inclined to accept new clients; the economy suffers. If a student can't count on getting a useful degree, he will be less inclined to enroll; education suffers. If you can't tell if charitable donations will actually be used to help people, your good judgment will keep you from giving; those in need will suffer. Fortunately, government regulations, laws, courts and enforcement punish actors like Trump who hack our systems with lies and abuses of trust. Eventually, the courts closed the fraudulent Trump Foundation and Trump University, and at least some workers whom Trump stiffed recovered some losses.

Tragically, in politics, it's not against the law to lie. We lack a coordinated coercive legal mechanism to address deceit. Instead, we depend on the mainstream media, and the consequent fact-checking and investigative reporting, to penalize politicians who abuse trust and spread lies. Politicians have powerful incentives to avoid this kind of coverage, because voters across the political spectrum would punish them if their lies were made public. Everything hinges on an implicit agreement among the citizens to have the media function as a referee in the political struggle between the two parties, as discussed in detail in Chapter 4.

But as that chapter recounts, trust in the media as a referee has deteriorated in recent years. Trump's attacks on the media as "fake news" and "the enemy of the people" have further undermined their credibility among many Republican voters. The media thus lacks the capacity, as things stand, to counter the destruction of trust, leaving us in a classical tragedy of the commons. Lacking any powerful public coercion toward truthfulness, or any agreed-upon penalty for lying, the United States political system faces a race to the bottom.

The degree to which lies were normalized under Trump came into stark focus during the release of the report by Robert Mueller investigating Russian meddling in the 2016 elections and related obstruction of justice, as starkly detailed in a *USA Today* article, "Sarah Sanders admits she lied about FBI trust in Comey—and other false statements revealed in Mueller report" (April 21, 2019). The report not only documented many of Trump's lies, but also how he directed others to lie for him, such as White House Counsel Don McGahn, whom Trump ordered to fire Mueller. McGahn refused, and when the story leaked, Trump ordered McGahn to lie about it (he again refused). Whitehouse spokespersons Sean Spicer and Sarah Sanders both confessed to deceiving the investigators, while several Trump campaign associates were convicted of lying under oath to investigators—a federal crime. The *USA Today* article listed them:

- Former National Security Adviser Michael Flynn pleaded guilty to lying about his interactions with Russian Ambassador Sergey Kislyak during the transition.
- George Papadopoulos, a foreign policy adviser during the campaign, pleaded guilty to lying about the nature and timing of his interactions with a source who told Papadopoulos that the Russians had dirt on Democratic

candidate Hillary Clinton.

- Trump's former personal attorney Michael Cohen pleaded guilty to lying to Congress about the Trump Moscow project.
- Trump's former campaign manager Paul Manafort lied to Mueller's investigators and the grand jury concerning his interactions and communications with Konstantin Kilimnik about Trump Campaign polling data and a peace plan for Ukraine.

The Race to the Bottom

A race to the bottom happens when trust starts to break down in a commons situation. Individuals look around, see other transgressors over-exploiting the resource, and then calculate that playing by the rules no longer pays off. They switch to a zero-sum strategy themselves, thus creating a downward, degrading spiral that dooms the whole commons. Trump has paved the way for a race to the bottom in US politics.

We already see commentators advocating that politicians adopt Trump's tactics. FrontPageMag.com, a website run by the conservative David Horowitz Freedom Center, published an article on November 11, 2016, entitled "5 Ways Trump Shows How to Win Elections." The piece advises Republican politicians: to go against the mainstream media; to appeal to the beliefs and emotions of white working-class voters; to "promise [voters] everything they want"; to "make them love you," with the implication that it doesn't matter if it's true or not; when challenged on anything, to double down instead of retreating; to engage in greater polarization and radicalization of your base; to court controversy and invite scandals, because "if you're running against the system, then scandals only make you stronger...Controversy isn't something to be feared. It's something to be embraced"; to channel "the voice of millions of angry Americans." No doubt, these represent highly effective ways to win elections—while further destroying trust and honesty in our political system.

Three Politicians Who Successfully Imitated Trump's Tactics
First: On May 24, 2017, Republican Greg Gianforte, a Montana politician running in a special election for a House seat, assaulted a reporter from *The Guardian*. Ben Jacobs was asking him questions about the Republican health-care plan when Gianforte attacked him (see PolitiFact.com, May 25, 2017, "Fact-checking Montana politician Greg Gianforte's account of clash with *Guardian* reporter"). Afterwards, Gianforte's campaign lied about the incident, claiming Gianforte first attempted to grab the recorder and then the reporter grabbed Gianforte's wrist, which led to the physical altercation. However, a Fox News team was in the room, and caught the assault on video. As Fox reporter Alicia Acuna recounted, there was no struggle over the recorder. Instead, "Gianforte grabbed Jacobs by the neck with both hands and slammed him into the ground behind him...Faith, Keith and I watched in disbelief as Gianforte then began punching the reporter...yelling something to the effect of, 'I'm sick and tired of this!'" Gianforte was charged with assault.

While a politician's assault on a journalist is disturbing, Gianforte's blatant lies (with the reporters recording the event!) is depressing. The fact that Gianforte easily won the subsequent election (despite the largest newspapers in the state retracting their endorsements) is downright demoralizing. A Fox News story on May 26, 2017 reported that a number of voters said the attack didn't influence their decision. One voter stated: "If you have somebody sticking a phone in your face, a mic in your face, over and over, and you don't know how to deal with the situation, you haven't really done that, you haven't dealt with that, I can see where it can...make you a little angry." How do you get from "a little angry" to punching a man in the face?

Second: In May 2017, Republican Kentucky Governor Matt Bevin tweeted that reporter Tom Loftus (who belongs to the Kentucky Journalism Hall of Fame) was "a truly sick man" for "sneaking around" Bevin's mansion in Anchorage, Kentucky. The *Courier-Journal*, where Loftus works, reported that he was researching an ethics complaint against Bevin who purchased the mansion for about $1 million below market price from a donor to his campaign—potentially a form of bribery (see *Courier-Journal* story on May 30, 2017, "Ethics Complaint Targets Bevin Over Anchorage Home"). The article described how Bevin bought the mansion for $1.6 million, but the home was assessed at $2.57 million. The house was previously owned by The Anchorage LLC, a company controlled by Neil Ramsey, who had donated extensively to Bevin and the Kentucky Republican Party. Bevin had Ramsey appointed to the Kentucky Retirement Systems board. Ramsey himself previously sold the house to Anchorage for $3 million, according to the sale price of the deed. A new assessment in April 2017 by the Jefferson County Property Value Administrator set the value at $2.9 million. In essence, Bevin purchased a property for at least $1 million less than its assessed worth, then attacked the journalist who uncovered the story as a "sick man." Trump's media-bashing made this a viable tactic.

Third: On February 8, 2019, Democratic Virginia Governor Ralph Northam confirmed he was pictured in a college yearbook photo of a man in blackface next to another in a KKK hood and sheet. Calling the photo "racist and offensive," Northam said in a statement: "I am deeply sorry for the decision I made to appear as I did in this photo and for the hurt that decision caused then and now. This behavior is not in keeping with who I am today and the values I have fought for throughout my career." He added, "I recognize that it will take time and serious effort to heal the damage this conduct has caused…The first step is to offer my sincerest apology and to state my absolute commitment to living up to the expectations Virginians set for me when they elected me to be their Governor." It was a textbook apology. However, as calls for his resignation mounted, Northam made a stunning reversal. The following day he announced, "I did not wear that costume or attend that party," claiming he had never seen the photo before, because he had not bought the yearbook. Although calls continued for him to resign, other scandals soon rocked the Virginia Democratic leadership. Polls were split in the weeks that followed, and as of May 2019, Northam appears to have survived. Politics aside, Northam's two statements are simply incompatible. Was he following Trump's tactic of simply changing his story, without explanation? (For example, see Trump's payments of hush money to porn star "Stormy Daniels," as detailed in "Not just misleading. Not merely false. A lie," in the *Washington Post* Fact Checker, August 22, 2018.)

Given Trump's successes in hacking the political system, we should not be surprised by these copycat behaviors from Democratic and Republican politicians. In following Trump's example, post-truth politicians further erode the public's trust, diminish the threat that media exposure will harm their careers, and undermine the social norm of punishing serial liars. Additionally, if citizens think their political leaders find advantages in lying, they too may feel it's normal to lie by creating and sharing deliberately deceptive information online.

What do political systems look like where the media does not play the role of referee and politicians face no consequences for lying? In countries like Russia, the media is usually owned or controlled by political parties who spread lies about their opponents and present their side only in glowing terms. Such nations often turn authoritarian, as Turkey has done in recent years. As governments grow more powerful, they crack down on the opposition, shutting newspapers, jailing journalists, and quietly ordering assassinations. They steal elections, with 90 percent victory margins for the winners. When governments do change, they do so via coup d'état or armed uprising. In sum, when the media can't bring to light the crimes of leaders as a credible referee, "Democracy Dies in Darkness" — which became the motto of the *Washington Post* in February 2017, the month after Trump took power.

Can we reverse this race to the bottom? To do so, the mainstream media and citizens must discover a new way to institute a system-wide "mutual coercion, mutually agreed upon by the majority of the people affected," as we would to solve any other tragedy of the commons.

A Strategy for Reversing the Race to the Bottom

To find effective strategies that solve the tragedy of the commons of truthfulness, we need to look again at what factors induce ordinary people to deceive, and what moves them to be truthful. Then we can turn to the specific case of post-truth politicians. In addition to the research on cognitive biases that facilitate deception described in previous chapters, other studies have emerged on motivators for honesty and dishonesty. A 2010 article in *Psychological Science* by Francesca Gino et al. showed that if people perceived others around them as behaving dishonestly, they were also more likely to behave dishonestly themselves; in turn, if they behaved dishonestly, they perceived others as more likely to behave dishonestly. These two patterns together, once they start, create a self-reinforcing spiral of deception.

For instance, consider social media sharing of viral deception. A person who spreads such deceptive content will perceive others around them as more likely to spread viral deception than is actually the case; likewise, if that person sees someone sharing misinformation, they will be more likely to share viral deception themselves, as that person's actions provide him or her with an implicit permission to do so. I can personally relate to that with my weight loss struggles: If I see someone around me eating a second helping, I am much more likely to eat a second helping than if no one around me does so.

Additionally, Nina Mazar and Dan Ariely's 2006 piece in the *Journal of Public Policy & Marketing* illustrated that people are more likely to lie if they believe it benefits their in-group. So, if someone sees an article favorable to their political in-group, they will be more likely to share it without doing any fact-checking, even if the article inspires some skepticism, compared to a neutral article. Promoting questionable content favorable to one's in-group both helps people feel like activists for their cause, and signals to others in their social media network an alliance around shared values, gaining them a sense of respect and approval.

Thus, any proposed solution needs to address both the perception of dishonesty by others and oneself, and also the perceived benefits to one's in-group from dishonesty.

Fortunately, we also have research on what causes people to avoid dishonest behavior from some of the same researchers. Two articles by Mazar et al. in 2008 in the *Journal of Marketing Research* show some intriguing findings: Reminders about ethical behavior made people less likely to lie; getting people to sign an honor code or other commitment contract to honesty before engaging in tasks involving temptation to lie increased honesty; making standards for truthful behavior clear decreased deception. In an interesting parallel to the environmental movement, those who chose to commit to recycling by signing a pledge were more likely to follow their commitments in comparison to those who just agreed to recycle, as shown by Richard Katzev and Anton Pardini's 1987 piece in the *Journal of Environmental Systems*. An article by Heather Mann et al. in *PloS One* in 2014 demonstrates that our likelihood of lying is strongly impacted by our social network, making it especially important to address social norms around deception.

For anyone interested in a more thorough analysis, Ariely summarizes and synthesizes the research on what moves us to lie and vice versa in his *The Honest Truth About Dishonesty:*

How We Lie to Everyone—Especially Ourselves. In a nutshell, he finds that what determines whether people lie or not is not some rational cost–benefit analysis, but a wide variety of seemingly irrational psychological factors. Crucially, our behavior around deception ties strongly to self-identity and group belonging. People generally wish to maintain a self-identity as essentially truthful and to act within accepted group norms, and so inducing a greater orientation toward the truth requires integrating truth-oriented behaviors into one's identity and group affiliation. The more of these factors a solution can address, the better.

Observing the misinformation, fake news, and post-truth politics rampant in 2016 during the US presidential campaign and the UK Brexit campaign, and aware of this research, a group of academics and concerned citizens—led by me—began to work on a project to uplift truthfulness in our public sphere. After all, we didn't want democracies in these and other countries to go the way of Russia and Turkey. Due in part to my Moldovan heritage, and my parents' decision to come to the United States to get away from the destructive lies and deceptions that dominated life in the Soviet Union, it was incredibly depressing for me to see such misinformation and post-truth politics emergent in my new home. In response, I felt driven to invest a great deal of my personal time and money into creating a truly effective initiative; an initiative that would get private citizens and public figures alike invested emotionally and personally into seeing and speaking the truth; an initiative informed by the success of the environmental movement that combined positive communal and reputational reinforcement of truthfulness together with penalties for deception. That initiative, which you found at the front of this book, and lives at the heart of it, is called the Pro-Truth Pledge.

Important Terms Referenced in This Chapter

Tragedy of the commons: when a group of people share a common resource — the commons — without any controls on the use of this resource, individual self-interest may lead to disaster ("tragedy") for all involved.

Race to the bottom: what happens when trust starts to break down in a "commons" situation.

Chapter 7

The Pro-Truth Pledge: Tilting the Scale Toward the Truth

The Pro-Truth Pledge plays a central role in the Pro-Truth Movement. The purpose of the pledge is to preserve the truth-and-trust commons from post-truth politicians and others who would pollute it for selfish gains with misinformation and lies. To move the needle toward truth requires addressing deception by both private citizens and public figures. Armed with accumulated research from studies on truth and lies, decision-making and cognitive biases, and successful pro-environmental interventions, a group of scholars and citizens—led by me—launched the Pro-Truth Pledge in December 2016.

The pledge asks signees to commit to 12 behaviors that research in behavioral science shows correlate with an orientation toward truthfulness. Private citizens who sign the pledge get the benefit of contributing to a more truth-oriented society. Public figures get more substantive rewards for signing the pledge, in the form of positive media and public recognition. The pledge crowdsources the truth by asking volunteers to evaluate the statements of public figures who sign the pledge and hold these figures accountable for sticking to their commitment. (For the most recent numbers of signers, see www.protruthpledge.org)

The Pro-Truth Pledge's Frequently Asked Questions (FAQ) webpage clarifies that the pledge only applies to knowable information about the public sphere. It does not address private speech, or spiritual speech, or personal experience: only public discourse. Thus, the pledge defines misinformation as anything that goes against verifiable facts. That may mean directly lying about the situation at hand, for instance when an athlete denies taking steroids that she was actually taking. It can mean lying by omission, as when a scholar publishes a study with a successful

The Pro-Truth Pledge

I Pledge My Earnest Efforts To:

Share truth

Verify: fact-check information to confirm it is true before accepting and sharing it

Balance: share the whole truth, even if some aspects do not support my opinion

Cite: share my sources so that others can verify my information

Clarify: distinguish between my opinion and the facts

Honor truth

Acknowledge: acknowledge when others share true information, even when we disagree otherwise

Reevaluate: reevaluate if my information is challenged, retract it if I cannot verify it

Defend: defend others when they come under attack for sharing true information, even when we disagree otherwise

Align: align my opinions and my actions with true information

Encourage truth

Fix: ask people to retract information that reliable sources have disproved even if they are my allies

Educate: compassionately inform those around me to stop using unreliable sources even if these sources support my opinion

Defer: recognize the opinions of experts as more likely to be accurate when the facts are disputed

Celebrate: celebrate those who retract incorrect statements and update their beliefs toward the truth

Fig. 7.1 The Pro-Truth Pledge (courtesy of Pro-Truth Pledge, www. protruthpledge.org)

experiment, while hiding the fact that he conducted 50 of the same experiments that failed, until by random chance one finally worked, a phenomenon known as *publication bias*. It can mean using made-up statistics to support one's argument. It can mean misrepresenting someone else's position in such a way that a neutral observer would have a completely twisted perspective of that position. It can mean insisting something is true despite lacking clear evidence that it is in fact true, especially after being challenged about the claim. It can mean sharing an article whose headline is at odds with the conclusions reached in the article. In general, misinformation is anything that conveys information in an obviously deceptive way that leads audiences to have a fundamentally wrong impression of the truth in any given matter.

In some cases, such misinformation is obvious, so that any reasonable external observer—in this case, fellow pledge-takers who evaluate each other—can see it. In other cases, it is less so. For those cases, the Pro-Truth Pledge calls on pledge signers to rely on credible fact-checking websites and/or on the scientific consensus. We consider credible any fact-checkers that have passed vetting by the Poynter Institute's International Fact-Checking Network and are listed as "verified signatories" on its website. Someone who takes the pledge will be considered in violation of the pledge if they make a claim that is similar to those rated as "mostly false" or "completely false" by one of these websites (they use different language, but you get the idea). In a case where credible websites disagree, for instance one calls a claim "mostly false," while another one calls it "mostly true," we will not consider the claim a violation of the pledge.

In some cases, fact-checking websites have not evaluated certain claims, but the claim will be opposed by scientific research. Since science is the best of all methods that we as human beings have found to determine the reality about the physical world, the pledge considers a clear scientific consensus as the third method that signees can use to determine the truth. For the purpose of the pledge, this consensus may come in the form of position statements by prestigious scientific organizations, or the result of meta-analysis studies, evaluations of a series of other prominent studies, which come to a clear determination. Since science evolves in part through individual scientists with expertise in a certain domain challenging the scientific consensus in that domain, those who are scientists do not have to abide by the scientific consensus in areas where they are experts. However, it is important to recognize that in areas where a scientist is not an expert, they are not exempt. For example, a scientist who is not a climatologist can be challenged for posting views against the scientific consensus on climate change if they imply that their expertise as, say a nuclear physicist, gives them credibility.

We do not expect perfection in sticking to the truth-oriented behaviors described in the pledge, which is why the pledge asks for "earnest efforts." It encourages all pledge-takers to support and encourage each other in pursuing truth-oriented behaviors, by highlighting opportunities for improvement in doing so by other pledge-takers and praising those who pursue such behaviors despite obstacles and temptations. At the same time, the FAQ text acknowledges that fellow pledge-takers cannot read one another's minds and see whether they actually dedicate "earnest efforts" to these behaviors or not. What may be easy to some people may be incredibly difficult to others, for all sorts of reasons; what may be glaring lapses in pursuing these behaviors may be invisible to others. Thus, where pledge-takers failed to engage in the 12 behaviors of the pledge, these are considered lapses, rather than violations of the pledge. Still, to ensure accountability, the pledge needs at least some clear and externally verifiable standards—something that all pledge-takers can agree on, could be externally verified, and should be avoided: statements deliberately meant to mislead, going against credible fact-checking sites, or going against the scientific consensus.

As part of signing the pledge, signees have the opportunity to receive the pledge newsletter and action alerts, to follow the Pro-Truth Pledge on social media, to ask all of their elected representatives to take the pledge, to be listed in a public database of pledge-takers, to join an online or in-person community of other pledge-takers, and to sign up to be a pledge advocate. The latter consists of any of the following: 1) promoting the pledge to other private citizens; 2) advocating for public figures to take the pledge; 3) monitoring and evaluating whether the public figures stick to their commitment. Furthermore, whenever they share a news article, signees are encouraged to add a sentence stating that they took the pledge and verify that they fact-checked the article. Pledge-takers are asked to share publicly with their networks about taking the pledge by email and social media (see, for example, Figure 7.2).

Fig. 7.2 Steven Pinker tweeting that he took the Pro-Truth Pledge (courtesy of Twitter)

Signees may add a logo on the back of their business cards indicating they took the pledge, to leave good impressions in the eyes of their business contacts. They are also encouraged to add a badge to their online presence demonstrating they took the pledge.

The pledge and these additional elements are designed to counteract the tendencies that cause us to lie. For instance, the first behavior of fact-checking before accepting information as true, the second behavior of avoiding lying by omission, and the fourth behavior of clarifying the difference between one's opinions and facts aim to address the need to create clear standards for truthful behavior. Signing the pledge itself serves a similar function to an honor code.

Joining online and in-person communities of pledge-takers, and promoting the pledge to one's existing social network, helps shift the orientation of one's social network toward the truth, decreases the perceived benefits to one's social network of sharing misinformation, and strengthens honesty-oriented group norms. So do some of the behaviors to which pledge-takers swear, such as asking people — including one's allies — to retract misinformation, and encouraging those around oneself to avoid using systematically unreliable sources of information (such as *Breitbart* on the right and *Occupy Democrats* on the left).

Committing to the pledge and engaging in the behaviors described there and all of the other surrounding behaviors strengthens one's identity as someone who orients toward the truth, and someone who identifies with other truth-oriented individuals. In other words, it helps to create a tribe of truth-seekers and truth-tellers that cuts across the partisan divide. Indeed, the Advisory Board of the Pro-Truth Pledge ranges from the founder of the Houston Tea Party Society Felicia Winfree Cravens and conservative Christian pastor Lorenzo Neal on the right, to businessman and progressive activist Michael Tyler on the left.

The behaviors to which pledge-takers commit also aim to address specific cognitive biases such as *confirmation bias*, our tendency to search for and accept information that aligns with our current beliefs. A major way to address confirmation bias involves asking people to consider and search for evidence that disproves their initial beliefs, as shown by Laura Kray and Adam Galinsky's 2003 piece in *Organizational Behavior and Human Decision Processes* and Edward Hirt and Keith Markman's 1995 article in the *Journal of Personality and Social Psychology*. The first behavior of the pledge asks people to take time to verify information before sharing it, by going to reliable fact-checking websites or evaluating the scientific consensus on any given topic. By taking time to verify this information, signees get an opportunity to evaluate the accuracy of their information and change their perspective if they do not find credible evidence supporting that information. This aspect of the pledge aims to address the extensive sharing of fake news, both by private citizens and by public figures.

In the spirit of anticipating errors, an important aspect of the 'choice architecture' approach to addressing cognitive biases, the pledge encourages signees to celebrate both others and themselves for retracting incorrect statements and updating their beliefs toward the truth, the twelfth behavior. Research by Philip Fernbach et al. in a 2013 *Psychological Science* article showed that people often hold extreme positions on complex topics due to a fallacious thinking mode termed *the illusion of explanatory depth*, an overconfidence in one's understanding of reality; the third behavior of the pledge of citing sources and the fourth behavior of distinguishing between one's opinion and the actual facts aim to help address this illusion.

Another problematic factor might be *group attribution error* and the *horns effect*, which causes people to censure irrationally those who do not belong to their in-group, and vice versa. To address this problem, the seventh behavior of the pledge asks people to defend others who come under attack for sharing accurate information even if they have different values.

The *Dunning-Kruger effect* is another cognitive bias where those who have less expertise and skills in any given area have an inflated perception of their abilities, related by Justin Kruger and David Dunning in their 1999 piece in the *Journal of Personality and Social Psychology*. To address this problem, the pledge calls on signees to practice the eleventh behavior of acknowledging that, when facts are disputed, the opinions and interpretations of experts on a topic are more likely to be accurate than those of non-experts.

Why would private citizens go to ProTruthPledge.org and sign the pledge? Signing the pledge gives them an opportunity to reject a 'post-truth' mentality, and help move our society toward greater honesty. This type of pro-social desire has been found to be a strong motivator in environmental efforts, according to a 1997 piece by Van Lange et al. in the *Journal of Personality and Social Psychology*. Furthermore, signing the pledge gives any individual who signs it greater credibility among their peers who know they signed it. The pledge encourages individuals who signed it to share about it on their social media and personal networks, and put a badge on their online presence indicating they signed it. They get access to unique resources available to signees, such as a search engine composed of credible sources verified as reliable by the pledge organizers. They also get to join a variety of closed communities both online and in their local area available only to pledge signees, where they can rely on the credibility of the information being shared by those who signed the pledge and also support and encourage each other in practicing behaviors advocated by the pledge. Peer support has proven helpful in maintaining desired behavior change in other contexts, such as health behaviors (as shown by Rick Zimmerman and Catherine Connor in a 1989 *Health Education Quarterly* piece). So we anticipate that similar support for signees of the pledge will help them maintain truth-oriented behavior.

All pledge-takers—private citizens and public figures—gain the benefits of cultivating socially beneficial habits of mind, word, and deed. All gain the pride and self-satisfaction of standing up for truth and fighting lies. All gain the benefit of being role models for others. All gain the benefits of building a more truth-driven public culture, and fighting the pollution of truth in politics. The latter forms a concrete social good for our society, and shows how the pledge aligns with the concept of libertarian welfarism.

Public Figures and the Pro-Truth Pledge

Public figures—politicians, journalists and others media figures, CEOs and other high-level organizational leaders, academics, clergy, authors, and others—get additional rewards for taking the pledge, since they have a stronger impact on our public discourse than private citizens. When they sign, they have the opportunity to share a paragraph about why they took the pledge and provide links to their online presence. The paragraph is then sent around in the pledge newsletter and posted on social media, as a way of providing a reputational reward for committing to truth-oriented behavior. Public figures also get their public information listed in a database on the pledge website and can post a badge on their own website about their commitment to the pledge, providing clear information about which public figures are committed to truthful behavior.

These rewards for public figures will grow as the pledge gets more popular, creating a virtuous cycle. The more private citizens and public figures sign the pledge and the more credibility it gets, the more incentives other public figures will have to sign it. While these early adopters will be most committed to honesty, later adopters will be more likely to do so out of a desire to gain a reputation as honest, and thus will be more likely to cheat. To address this problem, the pledge crowdsources the fight against lies. One of the volunteer roles for the pledge is holding public figures accountable. If a volunteer suspects that a public figure made a false statement, the volunteer would approach the person privately and ask for clarification. The matter can be resolved by the public figure issuing a retraction—everyone makes mistakes—or the volunteer realizing that the public figure's statement is not false. If the matter is not resolved, the volunteer would then submit the case to a mediating committee of vetted and trained volunteers. They would investigate the matter and give the public figure an opportunity to issue a retraction or explain why the statement is not false.

If the public figure refuses to do so, the mediating committee then assumes that the public figure lied, meaning they made a deliberately false statement, and rules the person in contempt of the pledge. This ruling would trigger a substantial reputational punishment. The mediating committee issues a media advisory to all relevant media venues that the public figure is in contempt of the pledge and puts that information on the pledge website. The committee also sends an action alert to all pledge-takers who are constituents to that public figure, asking them to tweet, post, text, call, write, meet with, and otherwise lobby the public figure to retract their words. A public figure who intends to lie is much better off not taking the pledge at all.

Given this accountability system, why should elected or appointed officials take the pledge if it restrains their activities? Officials need to be perceived as trustworthy by citizens. The pledge provides that credibility, due to the presence of the monitoring mechanism. Citizens can easily look them up in the pledge database. If the official has signed the pledge a while ago and is not in contempt, the citizen can assume the official has not made any deceptive statements without retracting them later. The official gets additional benefits because when the official signs up, his or her information is included in the pledge updates. This provides the official with a positive reputation for being honest and credible, and gets them more support. There is an additional benefit for elected officials whose opponent for office has not taken the pledge, since the pledge-taking official can raise questions about why the opponent does not wish to take the pledge. For those public officials who take it early-onward, the pledge thus offers a first-mover advantage, which often bears strong long-term competitive advantage, according to research by Roger Kerin et al. in a 1992 *Journal of Marketing* article.

What about political commentators, analysts, media figures, and scholars of politics, as well as policy experts? Why should they sign? They all need to be perceived as trustworthy by their audiences. The pledge provides them with that benefit due to the monitoring mechanism, and similarly to the officials described above, the longer they are signed up without being in contempt, the more credibility they get. Those who sign can also get a broader audience engaged with them since their information will be included in the pledge updates. Moreover, if their competitors do not sign the pledge, those who signed up will get a bigger audience, since audiences will start flocking to those deemed more trustworthy sources of news/analysis/ thought leadership. Thus, the first-mover advantage applies to these groups as well.

The Pro-Truth Pledge is also useful for organizational leaders in the corporate and nonprofit sectors. They too need to be trusted, both within and outside their organizations, as leading with integrity. The same evaluation mechanisms of the pledge that hold public figures accountable offer that benefit. To be clear, the pledge focuses on statements made by organizational leaders that have relevance for public discourse. One example might be claims about the application of public policy to their specific domains, for instance, minimum wage policy to employment by a specific corporation; another example relevant to public discourse might be the environmental harm done by a certain company; a third might be making sure to avoid misrepresenting data about gun deaths by nonprofits advocating for or against gun control.

The pledge encourages pledge advocates from inside organizations to provide information demonstrating evidence of deceptions by organizational leaders and will readily use such documentation in its evaluations of pledge violations. It also welcomes external stakeholders of organizations providing information about violations. Due to such monitoring by internal and external stakeholders alike, organizational leaders who take the pledge will have greater credibility than those who choose to avoid taking it.

Additionally, an organization as a whole may choose to commit to the pledge, which means all public statements made by the organization, and by employees of the organization in their official role representing the organization, would be evaluated for accuracy to the extent these statements impinge on issues of relevance to public discourse. For instance, a statement about the quality of a car by a car company—whether it really goes from 0 to 60 in 5 seconds—would not have much relevance for public discourse, while claims about the impact of government policy on the emissions of that car do bear relevance for public discourse.

As of spring 2019, several hundred politicians across the political spectrum have taken the pledge, whether state-level ones such as members of state legislatures Jamie Flitner (Wyoming), James White (Texas), and Ogden Driskell (Wyoming), or national politicians such as presidential candidate Beto O'Rourke and members of US Congress Dean Phillips (Minnesota), Matt Cartwright (Pennsylvania), and Marcia Fudge (Ohio). Over a thousand other public figures have taken the pledge, including globally known intellectuals Peter Singer, Steven Pinker, and Jonathan Haidt, religious leaders such as Pierre Whalon, Jim Burklo, and Lorenzo Neal, media personalities such as Ethan

Bearman, Andrew Keen, and Bob Fitrakis, and civic activists such as Bill Shireman, Andrew Hanauer, and Ricken Patel. Additionally, over a hundred organizations, whether news-oriented ones such as Media Bias/Fact Check, Media in Action, Columbus Free Press, and Fugitive Watch, or civic-oriented ones such as Stand Up Republic, Faith and Freedom Coalition Delaware, George Mason University Center for Climate Change, and BridgeUSA also took the pledge.

Beyond simply signing the pledge, there are several examples of the pledge changing the behavior of public figures (see Figure 7.3).

Fig. 7.3 Michael Smith's Facebook post, February 15, 2017 (courtesy of Facebook)

The 2017 Facebook post of a tweet by Donald Trump criticizing minority and disabled children in classrooms—which got a sizable number of Facebook shares—was made by Michael Smith, a candidate for the US House of Representatives in Idaho. After being called out on whether Trump really made the tweet, Smith went and searched Trump's Twitter feed. Unable to find the tweet in question, he then edited his post to say "Due to a Truth Pledge I have taken I have to say I have not been able to verify this post." He indicated that he would be more careful with future postings.

Second, a candidate running for the state house in Arizona,

Johnny Martin, also took the pledge. He made a misstatement during a public rally, and later posted on Facebook about the misstatement, retracting it and citing the pledge (see Figure 7.4).

Fig. 7.4 Screenshot of Johnny Martin's Facebook post with retraction (courtesy of Facebook)

Third, Republican Minnesota state legislator Dean Urdahl was challenged by his Democratic opponent, Justin Vold, to take the pledge during the 2018 election campaign (see Figure 7.5). Despite being in a very safe Republican district, which he won by over 67 percent

Fig. 7.5 Justin Vold's challenge to sign the pledge, and Dean Urdahl's acceptance (courtesy of Twitter)

in 2016, Urdahl took the pledge (and won in 2018 by over 69 percent).

Lastly, an example from the media: Brent Hatley, a senior producer of *The Howard Stern Show*, signed the pledge and then tweeted to his 45,000 followers about the impact it has had on him (see Figure 7.6).

Fig. 7.6 Screenshot of Brent Hatley's tweet (courtesy of Twitter)

Reversing the Tragedy of the Commons

As shown above, the pledge draws on research about what interventions make us most likely to behave honestly; it also uses findings on what helps address tragedies of the commons similar to what has been shown to work in campaigns for reducing water and air pollution. The pledge sets up default options of guiding signees into truthful behavior, anticipates errors by encouraging pledge-takers to retract statements that they cannot support through clear evidence, celebrates updating of beliefs, and creates incentives to promote honesty. The community support for private citizens and evaluative mechanism for public figures offers clear feedback. In short, it creates incentives for not polluting the commons of trust with lies, and holds pledge-takers accountable.

For many readers of this book, pledging to follow the 12 behaviors may not prove burdensome, and in fact may already represent what they already do in daily life. In fact, I have heard truth-oriented people say that they don't need to take the pledge because they already behave in these ways. I understand these sentiments: ideally, we would not need a pledge, as everyone would naturally behave in a truth-oriented manner. As one of the pledge signees, Stephanie Savage, states in her July 1, 2017 post on *Patheos*, "Our Enlightenment-era Founding Fathers would've wept to learn that a Pro-Truth Pledge was even necessary in our time." Unfortunately, as the research above showed, humans are not naturally honest, especially when they stand to gain from dishonesty for some of their other goals.

I'm willing to bet that readers of this book are much more likely to be honest than the average individual. However, we need to remember that those who are allergic to lies and already behave in a truth-oriented manner do so as a result of factors in our cultural upbringing and genes that helped shape our personality. We represent an unfortunately small slice of the population, as researchers like Ariely and others discovered. For people who already do not abuse the commons of truth and trust in our public discourse, the main benefit of taking the pledge consists of signaling — sending information to others about their commitment to such behavior, without giving anything up (for more on signaling, consult Brian Connelly et al.'s 2011 article in *Journal of Management*). For plenty of others, committing to the 12 behaviors would involve some effort on their part to avoid destroying the commons of truth and trust, for the sake of knowing that they are pushing other participants in public discourse to avoid such behaviors as well. In addition, all pledge-takers are encouraged to evaluate other participants, which helps motivate participation in the agreement, discourages those who intend to cheat from signing up, and maintains the strength of the accord.

The lessons for avoiding the tragedies of the environmental commons all apply in the truth-and-trust commons: creating or reforming institutions, offering trustworthy information, appealing to identity and group belonging, and changing incentives. These all provide important guidance for the pledge. The pledge itself serves as a new institution, and following research on the environmental movement, strives to treat all fairly and focus on transparency. Likewise, the pledge appeals to and strengthens one's identity as a truth-teller; it also encourages a shift in group affiliation to greater honesty, both with one's existing group ties and also via developing new ties to fellow pledge-takers.

The pledge combines a universal set of behaviors with local-level implementation and evaluation. Studies on the environmental movement showed that local-level accords have more likelihood of working effectively. This research helps inform the organizational structure of the pro-truth movement surrounding the pledge. Along with the ProTruthPledge.org website and virtual communities on Facebook, Twitter, and elsewhere, the Pro-Truth Movement focuses on setting up local in-person communities devoted to promoting truth and fighting lies at the local level. The aspiration of the Pro-Truth Movement is to have Pro-Truth Pledge organizers in each locale who coordinate various activities related to the pledge, such as getting private citizens to sign it, lobbying public figures to take it, and evaluating public figures who do take it. Moreover, the organizers help set up community activities around the Pro-Truth Movement. It really helps people to have a community of other truth-oriented individuals around them, who they can trust and bond with around fighting lies and promoting honesty in our public discourse.

At the same time, the pledge has an international reach. Anyone around the world may take the pledge, and people from six continents have already signed the pledge, mainly from democratic countries but also authoritarian ones such as Iran. In contexts like that one, signing the pledge mainly involves a personal commitment and voicing a desire to change the culture of public discourse, without much hope of shifting the behavior of individual government officials. A public figure from Iran who signed the pledge did so under his public pseudonym, Kaveh Mousavi, which he uses to blog about Iranian politics. He avoids his real name due to fears of political retribution. He wrote a blog on June 20, 2017 with the title "Why I Signed the Pro-Truth Pledge (And You Should Too)." In the blog, he states that "I signed the Pro-Truth pledge because I want to encourage skeptical and critical thinking, especially when it comes to politics and political behavior." Mousavi explains that "conspiracy theories are very prevalent among Iranians" and that "the regime likes to blame everything on foreign meddling" while "the opposition blame everything on a conspiracy of the regime." He states that "there's a strong link between a conspiratorial mind and a totalitarian mind" and adds "to me, having a pro-truth attitude and promoting skepticism in the place of credulity is an integral part of my activism as a pro-democracy reformist."

Fortunately, most signees live in a context where they do not have to use pseudonyms to avoid political repression. For example, the globally known moral philosopher Peter Singer lives in Australia, and his public statement about taking the pledge, which is on the Pro-Truth Pledge public figures page, says: "How can citizens make the right choice at elections if they are lied to, and don't know how to distinguish a lie from truth? Truth in the public arena is essential to a functioning democracy." Pierre Whalon states his motivation as follows: "As the Episcopal Bishop in a highly-visible post in Europe, it is essential that people know and believe that I always seek the truth, the facts, and the context of the materials I post online or give in my sermons." Turning to the US, news personality

Ethan Bearman, rated number 57 talk-show host in 2017 by *Talkers* magazine and guest star on prominent TV channels such as Fox News and CNN, wrote: "Facts matter and the truth matters...There are people who prey on others with falsehoods for monetary gain, political influence, and even pure malice. It is up to us to make sure the truth shines through the clouds of falsehoods."

Politicians who took the pledge share similar reasons for doing so. For example, Shane Sandridge, a Republican who ran and won in November 2018 for the Colorado state legislature stated that "fake news and misleading information is out of control in our country." Another Republican who ran and won in November 2018 for the Minnesota state legislature said he signed because "I believe the truth is important." Rob Sand, a Democrat who ran for and won the Iowa State Auditor office in 2018, stated that he took the pledge because "Like any case I pursued as a prosecutor, I base my actions as a candidate upon what the facts and evidence show. While we can have disagreements about what policies may be best, we must all first base our opinions upon the same facts." Rob Sand's official campaign picture on his Facebook page bore the logo of the Pro-Truth Pledge, an important demonstration of how useful he found it in his campaign.

These commitments by public figures and organizations speak to the question of reputation in the role of solving tragedies of the commons. A number of the public figures and organizations who signed up did so primarily or solely out of a desire to help fight lies and promote truth; for instance, people like Singer have a sufficiently high reputation that signing the pledge makes no substantial impact for them. Others have explicitly told me in private conversations that getting their name recognized represented a part of their motivations, showing that the reputational incentive matters.

In the end, it doesn't matter why people sign up, because

they are accountable once they do choose to take the pledge. Just as solving the environmental tragedies of the commons requires effectively identifying those who are environment-friendly, the pledge helps solve this problem for the tragedy of the truth-and-trust commons; we can have much higher confidence in those who did sign up, due to the presence of the evaluative mechanism. Like the "dolphin-safe" label for tuna, the pledge provides a clear and easy-to-understand sign for observers. The pledge website badge will increasingly serve as a signal of public figures and organizations that are truthful in their engagement with public discourse, in similarity to how the Better Business Bureau website badge offers proof of credibility in business practices for organizations.

Another challenge for addressing the tragedy of the commons in the environment relates to the lack of coordination around rewarding good actors, and punishing bad ones. The pledge coordinates rewards by distinguishing good actors, the public figures and organizations that signed the pledge and did not fall into contempt of the pledge, from ones who are ambiguous, the ones who fail to sign the pledge and thus do not have an evaluative mechanism to measure their credibility. While some of them may be good actors, others will be bad. For the good actors, the pledge offers increasingly powerful reputational boosts, as more and more private citizens sign up and become familiar with the public figures who took the pledge.

Furthermore, as pledge organizers approach public figures about signing up and certain public figures refuse to do so, more evidence will accumulate about potential bad actors. Right now, at the early stage of the Pro-Truth Movement, many public figures have not taken the pledge because they lack knowledge about it. In our experience, as soon as they find out about the pledge and gain a reasonable understanding of how it functions, a certain percentage of public figures sign up eagerly. As more time passes and additional public figures take the pledge, the remaining pool of public figures will consist more and more of bad actors. Those who want to distinguish themselves from the bad actors, even if they did not express early enthusiasm for the pledge, will decide to take it.

For instance, I have spoken to a prominent author and speaker who stated that he did not want to take on the effort of engaging in the 12 behaviors of the pledge until the incentives to do so were sufficiently high. These incentives involve both rewards and punishments. The former relates to a large number of private citizens taking the pledge, so that the public figure in question gets a bigger reputational boost from pledging. The punishment in this case involves increasing pressure from questions being raised about why the public figure has not taken the pledge despite being approached a number of times and also a number of other public figures of a similar stature taking the pledge, such as the peers of the author and speaker mentioned above. Through this process, we will over time move to a place where those who choose not to sign up do so mainly because they persistently abuse the common good of trust and honesty in public discourse, and do not wish to stop. We know from examples in the environmental movement that such figures and organizations will make the biggest efforts to obscure that information, either by making false arguments about why they do not wish to take the pledge or attacking the credibility of the pledge itself. The potential for such attacks explains why maintaining the nonpartisan and transparent nature of the pledge and its function is so critical.

Will It Work?

For the pledge to work, several things have to take place. Externally, private citizens and public figures have to take the pledge, and the pledge has to change their behavior. Internally, the organizational structure of the pledge needs to function, which includes promoting the pledge to private citizens and public figures, and managing all the aspects of the pledge, from the newsletter and social media, to coordinating the virtual and in-person communities, to evaluating public figures. For this organizational structure to work, the pledge needs to attract sufficient volunteer time and financial support.

It has proven pretty easy to get private citizens to sign. For in-person events, pledge volunteers simply attend political and community events and present the pledge as an opportunity to fight lies in public discourse. Other volunteers promote the pledge on social media, as well as content such as blogs, podcasts, TV and radio interviews, and books, such as this one. So many people are tired of viral deception and alternative facts that many willingly jump on the chance to do something about this problem.

Certainly, signing the pledge is a bigger task than signing a petition, as the pledge asks participants to change their behavior. Still, it's not atypical for a volunteer at a community event to get 50 signatures in a day, for instance Michelle Bell at the 2017 Comfest in Columbus, Ohio, or even more at a political event: Carl Baker gathered over 60 at the 2017 Tri-City March for Science. Additionally, many pledge-takers have had success by asking those they engage with in discussions on controversial topics, in-person or online, to sign the pledge and commit to sticking to it during the discussion, and refusing to have the discussion otherwise. Members and leaders of committees, clubs, fraternities, churches, and secular groups, and the employees and managers of companies, nonprofits, and municipalities, have encouraged others around them to sign the pledge for the sake of healthy discussions and decision-making within each. A percentage of all people who sign up choose to become volunteers for the pledge, and one of the volunteer roles involves signing up new participants. Thus, the pledge has a self-perpetuating dynamic, which makes it highly likely that it will continue to expand.

Further evidence of the promise of the pledge comes from positive media coverage. *Scientific American*, a major and well-respected journal, published an article on June 15, 2017 devoted to highlighting the pledge, entitled "How to Address the Epidemic of Lies in Politics." TV coverage of the March for Truth in Columbus, which had speeches devoted to the Pro-Truth Pledge, covered the pledge in a positive manner, linked on the website of the ABC Columbus affiliate in an article on June 3, 2017, "Columbus Marchers Ask for Truth in Politics." A host of podcasts and blogs devoted to the pledge have also depicted it in a beneficial light; simply google "Pro-Truth Pledge" to see these. This positive coverage should demonstrate to public figures the potential benefits they would get from signing on to the pledge.

Case Studies in Behavior Change

How strong is the evidence that signing the pledge creates behavior change in ordinary citizens? Three examples follow.

First, a private citizen, a retired US intelligence officer who prefers to remain anonymous due to his former occupation. He described to me in a May 26, 2017 email how, soon after taking it, he saw an article "that played right to [his] particular political biases" and his "first inclination was to share it as quickly and widely as possible. But then [he] remembered the pledge [he'd] signed and put the brakes on." The story turned out to be false, and "that experience has led [him] to be much more vigilant in assessing, and sharing, stories that appeal to [his] political sensibilities."

Second, a public figure, John Kirbow, a US Army veteran and member of the Special Operations community as well as an advocate for reason and science, wrote a blog post on June 6, 2017 on *Medium*, entitled "How the Pro-Truth Pledge has impacted me." In the post, he noted that "I've verbally or digitally passed on bad information numerous times, I am fairly sure, as a result of honest mistakes or lack of vigorous fact checking." He describes how after taking the pledge, he felt "an open commitment to a certain attitude" to "think hard when I want to play an article or statistic which I'm not completely sold on." Having taken the Pro-Truth Pledge, he found it "really does seem to change one's habits," helping push him both to correct his own mistakes with an "attitude of humility and skepticism, and of honesty and moral sincerity," and also to encourage "friends and peers to do so as well."

Third, a Christian pastor named Neal told me in a June 1, 2017 email exchange that "I took the Pro-Truth Pledge because I expect our political leaders at every level of government to speak truth and not deliberately spread misinformation to the people they have been elected to serve." He adds that "having taken the pledge myself, I put forth the effort to continually gather information validating stories and headlines before sharing them on my social media outlets."

What about *quantitative* research studies? As you already know, I have a behavioral science background, and so do a number of other academics who are involved in the Pro-Truth Pledge project. We tested one of the quantifiable mechanisms of the pledge, namely whether the pledge can help address the scourge of private citizens sharing fake news on social media. In our empirical impact evaluation, we decided to target Facebook, as the most popular social media platform. Our hypothesis was that taking the pledge will impact sharing on Facebook, both when people share news-relevant content themselves on their own Facebook profile, and when they engage in other venues on Facebook, such as Facebook groups or other people's profiles. To test this hypothesis, we conducted a study of people who took the pledge and engaged actively in sharing news-relevant content on Facebook (an average of at least once a week). Since these people already care about the truth—otherwise, they would not take the pledge—any difference between sharing behaviors before and after taking the pledge can be attributed to finding out about the pledge and taking it. We recruited 24 participants to fill out Likert scale (1–5) surveys self-reporting their Facebook engagement with news-relevant content on their own profiles and also with other people's posts and in groups before and after they took the pledge. We asked them specific questions such as:

> Before you heard about the Pro-Truth Pledge, to what extent did your behavior on your personal Facebook profile align with the Pro-Truth Pledge's 12 behaviors? Please give an estimate of 1 to 5, with 1 at lowest level of alignment to 5 being full alignment. Lowest alignment means sharing misinformation. Highest alignment means actively fighting lies and promoting truth. Remember that in this question, you are evaluating only your behavior on your personal profile, not your behavior in groups or in response to other people's posts.

Our results show that taking the pledge results in a statistically significant increase in alignment with the behaviors of the pledge, both on one's own profile on Facebook and when interacting with other people's posts and in groups. Specifically:

1. For sharing content on their own profile, 70.83 percent of participants (17 of 24 respondents) reported an increase of their pledge alignment after taking the pledge: 11 participants increased by one point on the alignment scale, 5 by two points, 1 by three points, while the remaining 7 maintained the same score.
2. For sharing content in groups and on other people's walls, again, 70.83 percent of participants reported an increase of their pledge alignment after taking the pledge: 12 participants increased by one point on the alignment

scale, 5 by two points, while the remaining 7 maintained their initial score.

We conducted a statistical test (the Asymptotic Wilcoxon-Pratt Signed-Rank Test, for those curious) and found that the results had strong statistical significance (the result is considered significant when the value of $p < .05$ and we had a value of $p < 0.001$). These results indicate that taking the Pro-Truth Pledge indeed clearly improves truthful behaviors in social media sharing, and thus the pledge is an effective intervention for addressing the scourge of fake news propagated by private citizens. Due to the statistical significance and the quality of the study, it was published in the high-quality peer-reviewed academic journal, *Journal of Social and Political Psychology* (you can see the study on the journal website, https://jspp.psychopen. eu/article/view/856).

One possible weakness of that first study was that it depended on participants self-reporting their behavior. We conducted a second study to determine specifically whether or not that might have significantly skewed the finding; the results of that second study indicated that it did not. Researchers examined the first ten news-relevant posts one month after study participants took the pledge and graded the quality of the information shared, including the links, to determine how closely their posts matched the behaviors of the pledge. They then looked at the first ten news-relevant posts 11 months before they took the pledge and rated those. The study found large, statistically significant improvement in pledge-takers' adherence to the 12 behaviors of the pledge, with the effect similar in size and scope to the first study, such as fewer posts containing misinformation and including more sources ($p < .0000001$) (see Figure 7.7). As with the first study, the second one's quality and statistical significance led to it being published in a top academic journal after peer review, *Behavior and Social Issues* (you can see the study on the journal website, https://firstmonday.org/ojs/index. php/bsi/article/view/9127/7551).

The fact that both studies went through academic peer review by anonymous peer reviewers with absolutely no stake in the Pro-Truth Pledge, and a strong stake in ensuring that only top-notch content was published in the academic journals for which they served as peer reviewers, says a lot about the quality of these studies. Of course, these studies are inherently limited due to small sample size and lack of random assignment. In the future, as funding becomes available, we intend to conduct a larger study with random assignments of one group of participants to take the pledge, and another to avoid taking the pledge, and then track their social media behaviors.

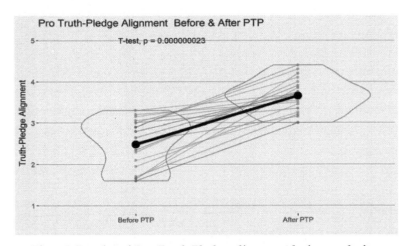

Fig. 7.7 Results of Pro-Truth Pledge alignment before and after taking the pledge for the second study (the one where researchers rated study participants, instead of relying on self-reporting). The thick black line shows the median. The lighter lines represent change among individuals. Note that every individual who took the pledge improved their sharing on Facebook to be more aligned with the pledge, some drastically.

The Pro-Truth Pledge and the Right–Left Divide

Even with all these sign-ups, and even if it does impact people successfully, the pledge may still founder on the ground of partisanship. An important part of the success of the environmental movement came from the efforts of advocates to reach across the political divide, even if liberals proved most enthusiastic about the pro-environmental message. While there is nothing inherently left-wing about the truth, in the current political context in the US and the UK of right-wing political forces using substantially more deception, left-leaning individuals will likely be most eager to support the pledge and the Pro-Truth Movement as a whole; in other countries, such as Turkey where the post-truth leader Recep Tayyip Erdogan is critical of many aspects of capitalism, those on the economic right would likely be more eager to support the Pro-Truth Pledge.

In all cases, pro-truth advocates have to make deliberate efforts to reach across the divide. While there should be no compromising on principles by taking it easy on public-figure signees who represent a minority perspective among pledge-takers, outreach to those who have less political motivation to sign up is crucial for the success of the project. In the US, for instance, pledge volunteers had success with going to conservative-leaning institutions such as Rotary clubs and similar venues to give presentations there: as an example, in a May 18, 2017 presentation at a Rotary Club in Hilliard, Ohio, pledge volunteer Susan Lear presented at a club where 25 percent of the audience signed the pledge afterward. We also had conservative public figures sign the pledge, for instance the Republican candidate for Congress John J. Baumeister, and the conservative podcast host John Wells, who stated in signing up: "The lifeblood of my program to which my name is attached and therefore all who I call and who call me, friend, those who trust me to be honest with them, and most importantly in the Earthly realm, my family rely on truthfulness in what I do. And of supreme importance, God is watching. And listening."

Such signings often come from a deliberate outreach effort to reach such figures, which needs to continue in order to ensure that the pledge, and the whole Pro-Truth Movement, does not fail by lacking solid representation across ideological divides. As stated above, in any specific local context, it will naturally draw people whose political group is losing support due to an opposing political group or groups using post-truth methods; it will also draw people whose political group is most strongly affiliated with values of reason and science. However, the Pro-Truth Movement may go off track by failing to act in a trans-partisan manner: that is, valuing truth above partisan politics, because all citizens have a stake in preserving the commons of truth. We need to go beyond our gut reaction of condemning those in political groups that oppose our own for lying while ignoring the deceptive behavior of those in our own group. We also need to go against our intuitions by finding and praising truth-oriented behaviors in those political groups opposed to our own. And we need the courage to censure those in our own groups who exhibit dishonesty.

To succeed, the Pro-Truth Movement must expend the extra effort needed to reach across the political divide, such as by putting in more energy into outreach toward those whose political group is not naturally attracted toward fighting lies. Doing so requires us to address our instinctive desire to associate only with those with whom we are most comfortable, namely those in our own political tribe. Another way the Pro-Truth Movement might go wrong is by failing to be especially welcoming and inclusive to new members who join after such outreach across the political divide. It is too easy to drive out members who represent minority political perspectives through failing to be considerate of their values and thus not helping them feel comfortable in the context of being a comparative outlier. Such participants have a great deal of value to the movement in several ways, such as demonstrating clearly its trans-partisan nature. Another key benefit involves these minority members being more capable of serving as Pro-Truth Movement ambassadors to their own political, ideological, and social groups, through being able to speak their language, knowing the key influencers, and having the personal legitimacy of belonging to those groups. Overall, the key for the Pro-Truth Movement is to ally around the behaviors described in the Pro-Truth Pledge, and more broadly to defend our democracy from the ravages of dishonesty and destruction of trust, despite our different values.

What Will It Take?

Internally, making the pledge work requires getting a host of supporters who care about fighting lies and promoting truth to contribute a combination of time, social capital, and money for this endeavor. The core organizers of the pledge, including myself, have donated substantial amounts of these three resources to start up the Pro-Truth Pledge, and the movement as a whole. Anyone who wants to join at the lowest level of participation in terms of time would go to www.protruthpledge. org, and take a minute to sign up. At a slightly higher level of involvement, one can follow the social media and updates of the pledge, perhaps for a half-hour a month. Still higher, maybe for an hour or two a month, one can participate in the online and in-person community activities. The next level, of one hour a week or more, involves various volunteer activities on behalf of the pledge. Contributing social capital involves telling friends, family members, social media connections, work colleagues, or members of one's church or secular group or other community or political organizations to which you belong about the pledge, and encouraging them to take it.

Readers interested in becoming a Pro-Truth Pledge volunteer or activist can find a free PDF of the Pro-Truth Pledge Activist Handbook at www.protruthpledge.org.

Finally, one can contribute financially, as the pledge is run by a 501(c)3 nonprofit, Intentional Insights, registered in the US. As a result, any donations made by US citizens are tax-deductible; foreign nationals who earn a percentage of their income in the US may claim a tax deduction against this income. Right now, the focus of the pledge project involves setting up organizers in all locales throughout the US, where the project started, while also expanding into other countries, starting with Canada and the UK. A key early test of the pledge will stem from the ability of pledge organizers to set up this in-person network around the US, and later in other countries around the globe. Indeed, a number of countries – such as the UK, Canada, Brazil, and others – already have activists promoting the pledge. Another vital test will come in the long term, when the pledge transitions from this early-adopter audience of the startup stage to a more mainstream audience. Will signees prove willing to contribute the resources needed to make this project sustainable in a manner that would enable the pledge to substantially impact public discourse? Will their efforts help create a Pro-Truth Movement that makes "post-truth" a brief moment that blemished our democracies, before we decisively turned ourselves toward the truth?

In conclusion, the Pro-Truth Pledge shows promise as a tool combining crowdsourcing with behavioral science to fight lies and promote truth in politics. While early adopters have exhibited enthusiasm, the pledge project requires setting up a network of local-level organizers and in-person communities to succeed in the medium term, and a transition toward a mainstream audience that might be more skeptical and less receptive to the central message of fighting lies and promoting truth compared to early adopters. To overcome such skepticism, pledge advocates need to overcome their gut reactions and show trans-partisan behavior, as well as to model the 12 tenets of the pledge themselves.

Moreover, they need to have effective ways of addressing

disagreements with other truth-oriented people, with whom they have a shared commitment to the truth but differences in values and also differing opinions about what methods to use in order to reach mutual goals. These disagreements will not be matters of fact but interpretations of fact, and thus the pledge itself, while helpful, will not provide sufficient guidance. To address these differences of opinion with other people whom you trust to orient toward the truth, the first step is to encourage them to take the pledge if they have not yet done so. Next, pro-truth advocates would be well advised to adopt the strategies of rational communication and collaborative truth-seeking, the topics of the next two chapters.

Fig. 7.8 The Pro-Truth Logo, available for use on social media for pledge-takers (www.protruthpledge.com)

Pro-Truth Pledge Links

To sign or donate: www.protruthpledge.org

To volunteer or become a Pro-Truth activist: www.protruthpledge.org/volunteer

For a free PTP activist handbook: www.protruthpledge.org/handbook

Important Terms Referenced in This Chapter

Publication bias: when a scholar publishes a study with a successful experiment, while hiding the fact that he conducted 50 of the same experiments that failed, until by random chance one finally worked.

Illusion of explanatory depth: an overconfidence in one's understanding of reality.

Confirmation bias: our tendency to search for and accept information that aligns with our current beliefs that it is in fact true, especially after being challenged about the claim.

Group attribution error: assuming one person's attitudes and behavior accurately represent the attitudes and behavior of a group to which the person belongs.

Horns effect: when we dislike one aspect of a whole, we let this dislike color other aspects of that whole. This dislike may apply to a person, an ethnicity, a political party or a nation.

Dunning-Kruger effect: the tendency of people who have less expertise and skills in any given area to have an inflated perception of their abilities. (More bluntly, this describes people who are too stupid to know how stupid they are, so they falsely think they know more than they do.)

Chapter 8

Rational Communication and the Backfire Effect

Imagine you've emailed someone to propose a phone meeting about the Pro-Truth Pledge and the Pro-Truth Movement as a whole. The person has expressed enthusiasm, and you've set up the call. After exchanging pleasantries and a bit of small talk, you get into the subject of the meeting. The person you're trying to convince to join the movement starts the conversation by talking about his perspective of "truth in politics." He discusses the 2016 US presidential election and says: "Trump was the one candidate that was speaking the truth that a lot of people in this country did not want to hear."

How would you feel? Would you be aghast? Would you start arguing with that person, trying to convince him that, in reality, Trump had lied way more than Clinton? After all, the facts would be on your side about Trump's lies. You could cite so many articles and analyses, such as the well-regarded fact-checking column of the *Washington Post*, which gave Trump a rating of Four Pinocchios (meaning "totally false") for 57 of 91 statements by Trump that the column checked (that is, 63 percent).

It's tempting to throw numbers at the person you're talking to in an effort to convince them head on that they are misinformed. However, behavioral science research suggests that it doesn't work. In fact, it's exactly the wrong thing to do. Too often, this approach triggers the *backfire effect*. When people are presented with information that challenges their beliefs, they tend to defend their positions, and by arguing for them they get more convinced their original beliefs are true. This has huge implications for anyone seeking to engage others in political discussions, especially across the partisan divide. This finding may seem counterintuitive to you, as it did to me when I first learned about it. However, the more I recalled discussions I'd had with people before learning about this research, the more I saw the point. Leading with the facts failed to convince most of my conversation partners. So how *do* you deal with people who express beliefs that are clearly at odds with the facts?

Let's go back to our example, which is close to a real situation in which I found myself. That real situation was in a much more high-stakes environment than a simple phone call. It was the start of my interview on *The Douglas Coleman Show*. Douglas Coleman has a sizable social media following of over 33,000 on Twitter and 17,000 plus on Facebook (as of July 2017). While I've done several radio and podcast interviews with conservatives, I always knew they were conservatives, and I prepared for that in advance. However, Coleman's social media and bio descriptions offered no clear signals in advance of his Trump-friendly perspective. So you can bet I was surprised by Coleman's claims of Trump's truthfulness.

What happened in the interview? Did it deteriorate into a shouting match? Well, no, though perhaps it could have. I didn't start throwing the facts about Trump's lies at Coleman. I quickly switched gears into a different mode of engagement, and sought to achieve emotionally intelligent communication instead. Validating Coleman's emotions, and mirroring his wording while subtly redirecting our conversation, I looked for and defined common ground and suggested potentially shared goals with which I thought he might agree. I laid out the Pro-Truth Pledge, and described the Pro-Truth Movement as an effective way forward to fight lies, and promote truth in politics. By the end of our conversation, Coleman committed to the Pro-Truth Pledge. He did so even though he must have realized that the Pro-Truth Pledge has the potential to harm the political prospects of Trump and other politicians he supports who rely heavily on post-truth methods. Soon after our interview, he tweeted about it to his Twitter followers (see Figure 8.1).

Fig. 8.1 Douglas Coleman's tweet about taking the Pro-Truth Pledge
(courtesy of Twitter)

This chapter lays out the science and the tactics that can help you communicate rationally and avoid the backfire effect with people who express beliefs at odds with the facts, as long as you are able to find some overarching goals or values that are shared with the other person. By communicating rationally, I do not mean communication that relies solely on reason or logic. Instead, I use the behavioral science definition of rational communication. That is, *communication that uses accurate information to make wise decisions about how to communicate, and thereby to reach your goals by getting your message across.*

The Science Behind the Backfire Effect

The *backfire effect* stems from *confirmation bias*—the tendency to look for and interpret information in ways that accord with one's existing beliefs. When confronted with information that conflicts with existing beliefs, rather than experience discomfort, people search for a way to prove themselves right. The more intensely they are forced to defend their original position, the more strongly committed they feel to it after the argument.

The research that brought this phenomenon to light was a study by Brendan Nyhan and Jason Reifler (reported in their 2010 *Political Behavior* article). They were seeking to learn whether providing corrective information to people who hold incorrect beliefs would reduce their misperceptions. Specifically, Nyhan and Reifler wanted to study the most typical way that people receive corrective information—in news reports that present both sides of an issue. Unfortunately, as Chapter 4 explained, news reports usually follow the journalistic practice of *false equivalence*: treating the two sides of a controversy as equal, even if one side has all the facts correct, and the other side merely presents misinformation. To mimic this real-life situation, the experimenters provided the study participants with mock newspaper articles that contained statements from political figures reinforcing misperceptions on three hot policy issues: 1) weapons of mass destruction in Iraq prior to the US invasion of Iraq in 2003; 2) federal policy on stem cell research; 3) the effects of tax cuts on tax revenue. Some of the articles included a corrective statement immediately following the misleading statement from a politician; other articles did not.

For instance, one of the news articles had a misleading quote from George W. Bush that might lead readers to believe that Iraq had a huge weapons-of-mass-destruction (WMD) program before the invasion, but hid or destroyed the weapons right before the arrival of US forces. In some of the articles, the quote was followed by corrective information in the form of the Duelfer Report (the highly authoritative report from the Iraq Survey Group organized by the Pentagon and Central Intelligence Agency to hunt for WMD in Iraq, which found only a very small amount of time-expired chemical weapons that offered a negligible military threat). The study asked participants who had read the article whether they agreed with the following statement: "Immediately before the U.S. invasion, Iraq had an active weapons of mass destruction program, the ability to produce these weapons, and large stockpiles of WMD, but Saddam Hussein was able to hide or destroy these weapons right before U.S. forces arrived."

Study participants were not asked for a yes–no answer, but for an answer on a scale ranging from "strongly disagree" (1) to "strongly agree" (5). On average the corrective statement did not cause a statistically significant change in incorrect beliefs.

However, the researchers also divided their subject pool by ideological beliefs, using a 7-point scale ranging from strongly conservative (3) to strongly liberal (-3). They found that providing corrective information to subjects who held strong ideological beliefs did have a statistically significant impact. Providing very liberal subjects (-3) with corrective statements that accorded with their ideological perspective (in this case, the information from the Pentagon and CIA that Iraq did not have large stockpiles of WMD) resulted in a statistically significant reduction of incorrect beliefs. Those who described themselves as liberal (-2), slightly liberal (-1) or centrist (0) had no statistically significant belief change. What happened with those who identified themselves as slightly conservative (1), conservative (2), and strongly conservative (3) was the most surprising finding, and perhaps the most depressing for those who believe explaining the facts helps people correct their opinions. When provided with clear and authoritative corrective information from highly credible sources that went against their ideological perspective, conservatives in the study actually showed a *stronger* belief that Iraq had a big WMD program and stockpile compared to subjects in the control condition, who only read the misleading quote from Bush without the data from the Duelfer Report. The correction *backfired*, resulting in a worse situation from the perspective of people having correct beliefs than giving no correction at all!

The backfire effect thus shows the danger of just providing facts in the hope that doing so will cause people who hold ideologically motivated irrational beliefs to change their minds. Another experiment described in the same study found that liberals are also not very likely to change their minds when provided with accurate information that does not accord with their worldview, so we should not suppose that this is a phenomenon that only happens with conservatives. However, other authors, such as Thomas Wood and Ethan Porter in a 2016 SSRN paper found that conservatives tended to respond less readily than liberals to corrective information.

So, what do you do if you have corrective information and you don't want to trigger the backfire effect in others? In the course of their research, Nyhan and Reifler also found some helpful insights on the backfire effect, and even some good news. In a manuscript they submitted for publication in 2015 they hypothesized that people reject corrections of their beliefs when they perceive the correction as a threat to their sense of personal identity, self-worth, and worldview. They also posited that compelling presentations of accurate information should reduce misinformation. To test the latter hypothesis, they showed that information presented in a visual format reduces misperceptions more than equivalent information presented as text, thus proving the efficacy of using compelling visual imagery to encourage accurate beliefs. A moment of reflection might explain why this is so: when we are taking in new information via text, if we disagree and it makes us uncomfortable, our eyes can easily flit over the words without really taking them in. But, when we see visual information, especially photographs or data that show clear trends, we can't help but take it in (though this is not the case for complex graphs and data sets).

Nyhan and Reifler tested this idea by evaluating whether

self-affirmation would increase people's ability to correct their mistaken beliefs. They hypothesized that starting with a self-affirmation exercise that supported people's self-worth would reduce the sense of threat to their worldview and personal identity when corrective information was given to them. They hoped this approach would decrease the psychological costs of internalizing uncomfortable facts and updating beliefs. The experiment focused on evaluating people's beliefs about whether the Iraq surge (the large increase in US troops by the Bush administration after the 2006 election) proved effective in decreasing civilian deaths and attacks by insurgents against the US-led coalition forces. Evidence shows that it did. The study participants were given information about the surge and its impact, and then asked to evaluate on a 5-point scale whether attacks "decreased substantially" (1) or "increased substantially" (5).

The specific intervention used by the researchers for self-affirmation asked participants to choose a value important to them from a list of values, and then write about some past experience when the value was "especially important to you and made you feel good about yourself." This exercise might sound silly to some readers, but it worked. Since the surge resulted in better outcomes, subjects who had advocated for withdrawal had the most to lose by looking at the evidence. But if they also engaged in the affirmation intervention, they ended the experiment holding more accurate beliefs.

While this aspect of the study addressed liberal bias, since liberals tended to be most skeptical about the surge, the manuscript also described a similar intervention for self-identified Republicans who believed that "global warming is just a theory." When asked to engage in self-affirmation, these conservatives proved more willing to update their beliefs and accept the reality of climate change.

Self-affirmations work best for situations where people

already know of some facts that go against their incorrectly held beliefs. They work less well when people are presented with new information that counters their *existing* incorrect beliefs. This outcome is exciting, since on most issues of political relevance in the real world, people do tend to know of some facts that contradict their beliefs. However, they usually just ignore those facts rather than try to square them with their worldview, which can feel uncomfortable. Thus, tactics to reduce the psychological costs of accepting new and uncomfortable factual information (even something as simple as making people feel good) have evidence-based backing as to their effectiveness. These links between identity, emotions, and the backfire effect have been confirmed by researchers other than Brendan Nyhan and Jason Reifler, as described in a 2016 article by Gregory Trevors et al. in *Discourse Processes*.

How You Can Engage in More Productive Political Conversations

First, resist the all-too-human temptation to convince the other person head on that he or she is wrong. Remind yourself that when presented with the facts that don't fit their worldview, most people would rather fight than switch. You will mostly end up strengthening their commitment to their wrong thinking.

Second, engage them on the level of values instead of information. Allow them to express not just what they believe, but something positive they did that affirmed their values. Increasing their sense of self-worth makes it easier for them to hear new information as less threatening. Keep in mind that if you demonstrate genuine respect for what the other person values, they are less likely to perceive you as a threat, and your new information as a hostile attack. If we're honest with ourselves, isn't that often what we do in political arguments: attempt to beat each other over the head with facts that support our case, in order to make the other person look wrong or uncaring? That's a sure way to trigger the backfire effect.

Third, rather than put forth your new information aggressively, as a *fact you know about the world*, reframe your information as something you have heard from a reliable source—a source the other person would find reliable, too. Invite them to consider what this fact would mean if it were true: "So, how would this information fit with your current thinking, if it were true?" Reframing difficult-to-believe information as a hypothetical situation gives the other person a chance to consider the information and how it fits with their worldview without being threatened by it. If you can allow them the psychological space to reject it, without forcing them to argue the point, you are much less likely to trigger the backfire effect. And, as a valuable byproduct, you are more likely to have a civil conversation and a better relationship when you part company.

Three Rs to Avoid Triggering the Backfire Effect

Resist the urge to start with fact.

Respect the other person's values, and ask them to talk about that instead.

Reframe your information in hypothetical terms, so the other can consider it safely: "What difference might it make if this new information were true?"

Emotional and Social Intelligence

The research findings we just reviewed have a wide relevance to the vital question of how best to handle conversations on controversial subjects. To sum it up: the findings suggest that people are more likely to feel good about your interactions with them, and pay heed to what you have to tell them, if you communicate in a way that they don't experience as threatening to their worldview, sense of identity, and self-worth. This should not come as a surprise. There is a lot of research on effective communication that points the same way, using the concepts of *emotional intelligence* and *social intelligence*. In a classical 1937 article in *Psychological Bulletin*, Robert Thorndike and Saul Stein defined social intelligence as "the ability to understand and manage people." Emotional intelligence, to quote Peter Salovey and John Mayer, who coined the term in a 1990 piece in *Imagination, Cognition and Personality*, refers to a particular kind of social intelligence that involves "the ability to monitor one's own and others' feelings and emotions, to discriminate among them and to use this information to guide one's thinking and actions." Daniel Goleman pulled together the extensive research on these topics into a comprehensive overview in his 1995 book, *Emotional Intelligence: Why It Can Matter More Than IQ*, and again in 2006 in another book, *Social Intelligence: The New Science of Human Relationships*.

Awareness and regulation of one's own emotions represents one of the most fundamental skills included in the concept of emotional intelligence. When hearing statements that we do not like, we tend to perceive them as a threat: to our worldview, our identity, or maybe to a 'tribal group' with which we identify. Our brain goes into overdrive, releasing cortisol (the stress hormone) and preparing us for a 'fight or flight' situation. As a result, regardless of the accuracy of the statement itself, we tend to have either an aggressive response, such as arguing against it; or a defensive response, such as closing down the discussion and ignoring the unlikeable statement. When speaking to people who hold beliefs that are irrational, it's highly likely that we'll encounter these kinds of aggressive or defensive responses. Consequently, we need to prepare ourselves well for such conversations, keeping these likely patterns of behavior in mind. It's also helpful to be in a well-rested mental state. We'll need mental alertness and nimbleness, and lots of willpower.

To succeed, we'll need self-knowledge and self-discipline too. In practice this means we need to develop skills at being fully aware of our own experience of aggressive or defensive emotions when we hear statements that we do not like. The easiest way to accomplish that involves paying attention to the bodily sensations that usually accompany our perceptions of threat, and the consequent emotions: anxiety, frustration, anger, and resentment. Each person exhibits these emotions in different ways. For me, they involve a wave of heat rising up in my shoulders, a prickling sensation in my head, agitated movements and speech, impulsiveness, rapid breathing, increased sensitivity to sound, and—if intense enough—a strong sense of fatigue. Others report increased sweating, sensitivity to light and other forms of sensitivity, tapping and fidgeting, clenching hands, grinding teeth, growing headaches, and many other symptoms. Awareness of uncomfortable emotional body sensations is the first necessary step in addressing them.

When we notice these physical sensations, we need to deploy self-regulation techniques to calm down. There's abundant research evidence to show that making decisions in an emotionally excited state results in bad decision-making. People take more risks, not always wise ones; and they don't behave according to their own ideal vision of themselves. We've probably all experienced this at one time or another. (The research on this can be found in a 2006 article by Dan Ariely and George Loewenstein in *Journal of Behavioral Decision Making*, and also a 2006 piece by Loewenstein and Jennifer Lerner in the *Handbook of Affective Science*.)

Most techniques for self-regulation to address this problem try to help us develop better conscious control of what we say and do. The techniques typically work by delaying responses so we have time to think, or by distracting us from the perceived threat. Some good techniques include deep breathing: take ten deep breaths, with each one involving three seconds to draw in a deep breath and five seconds to breathe it out.

Meditating is an excellent strategy (though it's not something you can do in the heat of the moment): take 5 minutes to just close your eyes, sit in a relaxed position, and focus on your breath as it goes into and out of your body. For those who want to read up on the science behind meditation, I recommend Jon Kabat-Zinn's 1990 *Full Catastrophe Living: Using the Wisdom of Your Body and Mind to Face Stress, Pain, and Illness.* Deep breathing and meditation work particularly well for those who experience defensive responses. Another helpful technique is focusing your attention directly on the uncomfortable sensation. Our natural tendency in dealing with physical and emotional discomfort is to divert our attention away from it, that is, take our mind off it. Although focusing directly on the sensation initially intensifies the discomfort, it can also "dissolve" the discomfort shortly thereafter, though this usually takes some training.

For those who feel aggression, a good technique is clenching your fists or toes and relaxing them. Clench for three seconds and relax for another three seconds, ten times. Another way to work out your aggression is by doing some exercises: the punching bag in my basement gets a lot of use during the winter, and the weeds in my garden suffer in the summer. In face-to-face communication, or on the phone such as during my conversation with Douglas Coleman, deep breathing and clenching are accessible, while meditation and exercises are not; the latter two can be easily done in other forms of communication, such as emails or social media discussions that do not have to take place in "real time." In fact, one of the gifts of the Internet is you can write an email or text, and then sleep on it. As a general rule, never hit the send button while you are angry.

While you may already be aware of your emotions, and capable of managing them to some degree, these are challenging skills to develop. To give ourselves the best chance of communicating effectively, we should assume that the other person—the one holding irrational beliefs—does not have those skills. They are likely to have strong and immediate defensive or aggressive responses when you make statements they don't like.

So how do you deal with this situation? Be sensitive to the emotional charge some statements will have for certain people. Instead, find a way to communicate accurate information while avoiding the phrases that will provoke an immediate aggressive or defensive response. Yet in political conversations, people do this again and again, right up to the highest levels of public office. When President Trump shut down the government in late 2018, insisting he would only reopen it when Congress authorized $5 billion to build a border wall, the Democratic leadership called the move a "temper tantrum," and the wall "immoral." Trump— never one to shy away from name-calling—tweeted back that Speaker Nancy Pelosi was behaving "irrationally." Adding: "And by the way, clean up the streets in San Francisco, they are disgusting!" (@realDonaldTrump, January 20, 2019). Clearly, this approach ratchets up the emotions, drives people apart, and makes clearheaded communication next to impossible.

Avoiding emotionally charged language requires developing your *empathy*: your ability to understand how other people feel. Empathy is often confused with sympathy, meaning sharing the person's feelings, but it's not the same thing. Also, empathy is often confused with compassion, which is caring about the misfortunes of other people. Having empathy is indispensable for being able to communicate effectively about emotionally charged topics in such a way as to help people update their beliefs with truthful information, nudging their perceptions closer to reality.

A first step to developing empathy involves imagining placing yourself in the other person's shoes. Given the other person's background and beliefs, how is that person likely to feel if they heard what you're about to say? Might they feel any sense of threat to their worldview, identity, "tribe," or perceptions of self-worth? In doing so, please be on your guard against the *false consensus effect*. That's our tendency to overestimate how far other people share our characteristics, beliefs, and emotions.

Kathleen Bauman and Glenn Geher showed how significant this is, in a 2002 article in *Current Psychology*, and earlier Gary Marks and Norman Miller in a 1987 *Psychological Bulletin* piece. Try hard to avoid making assumptions; instead, use curiosity and gentle questions about the perspectives that the people you're speaking with have on the topic you have in mind. But don't ask so many questions that it will feel to them like probing or pressure.

To help you imagine how the other person might feel, consider reading some books describing the worldview and self-identity of people who hold differing ideologies. Two good research-based books to start with: Jonathan Haidt's 2012 *The Righteous Mind: Why Good People Are Divided by Politics and Religion* and George Lakoff's 1997 *Moral Politics: What Conservatives Know That Liberals Don't*. When engaging in face-to-face conversations with people who hold differing ideologies, pay particularly close attention to signs of negative emotions in their facial expressions. We all have some idea of what these are, but we can all learn quite a lot more from those who've studied the subject systematically. Paul Ekman's 2003 *Emotions Revealed: Recognizing Faces and Feelings to Improve Communication and Emotional Life* provides a wealth of valuable insights. With those insights in mind, here are some pointers: on the phone, strive to note changes in tone; in online discussions, pay attention to cues such as changing pattern of engagement, such as use of emojis and length and timing of comments.

Our ability to understand other people's feelings is often hindered by the *interpersonal empathy gap*, a cognitive bias where we make mistakes about the intensity of other people's emotions, usually underestimating it. Leaf Van Boven and colleagues demonstrated in a 2013 article in *Advances in Experimental Social Psychology* that people typically underestimate the impact of emotions in influencing other people's judgments, as well as in influencing their own. We typically don't sufficiently appreciate the pain of social suffering, or its effect on outcomes. The interpersonal empathy gap is especially problematic from the perspective of the backfire effect: if we don't appreciate how distressed or provoked somebody feels when force-fed information that's contrary to their prior beliefs, we're unlikely to succeed in modifying those beliefs.

An article in *Social Cognitive and Affective Neuroscience* by Jennifer Gutsell and Michael Inzlicht published in 2011 showed that people tend to show less of a spontaneous understanding for other people's sadness if they perceive those people as not being "one of us," but as members of an out-group. Gutsell and Inzlicht measured the brainwaves (electroencephalographic alpha oscillations) of study participants when these participants were observing those they perceived as part of their in-group or out-group—which mostly meant those people they liked, and those they did not. When observing in-group members who expressed sadness, the measurements of participants' brainwaves showed strong activation patterns, suggesting that the participant's brain was paying attention to the signs that the in-group members were sad. But when observing out-group members, subjects showed much weaker activation. That's not a surprise: most of care more about the feeling of close family, close friends or close colleagues. If, however, we want to have meaningful communication with people who neither share our views, nor belong to our in-group, the research suggests we need to focus especially hard on empathizing. This will often be the case when conversing with people who hold irrational beliefs (that is, the beliefs *of others* that *we* consider irrational).

Once you can understand the other person's feelings, the next vital step is to convey your message in an emotionally and socially intelligent manner. One of the best works about this that's grounded in serious research, Marshall Rosenberg's 2003 *Nonviolent Communication: A Language of Life,* offers a wealth of valuable guidelines and suggestions. One suggestion is to *echo* what the other person says, meaning paraphrasing what the other person has said in a short summary using your own words. That shows the other person you're respectfully paying attention to what they have to say. As part of echoing, aim also to echo the other person's emotions, whether the person states them or does not state them: for example, you might say "I can see you're very concerned that such-and-such an outcome might occur."

Doing so helps the other person feel emotionally validated and heard. Remember, while the person's beliefs may be irrational, their emotions about these beliefs are real: we have to understand them and act according to that understanding. By showing that you heard and understood that person's ideas and beliefs, while also acknowledging the reality of their emotions, you help that person feel respected, good, and reduce the risk that what you have to say will be perceived as a threat. Doing so is helpful, and often indispensable, for connecting with others, and helping them update their understanding by means of truthful information.

To be clear, by "echoing" Rosenberg doesn't mean endorsing, or appearing to endorse, false beliefs the other person may hold. If they say "people have not contributed significantly to global warming," it would be going against reality to agree with that, and thereby possibly reinforce that person's state of misinformation. However, you might say, "I understand: you're skeptical about the scientific evidence that industrial production is causing climate change," thus showing them that you heard their message, without stating in any way that their message accurately reflects reality. Then, you can, for example, inquire into why they would think it problematic if industrial production did lead to global climate change. At that stage, perhaps you would uncover that their underlying fears come from economic security concerns: they might not want carbon emission limits to undercut job growth. Now, with that information about their emotional concerns, you can have a much healthier conversation, for example about the benefits of green energy.

Echoing has many benefits. It helps address the *illusion of transparency*, our tendency to believe that other people understand us better than they really do (as Thomas Gilovich and colleagues showed in 1998, in an article in the *Journal of Personality and Social Psychology*). A related kind of error, called the *curse of knowledge*, refers to the fact that most of us often forget that others do not have the knowledge and understanding that we do (described by Susan Birch in a 2005 piece in *Current Directions in Psychological Science*). This curse affects both the content of the interactions, and the skills needed for effective communication. Overestimating what others already know and understand can make us forget to include in what we say enough appropriate information about the context so that others can understand our perspective and the content we are trying to convey. Because of all this, it's better to over-communicate rather than under-communicate about your message and the context behind it.

It's best to assume that your conversational partner does not possess the rational communication skills described and advocated here. You'll need to assume responsibility for the unspoken interaction between you and your conversational partner, such as what influences whether your conversational partner can comfortably pay attention to what you have to say. Psychologists call such "unspoken interaction" ("unspoken" because it's implicit, not explicit, in what's said in the conversation) the *meta-conversation*.

In addition to echoing, you'll need to convey your own emotions to the other person so as to help them be emotionally attuned to you. Your success will lead to them perceiving you as authentic, and opening up to you, being vulnerable and willing to listen—really listen. Conveying your own emotions to other people involves a broad skill set usually called *charisma* or *personal magnetism*. Charisma is often seen as a talent that you either have or don't have. However, there's a lot of research that shows such magnetism mostly involves a range of strategies and techniques that you can master with study and practice. The research was well summarized by Olivia Fox Cabane in her book *The Charisma Myth: How Anyone Can Master the Art and Science of Personal Magnetism*, published in 2013. She advocates listening actively to the other person, and learning to read their emotional state, echoing their points and validating their emotions— methods we've already discussed. She offers other useful tactics as well, which I summarize here:

- Pausing for two seconds before responding
- Lowering the intonation (but not the volume) of your voice at the end of sentences
- Nodding when the other person speaks, but not more than once or twice a minute
- Noticing physical and emotional discomfort and addressing that intentionally before and during conversations; putting yourself into a good mood before talking to the other person, and helping the other person feel good as well
- Subtly mirroring the other person's body language, vocal tone, and terminology, to convey to the other person that you are part of their in-group
- Avoiding interrupting
- Adapting to the other person's communication style
- Expressing appreciation for other people; using language that conveys warmth and kindness toward them; having open body language: avoid crossing your arms on your chest, keep eye contact, and maintain a friendly facial expression
- Being concise, delivering maximum impact with every word

- Varying your tone to emphasize important points
- Conveying vulnerability through tone and body language.

All of these ideas concern *how* the conversation is managed. Other contributions have been more focused on *what* is said, more than *how*. Research by Chip and Dan Heath, described in their 2007 book *Made to Stick: Why Some Ideas Survive and Others Die*, points to benefits from using stories that have emotional narratives and characters with which the other person—not you—can relate. For the same reason, it's desirable to use language, and supporting points or examples, which will be comfortable for the person to whom you're speaking. While the research by Chip and Dan Heath focused on everyday life, and on the business environment, more recent research shows that similar considerations apply to more politically sensitive conversations. An article in the journal *Science* by David Broockman and Joshua Kalla in 2016 showed that effective conversations can have long-term impacts on people's views about politically sensitive issues such as transphobia. The study showed that ten-minute conversations with door-to-door canvassers who were trained in effective communication techniques reduced transphobia for at least three months.

Communicating the way that I'm recommending sounds like a lot of work, right? Well, yes, it is. I remember learning all of these skills one by one over time, and I still would certainly not consider myself a master at any of them. However, I've had a lot of such conversations, because I know they're necessary and important. The techniques I've described in this chapter helped a lot: both the psychological research and my own experience of activism have convinced me of their effectiveness. To sum it up:

Put Empathy Before Information: Five Es to Help You Communicate Rationally
E1. Emotional states: Become aware of your emotional states and

learn to manage them (especially aggression). Own them; don't let them own you.

E2. Empathy: Tune in, and turn it on. Develop your capacity to tune in to what others feel, and learn to turn it on especially when speaking with those who are not of your "tribe."

E3. Eschew emotionally charged utterances. Use your empathy to avoid statements that will trigger difficult emotions in your conversation partners

E4. Echo what you hear the other person saying, so that they realize you are listening to them and getting their messages.

E5. Express your own emotional reality using the techniques of charisma, so that you build an authentic connection with the other person.

A Case Study in Rational Communication

I've had numerous successful conversations using these techniques to change people's minds when they held irrational beliefs that are at odds with their goals. After getting practice in day-to-day conversations, I began to go on radio shows and do podcasts. These are high-stakes environments with little room for error. Let's return to my radio interview with host Douglas Coleman, mentioned at the start of this chapter. For readers who want to listen to the interview as they read along, here's the link: https://www.youtube.com/watch?v=Vkyu538T4ts

Around 16 minutes and 45 seconds into the clip, Coleman said that Trump "spoke the truth that many people did not want to hear." I had to shift gears very quickly, reassessing the whole shape and course of the interview. I updated my evaluation of the situation, and my intended approach, in order to effectively target Coleman's conservative audience. My response—in this and all other similar interviews—had to walk a fine line. I had to avoid inspiring defensive or aggressive responses by making the other person feel wrong or threatened, while still conveying my points effectively. Around 16:55, you will find my response.

I first echoed Coleman's point, saying that Trump had indeed expressed many ideas that people in this country did not want to hear. That created an immediate atmosphere of agreement between Coleman and me on something and helped him feel good about our interaction, validating his emotions. At the same time, I avoided saying anything untruthful or inaccurate: the plain statement that Trump said many things that plenty of people in the US did not want to hear is very accurate. Going onward, as part of that same response, I talked about Trump speaking to people's guts, their emotions, and discussed how some people thought he was authentic. The point about Trump's authenticity is something that conservatives often bring up as a point of pride, and I thought that Coleman might be gesturing at this in his original comment. Of course, I didn't have the opportunity to use gentle questioning and curiosity here on the radio show, but my experience in these sorts of interviews enabled me to have a pretty good assessment of what Coleman's perspective would probably turn out to be. While I wanted to make sure to acknowledge the perception of Trump as authentic, I also aimed to highlight how perceptions of authenticity came from speaking to people's guts, not reason. I was willing to let audience members judge for themselves whether they think that's a good idea.

Naturally, I could not leave unquestioned the idea that Trump spoke the truth: if I had done so, I'd have done more harm than good. So, after my two initial comments designed to help Douglas Coleman be comfortable with the conversation, at around 17:05 I stated that we need to be careful about what we mean by "truth." Gently nudging the conversation toward the definition of the truth that I wanted to use, I posed the rhetorical question of whether Trump actually described reality on the ground, whether he conveyed the facts. I then provided the answer myself: sometimes he did, and sometimes he didn't. To lessen the sting of that comment, I made sure to then quickly say that Clinton sometimes conveyed the facts, and sometimes did not. Then, I went on to say that we can discuss—if Coleman wishes—how to compare who is more truthful. I made sure to finish with a statement that again echoed Coleman, stating "there are certain truths, like you say yourself, that Trump was expressing that other politicians were not expressing." Coleman responded at 17:37, and the first thing he said was "right." Probably he was pleased by my near-quoting of his words. He then began to discuss the difference between objective, scientific truths—the facts—and personal, subjective truths, specifically bringing up belief in what is written in the Bible as an example of the latter.

Starting my response at 18:13, I agreed, and emphasized that we need to differentiate the truth about physical reality from the truth about personal beliefs. That set up a really good basis for the rest of our conversation. Coleman at around 19:00 steered the conversation to the Pro-Truth Pledge, and asked whether the goal is to get politicians and other public figures to describe their beliefs accurately, or to speak the truth about the issues. My response was that we can't read people's minds and thus are unable to verify whether they accurately report their beliefs. However, we can verify the facts about the issues, what Coleman referred to as "scientific facts." Again, I used Coleman's own language. As the discussion moved on, I used a number of conservative-friendly talking points, for example disparaging the myth spread mainly by liberals that the September 11 terrorist attack was an inside job by George W. Bush. Whenever I brought up mainstream news sources, I focused on conservative ones such as the *Wall Street Journal*. My comments emphasized how the Pro-Truth Pledge offers an opportunity to fight myths from the liberal side that lack a factual basis, while omitting to mention that most myths come from conservatives, and that many of the attacks on mainstream news sources stem from the right. This made sense, since my goal was to establish the pledge as a tool for fighting myth, not blaming one side or the other for creating them in the first place. The conversation flowed very smoothly after that, and by the end of the conversation, Douglas Coleman decided to take the Pro-Truth Pledge.

I used these rational communication techniques in many other interviews with conservative radio show hosts on topics ranging from Trump's firing of FBI Director James Comey, and the baseless allegation that Obama wiretapped Trump Tower, to Muslim terrorist attacks. In these cases, and others, the hosts were able to shift their views at least somewhat. I believe it's likely that the conversations swayed some of the audience to change their perspectives as well. Do conservative radio show hosts like Coleman feel hoodwinked and recant their agreements with me later? My experience so far indicates that's not the case. (For a fuller analysis of three additional interviews, you can find a free PDF download at www.protruthpledge.org/book-interviews.) Given the scientific basis for the effectiveness of these rational communication methods, my hypothesis is that they will prove as effective for you as they have for me—and will be much more productive than just plain arguing.

How Can *You* Practice Rational Communication?

Remember, rational communication does not mean arguing facts first. Rational communication means to think rationally about the psychological reality of the other person, especially if they believe irrational ideas. If you argue facts first, you will most likely create a *backfire effect*, further entrenching the other person in their irrational ideas. To be rational means to use *empathy before information*. Take the time to understand their values, in a curious and respectful way. Create a sense of common goals for the conversation, so that the discussion of the facts works toward a common purpose. Make sure you do not threaten the other person's sense of self and worldview. Then introduce information in such a way that they can consider it in a "what if" hypothetical manner, so they can see whether or not new information fits together with their worldview. Here's a quick summary of these techniques.

Seek first: to understand the other's worldview
- Try to prepare for the conversation by figuring out the person's beliefs, worldview, and position on the issues in advance, to minimize being surprised during the interaction.
- Do *not* lead with facts and logic. Though tempting, you will likely trigger the backfire effect. The result reinforces the other person's existing beliefs.
- Work hard to avoid threatening their worldview, identity, group belonging, and self-worth, or arousing feelings of defensiveness and aggression; this will likely trigger the backfire effect.
- Echo their points and use their language, to help them feel heard and understood.

Seek second: to understand the other's emotions
- Acknowledge that their emotions are real and valid, without necessarily agreeing with their conclusions and course of action.
- Use empathy to model their emotions, and as needed, use curiosity and subtle questioning to figure out what they value.
- Use self-awareness and self-management techniques to regulate your own emotional responses and avoid triggering defensiveness.

Seek third: to find common goals and values
- Connect your values and long-term goals to theirs. This puts you both on the same side, making you both part of the same social group (remember, we all share much

more than we intuitively assume, such as caring for our families, wanting safety and security and happiness).
- Work to find other areas you agree on—if they are nodding their heads and saying "right," and "yeah," you're probably on the right track.
- Get on the same page by discussing how the things you both value can be destroyed by the harmful effects of false beliefs.

Seek fourth: to find a common ground of facts and logic
- Only at this point should you use facts and logic.
- Be sure you reference sources credible to you both. At the same time, don't be dismissive of sources that the other may find credible. Read those sources, and if you have doubts, express them in factual, not emotional terms (how are the claims in that source verified, are the claims reported in other media, and so on).
- Avoid forcing the other to admit they are wrong, or you will again trigger the backfire effect.
- Stay open-minded. If the other person has facts or logic on their side, are *you* flexible enough to change your mind? (If not, then you are engaged in a power struggle, not a search for truth.)

Seek fifth: a course of action you mutually agree on
- Once you find common ground, is there a course of action that aligns with both of your values and goals? This shifts the conversation from who was right or wrong to, "what can we both do about it?"
- If you can agree on a course of action, use positive emotional reinforcement so that the other person associates your mutual accomplishment with truth and reason, and can integrate these into their own identity. For example, if they updated their thinking, sincerely praise them for it.

If you updated your thinking, thank them for helping you see reality more clearly.

- A sense of alignment gives you the positive feeling you are on the same side, if only about this one thing. Enjoy that moment with the other person. It will remind you both that the "other" is not the enemy.

Please experiment with these five steps in your own political conversations, including with close friends and family members. Indeed, one of the worst features of a politically polarized society is that people stop talking to each other. Without conversations across the political spectrum, it's all too easy to assume the worst motives of the "other side." Because we fail to understand each other, we impute motives to them, that: they are "stupid," they "hate America," and so on. Even if you don't succeed in changing another person's mind, you will better understand their thinking, and you will leave an impression of openness and willingness to communicate, which is desperately needed.

Important Terms Referenced in This Chapter

Rational communication: communication that uses accurate information to make wise decisions about how to communicate, and thereby to reach your goals by getting your message across.

Backfire effect: happens when people are presented with information that challenges their beliefs. People tend to defend their positions, and by arguing for them they get more convinced their beliefs are true.

Confirmation bias: a tendency to look for and interpret information in ways that accord with one's existing beliefs.

Social intelligence: the ability to understand and manage people.

Emotional intelligence: the ability to monitor one's own and others' feelings and emotions, to discriminate among them and to use this information to guide one's thinking and actions.

False equivalence: treating the two sides of a controversy as equal, even if one side has all the facts correct, and the other side merely presents misinformation.

False consensus effect: our tendency to overestimate how far other people share our characteristics, beliefs, and emotions.

Interpersonal empathy gap: a cognitive bias where we make mistakes about the intensity of other people's emotions, usually underestimating it.

Meta-conversation: the implicit, unspoken interaction in a conversation.

Illusion of transparency: our tendency to believe that other people understand us better than they really do.

Curse of knowledge: the fact that most of us often forget that others do not have the knowledge and understanding that we do.

Echoing: in a conversation, paraphrasing what the other person has said in a short summary using your own words.

Charisma: "personal magnetism"; the ability to convey your own emotions to other people in a way that attracts or "charms" them, and thus more easily influence them.

Chapter 9

Collaborative Truth-Seeking Instead of Argument

Heated, emotional arguments between people who share similar values and goals are very common in primary elections. The 2016 US presidential primaries witnessed bitter fights among advocates of candidates perceived as more moderate and more radical. On the Republican side, moderate candidates included Jeb Bush, John Kasich, and Marco Rubio, while Ted Cruz and Donald Trump offered a more radical departure from the center. For Democrats, the choice was between the more moderate Hillary Clinton, and the more radical Bernie Sanders. Political activists who shared the same goals of advancing their party's political values often spent more time and energy fighting each other than the opposing party's candidates.

These struggles were also quite costly in the general presidential campaign. For example, according to a *Washington Post*–ABC News tracking poll published five days before the election, only 82 percent of former Sanders supporters intended to vote for Clinton, despite the two sharing very similar political values, especially compared to their opponent. Compared to the less bitter 2008 Democratic primary between Barack Obama and Hillary Clinton, when 47 percent of former Clinton supporters said they were "very enthusiastic" about endorsing Obama, only 32 percent of those who supported Sanders described themselves as "very enthusiastic" about supporting Clinton. Given that 60,000 votes in several key states decided the 2016 election, we can deduce that this lack of support from former Sanders supporters likely helped decide the election against Clinton.

Such harsh struggles result in part from our conception of arguments and debates as a form of conflict. In the first chapter of their 1980 book *Metaphors We Live By*, George Lakoff and Mark Johnson highlighted how our conception of arguments as a form of warfare results in a highly divisive and unnecessarily conflictual approach to disagreements. This perception of disagreements as fights is particularly problematic for emotionally charged issues: we are unlikely to break off friendships or stop talking to family members over whether vanilla or chocolate is the best ice cream flavor (although I will personally never understand those who prefer vanilla).

Fortunately, we can use less intuitive conversational strategies to figure out the truth in situations of disagreement. This chapter lays out the tactics of the broader strategy of collaborative truth-seeking, which shifts disagreements from wars to cooperative explorations where all participants seek to find the truth as a shared goal. Generally speaking, collaborative truth-seeking has much better outcomes with emotionally charged topics than argument. All those who wish to advocate for truth and reason in politics would benefit greatly from modeling collaborative truth-seeking when engaging with each other, and also adapting elements from this set of tactics for other situations where they are striving to resolve disagreements with people who share similar values and goals.

The Problem with Debates

I'm good at arguments, always have been. As a teenager, I remember myself being one of the best in my school at debates. Hanging out with other intellectually-oriented kids in the math team, otherwise known as the "nerd club," we argued constantly. It was our way of competing, establishing dominance, and feeling good about ourselves. We showed off in class by trying to give the best answers and nitpicking the answers given by other students. Sure, we got beaten up after school by the jocks, but we beat them in class and the teachers loved us. We weren't as cool as the jocks, but we were much smarter, and that's what really counts, right?

My experience matches that of many others who found pride and meaning in their high intelligence and debate skills. It was only after I started to read the research on debating that I realized the problem with debates. A particularly relevant book is Robert Kurzban's 2012 *Why Everyone (Else) Is a Hypocrite: Evolution and the Modular Mind*. According to Kurzban, we evolved the capacity to argue not with the intention to figure out the truth, but with the intention to win for our own side in social conflicts within tribes on the ancient savannah. While the thesis is disputed by others in the field of behavioral science, it helped me realize some problematic aspects of debating.

Debates are all well and good when more intelligent individuals hold correct beliefs. On the whole, higher intelligence makes it more likely. Still, smart people often hold inaccurate beliefs. Higher intelligence does not mean that people will not fall for the cognitive biases described earlier in the book, although it does make it somewhat less likely for most biases, as shown by Keith Stanovich and Richard West's 2008 article in the *Journal of Personality and Social Psychology*. However, more intelligent people tend to be more vulnerable to a specific set of biases, such as the *bias blindspot*, thinking that other people have more cognitive biases than oneself, related by West et al. in a 2012 *Journal of Personality and Social Psychology* piece.

I know many reason-oriented people who posit that debates are the best way of figuring out the truth. However, let's be honest with each other. How many times have you argued for a position you had doubts about? Heck, I remember arguing in school for why Coke was better than Snapple as part of a class debate, and winning that debate—and I much prefer Snapple to Coke (Snapple did not pay me for this endorsement). In fact, many of my classmates were genuinely shocked afterward that I actually argued so well for a position that differed from my own. Indeed, there's a reason that rhetoric is a skill taught in college classes, and why publishers print so many books about how to win arguments. Debating is a skill, and while winning a debate is easier if you have the truth on your side, skilled debaters can easily win over those who have weaker skills, even if the other's perspective is closer to the truth. In fact, research shows that participating in debates does not reduce certain cognitive biases, such as the tendency to look for and evaluate evidence with a bias toward one's current opinion, reported in a 1986 unpublished manuscript by David Perkins et al.

In addition to winning the argument for their side, people have many other motivations for debate besides seeking the truth. Some debate as a mode of entertainment and enjoyment. To me and plenty of other people, it feels exciting and fun to cross intellectual swords with a worthy opponent, to parry and riposte. There's nothing like finding weaknesses in my opponent's arguments and striking hard, piercing his defenses and landing a solid blow, while blocking his attacks on my weak points.

Did you notice all of the metaphors I used for debate as warfare in the above paragraph? If not, it's because the structure of our language leads us naturally to accept such metaphors as appropriate. If we think of debate as a fight where we win or lose based on whether our argument prevails, we are not very likely to seek out the truth. How easy do you think it is to acknowledge a worthwhile point made by an opponent in a debate if I am seeking to protect myself from his strikes while marshaling my forces to make a strong counterblow?

These problems with debates don't mean we should never argue—far from it. I still participate in debates for fun. But I no longer fool myself that debating helps me figure out the truth. Instead of debating, I pursue collaborative truth-seeking as a means of being "actively open-minded"—a term Jonathan Baron used in a 2015 piece in *Current Opinion in Psychology,* in which he demonstrates this state of mind is vital for improving functioning democratic systems.

From Winning to Collaborative Truth-Seeking

To move away from the conflict-laden emotional and intuitive associations we have with debates, we can apply what behavioral science calls *reframing*. *Reframing* involves changing our mindset in an intentional manner to get a different perspective on a topic: in this case, a perspective better aligned with our truth-seeking goals. Adam Altera et al., in a 2010 article in *Journal of Experimental Social Psychology*, demonstrated that reframing a situation from a threat to a challenge improves performance. Additionally, research by Rebecca Ray et al. published in 2005 in *Cognitive, Affective & Behavioral Neuroscience* showed that reframing one's thinking patterns decreases negative thoughts and increases positive ones.

So, what happens when we reframe win/lose political debates as a collaborative search for the truth? We transform our opponent into our partner. We replace the threat of being defeated with the challenge and opportunity to gain something valuable (a better grasp of the truth). This decreases our negativity toward our conversational partner and increases positive emotions. However, to make this reframing work, we have to make sure that all participants sincerely focus on finding the truth as a victory for all, instead of their side winning. Likewise, we have to get participants to emphasize collaboration over conflict, and to listen and address the emotions both of ourselves and of others in the conversation.

Now, collaborative truth-seeking should be used only in certain contexts. First, all participants need to have a commitment to finding the truth as a shared goal. Other techniques, as described in Chapter 8, are more applicable to situations where you seek the truth, but believe that your conversational partners aim only to win. Second, participants should already have a certain basic level of mutual trust in each other, or at least the willingness to build that trust during the conversation. Third, participants need to be capable of at least a minimal level of emotional management and empathy, so as to notice and address their own emotional turmoil and also understand and validate the emotions of those with whom they are conversing.

Some important features of collaborative truth-seeking, which are often not present in debates, are: focusing on a desire to change one's own mind toward the truth; maintaining curiosity; being sensitive to others' emotions; striving to avoid arousing emotions that will hinder updating beliefs and the discovery of truth; and trusting that all other participants are doing the same. These contribute to increased social sensitivity, which, together with other attributes, correlate with accomplishing higher group performance on a variety of activities, according to research by Muriel Niederle et al. published in *Science* in 2007.

Strategies for Collaborative Truth-Seeking and a Case Study

Let's return to the beginning of this chapter, and outline some strategies for collaborative truth-seeking using the example of a conversation between two supporters of different primary candidates. I will use a case study of a conversation in January 2016 between supporters of Sanders and Clinton, since there were only two major candidates for the Democratic presidential nominee, which presents fewer complications than the multiple candidates for the Republican nomination.

Before the Conversation: Collaborate on Building Trust
First, you will want to pursue a series of strategies for building trust in pursuing this emotionally charged topic. Start by cultivating an intellectual, collaborative relationship with the other person, where you set shared goals and express a mutual desire for learning and updating beliefs. Taking the Pro-Truth Pledge represents an excellent way of doing so: consider

asking all participants to take this step before engaging in the conversation.

Thus, the two advocates for each candidate would first share that they are engaging in the discussion to help themselves and each other orient toward the truth and learn more about the topic at hand, rather than to convince each other of their own perspective. Doing so takes advantage of the strategy of *priming*, where we set up a context that helps us orient toward a certain outcome, as shown by Stanovich and West in a 1983 piece in the *Journal of Experimental Psychology*. Then, they would outline the shared goal they would pursue in the conversation. For example, a shared goal might be for each supporter to improve their perspective on which candidate to vote for in a way that would most likely lead to the kind of public policy they would like to see.

Following that, you would establish a shared language, by making sure to define terms and decide on what constitutes credible evidence, keeping in mind that, as discussed earlier in the book, reputable fact-checking organizations and the scientific consensus should always represent the first line of evidence. So, for instance, both participants may decide that they do not want to consider what each candidate states as credible evidence, since they both are saying things that will increase their likelihood of getting elected, and thus are not necessarily aligned with the truth. Or they may decide to trust different candidates to a different extent, based on a mutually agreed-upon evaluation of the credibility of each candidate. If you cannot agree on a shared language and standards of evidence, at the very least on the baseline of the first line of evidence as stated above, it may be wise to stop at this point, as the collaborative truth-seeking approach will likely not work out for the conversation you are about to have.

Next, you would deepen the relationship by showing vulnerability, a central factor of cultivating relationships, as described in *Development and Vulnerability in Close Relationships*, a 2013 edited volume by Gil Noam and Kurt Fischer. To do so requires the very counterintuitive tactic of deliberately opening yourself up to potential attacks by your opponent by sharing the weaknesses and uncertainties of your position, your own personal biases, and how your social context might impact your perspective. Doing so helps you prime yourself to know what you need to set aside for the sake of collaborative truth-seeking, and ensures that your opponent has greater trust toward you and also empathy for your viewpoint.

For instance, let's say the Clinton supporter describes how he is tired of the long succession of male presidents, and is eager to see a female president in office. He might acknowledge that this does not have much to do with the conversational goal of determining which candidate would be best suited for putting his personal values into public policy, and needs to set that bias aside for the sake of collaborative truth-seeking. Another point he might share is a concern with Clinton's rather aggressive foreign policy stance, which doesn't fit his personal view of America's role in the world. The Sanders supporter might share that she was an activist protester in the 1960s, and feels a strong connection to Sanders because of his own involvement in those protests. She can also describe her concern with Sanders' strident attacks on Wall Street, which might undermine his capacity to work with the important finance sector of the American economy once in office.

Finally, you need to express trust in your conversational partner by asking them to pause the conversation if they perceive something going wrong, if they are experiencing excessive emotional stress, or if they perceive you as slipping into debate mode instead of collaborative truth-seeking. Doing so requires enough skill and intentional awareness to notice a problem and the willpower to leave an engaging discussion about Sanders and Clinton, and instead discuss the shape of the conversation and how to get it back on track. This tactic is known as going "meta," as it implies rising above the object-level conversation and going to the higher, meta-conversation level.

A useful strategy here is to agree on an unmistakable non-verbal signal or "safe word." I have good experience with using a hand signal of a triangle, invented by Max Harms. It is made by putting one's hands at the level of one's chest and extending thumbs on both hands together until they touch at the tips in a horizontal position. Then, extend the index fingers on both hands upward at a 45-degree angle until the two fingertips touch together in a triangle. This signal works well, since it visually implies going above the conversation, and cannot be mistaken for anything else, even in a heated discussion. For a verbal signal, I suggest saying something like "let's take a pause." While these are good defaults, I suggest you work out what feels comfortable to you and your conversational partner.

During the Conversation: Emotional Management

Almost everyone who starts engaging in truth-seeking has difficulty avoiding slipping into debate mode. It's natural to do so, as that is our autopilot approach to addressing disagreements. Changing mental habits is difficult, particularly in situations with charged emotions. So, the first set of tactics is informed by research to help manage your own emotions well and address the emotions of your collaborator in the conversation. These tactics are inspired by studies described in books on emotional and social intelligence by Daniel Goleman and nonviolent communication by Marshall Rosenberg, as well as cognitive-behavioral therapy, whose research backing can be seen in a meta-analysis by Andrew Butler et al. in 2006 in *Clinical Psychology Review*. (These are similar to the emotional management techniques described in Chapter 8, but with some important differences.)

Focus first and foremost on intentionally gaining awareness

of your emotions and managing them. You are responsible for your own feelings, so do whatever you need to do to get into a calm and relaxed state before talking about the emotionally charged topic at hand. My personal preference is a combination of meditation and exercise, both supported by studies as helping gain calmness and emotional stability (for research on meditation, see Shauna Shapiro and Roger Walsh's 2003 article in *The Humanistic Psychologist* and, for exercise, Jerome Smith and James Crabbe's 2000 piece in the *International Journal of Sport Psychology*).

During the conversation, notice when certain statements by your conversational partner trigger negative emotions. You may notice this triggering through observing physical symptoms: your movements getting quick, your breathing and/or heart rate becoming rapid, your thoughts flowing quickly, a feeling of heat or tension in your shoulders or head, an experience of a tightness in your stomach, and other physical experiences particular to you. These symptoms correlate with the fight-or-flight response of the sympathetic nervous system, which is gearing up to get you out of danger by flooding you with the stress chemical cortisol, whether by shutting down and withdrawing from the conversation or attacking your opponent, instead of orienting toward the truth.

At that point, use emotional management strategies to calm yourself. I suggest two highly effective strategies drawn from cognitive-behavioral therapy. One effective cognitive emotional management technique is positive self-talk. Remind yourself that your aspiration is to orient toward the truth and update your beliefs, rather than protect your current beliefs. Remind yourself that you win by getting as close to the truth as possible, not by convincing the other person to share your beliefs. A second technique is self-talk about your partner. Remind yourself of their agreement to seek the truth with you, and that they will respect you more for seeking the truth than for defeating them. Another behavioral tactic is deep breathing: take 3 seconds to breathe in deeply, hold your breath for 2 seconds, then take 5 seconds to breathe out. By combining these cognitive and behavioral tactics, you are signaling to yourself that there is no actual danger, and turning on your parasympathetic nervous system, getting the cortisol out of your body and getting you calm and relaxed. You can also consider asking for a brief time-out for a few minutes to cool down and address heated emotions. Use that time to meditate, take a walk, do some stretches—whatever helps you cool down.

For instance, say the Clinton supporter started expressing concerns about Sanders' stance on guns. Sanders has been criticized by more left-leaning Democrats for his relatively centrist stance on gun control, one of the few issues where he is more moderate than Clinton. The Sanders supporter would personally prefer Sanders to have a much more stringent gun-control policy, and this is one of her few concerns with Sanders. She might start to feel overwhelmed and defensive, shutting down instead of listening. This is a perfect time to use the emotional management strategies above to grow calmer. It's much more important to take things slow and stay calm rather than try to rush through and ignore such feelings.

Besides managing your own emotions, help the other person maintain their emotional stability. After all, this is a collaboration, not a fight. It's in your best interests to ensure that your partner is as capable as possible at working well with you to get closer to the truth. To do so, help the person feel respected, heard, and understood. Validate that person's emotions as real and legitimate, even if they do not appear to reflect the actual reality of the situation at hand. Remember that our gut reactions about the world are frequently mistaken, yet we are still experiencing these reactions, and they are powerful things indeed. Strive to avoid arousing defensive and aggressive responses by not coming across to your collaborator as a threat, instead presenting yourself as an ally in the common endeavor of truth-seeking.

To ensure the person feels respected, engage in active listening. Take turns speaking, without interrupting unless you need to go meta, and focus on what the person is saying, instead of waiting to speak or simply assuming they are saying the same things that other people who support the same position might say. You are listening to hear and understand what the person is saying, not merely frame a response. Empathize with the person by striving to notice the kind of emotions that might be underlying what they are saying. Echo the essence of what the person said. Use your own words, but make every effort to state their position in a way they would agree with. Seek a resounding "yes!" in response to your paraphrasing. This is to signal to the person that you hear and understand them. In your echoing, include references to any emotions the person indicated that they are feeling. Doing so will help validate the other person's emotions, and help establish you as an ally in the conversation.

For instance, the Sanders supporter should echo the concern of the Clinton supporter about gun control. For instance, she might say, "You have a real concern about Sanders' stance on gun control, and you feel worried that he would not be as firm as you would want him to be if he were making policy." Doing so does not in any way oblige the Sanders supporter to change her beliefs about Sanders, but simply acknowledges the reality. This basic respectfulness—of listening, empathizing, echoing, and validating—will deepen the quality of your collaboration.

After the person speaks and you echo and validate, take your turn to speak. Make sure to use language that conveys humility and willingness to update beliefs. Use "I" statements, and steer away from making definitive statements about reality. Likewise, avoid words that might be perceived as hostile by the other party—be diplomatic toward the other person to decrease negative emotional arousal. Make your statements as specific and clear as possible, define possibly confusing terms, and provide credible evidence for any points you make. Convey an attitude of curiosity and use questioning to help signal your desire to learn, to collaborate, and to orient toward the truth. Use probabilistic thinking and language to help get at the extent of disagreement. For instance, avoid saying that X is absolutely true, but say that you think there's an 80 percent chance X is true.

As an example, the Sanders supporter should not say that "Clinton is not trustworthy." Rather, she would be much better off saying that "I am worried that Clinton is too private, by which I mean she does not share all the information that I believe she should share for the public to make an informed decision about her candidacy. For example, I still don't know what happened with her email servers, and I believe she took much too long to apologize for using a private email server while serving as Secretary of State. I also know that the *Washington Post's* Fact Checker column, which is well-known as reliable, has revealed that Clinton lied when she said she landed in Bosnia under sniper fire. I am anxious that as president, she would still be too private for the benefit of the country, and might lie to gain political advantage. Moreover, I don't know what other things she might be hiding. I still think that maybe about a third of the time she's concealing some important information that would cause me to perceive her in a more negative light if revealed. In fact, I have a feeling she would set policy the way I would want her to about 60 percent of the time, and with Sanders I believe it's closer to 90 percent. My confidence would be higher if I had a more positive perspective of Clinton's trustworthiness. Can you help me figure out whether my current perspective aligns with reality?"

During the Conversation: Truth-Seeking Instead of Debating
To avoid slipping into debate mode in response to your collaborator's points, practice *steelpersoning*. This is in contrast to the term *strawmanning*. Strawmanning is an underhanded

tactic in debates where opponents attack a very weak version of their opponent's points—a "straw man." By contrast, steelpersoning involves strengthening your opponent's points into the strongest possible version. Since your goal is to find the truth, you both benefit through doing this. As a case in point, the Clinton supporter might give more instances of Clinton hiding information of relevance to the election, such as whether donors to the Clinton Foundation received additional access to the State Department when Clinton served as Secretary of State.

Another good tactic to help you avoid debate-style engagement is to be in *charity mode*, which means trying to be more charitable to others and their expertise than seems intuitive to you. Our intuitions are a bad guide to seeking the truth when the person with whom we are in discussion has a perspective different from our own. For instance, if someone says something that seems wrong to you, check to make sure that is what the person actually said: you might have misheard things, or the person might have misstated something. Moreover, you can deliberately invoke charity mode for points that you think are tenuous but deserve to be said.

Consider what happens when the Sanders supporter hears the Clinton supporter say that Sanders is idealistic. The natural and intuitive reaction to this among some Sanders supporters might be to become defensive, because they think that the Clinton supporter believes that Sanders will never be able to get anything done even if he does get elected. Rather than making this assumption, and responding with this in mind, the Sanders supporter would be much better off using curiosity and being charitable, asking the Clinton supporter what he meant. For instance, the Sanders supporter may ask for a clarification as follows: "When I hear you say Sanders is idealistic, I notice I have an assumption of what you mean by that. Could you expand on that so I can make sure I'm understanding you correctly?" The Sanders supporter might be surprised to learn that the Clinton supporter thinks that the idealism is noble, and that more politicians should be idealistic like Sanders.

The Clinton supporter might ask for charity mode before offering potential criticism that might be upsetting, such as saying that he perceives Sanders as inauthentic because he changed his position on gun control in time for the election. In this case, asking for charity mode might involve phrasing such as: "I'm having trouble articulating my thoughts, and I'm worried the way it comes out might make you upset. I'd like to try to say what I'm thinking and just ask you to give me as much credit as you can for wanting to do and say the right thing; then maybe you can help me figure out what's really going on." Making such a request for charity mode prior to making a statement likely to inspire antagonism will help your conversational partner prepare for negative emotions and decrease the triggering in your conversational partner.

Another good technique for collaborative truth-seeking involves using what the Center for Applied Rationality terms the *double crux technique*. In this technique, two parties who hold different positions each write the crucial reason—the crux—for their position. This reason has to be the key one, so if it was proven incorrect, the person would change their perspective. Then, they would look for ways to test the crux—conduct experiments, real or hypothetical, or see if you can find examples that might address the crux. For example, the Sanders supporter might believe that Sanders is very honest, and would not make false statements; the experiment might involve evaluating Sanders' statements for misinformation, or going to a credible fact-checking website such as *PolitiFact* or Factcheck.org or *Snopes* to see whether they have a history of Sanders' past statements. If a person identifies more than one reason as crucial, you can go through each as needed.

Throughout your conversation, acknowledge any points you updated, and thank your conversational partner for helping you update. In the example above, a quick check of *PolitiFact* will show that Sanders did make some false statements. This offers a good opportunity for the Sanders supporter to share that she updated on this point, and express her gratitude that the collaborative truth-seeking conversation helped reveal a flaw in her evaluation of reality, thanking the Clinton supporter for helping lead to this realization. Such a statement of updating and expression of gratitude strongly reinforces trust, vulnerability, and a commitment to truth-seeking as opposed to partisanship.

As a more complex example of the double crux technique, the Clinton supporter might say that his values are overall closer to those of Sanders, but he doesn't think Sanders is as electable, thus making Sanders less likely to succeed in realizing the Clinton supporters' desired values (remember, the conversation took place in January 2016, and the outcome was not known). The Sanders supporter might respond that perhaps Sanders is less electable according to polls, but he may still have a better shot at translating the desired values into public policy.

As an experiment, the two supporters might use a decision-making structure informed by a combination of probabilistic thinking and multiple attribute utility theory, described by John Butler et al. in a 2001 article in *Management Science*. This decision-making structure involves rating and weighing the various qualities of each candidate to choose the best option. For the two candidates, the Sanders and Clinton supporters might decide that they want to evaluate three qualities—alignment with their values, electability, and anticipated effectiveness in policy making—all of which they decide are equally important to achieving their stated goal in this collaborative truth-seeking conversation of seeing which candidate would best make their public policy goals a reality.

Each supporter would rank the two candidates on all three qualities, on a scale of 1 lowest to 10 highest. The Sanders supporter ranked the two candidates as follows: (1) alignment:

Clinton 7, Sanders 9; (2) electability: Clinton 9, Sanders 8; (3) effectiveness: Clinton 6, Sanders 9. Adding up the points for each, Clinton got 22, and Sanders 26. The Clinton supporter ranked the two candidates as follows: (1) alignment: Clinton 7, Sanders 9; (2) electability: Clinton 9, Sanders 6; (3) effectiveness: Clinton 8, Sanders 7. Adding up the points for each, Clinton got 24, and Sanders 22. The two talked further about the results, and the Clinton supporter decided that he had unfairly penalized Sanders' electability, and revised it to 8. At this stage, for him Clinton and Sanders both got 24, and he updated his beliefs to being much less sure he should vote for Clinton in the primaries.

After the collaborative truth-seeking conversation is over, discuss any points on which you might have updated your beliefs. Doing so helps both yourself and the other person see clearly the benefits of collaborative truth-seeking and serves as a way of honoring and respecting the other person's efforts. Then, check if your collaborator wants any suggestions for improvements. Often, an outside perspective is quite valuable for helping improve our ability to engage in collaborative truth-seeking. Finally, share your gratitude to the other person for engaging in the effortful task of collaborative truth-seeking with you. This approach is not intuitive and takes an emotional toll. So, make sure to acknowledge and appreciate the effort of the other person, as well as your own. Remember always that truth-seeking is a journey, not merely a destination, and that while you have traveled to where you are right now with this person, note that further evidence will change your mind.

In summary, engaging in collaborative truth-seeking goes against our natural impulse to win in a debate, and is thus more cognitively costly. It tends to take more time and effort than just arguing, and it's far too easy to slip into debate mode, which comes so naturally. It works best when discussing issues that relate to deeply held beliefs and/or ones that risk emotional triggering for the people involved. However, collaborative truth-seeking should not be used to create a community oriented toward avoiding upsetting others at all costs, which might result in important issues not being discussed candidly. After all, research shows the importance of disagreement in order to make wise decisions and to figure out the truth, as in James Surowiecki's 2005 *The Wisdom of Crowds*. Of course, collaborative truth-seeking is well suited for expressing disagreements in a sensitive way, so if used appropriately, it might permit even people with triggers around certain topics to express their opinions. Finally, collaborative truth-seeking is a great tool to use to discover the truth and to update our beliefs, as it can get past the high emotional barriers to altering our perspectives due to our cognitive biases.

Notes for Collaborative Truth-Seeking Conversations

Here's a quick summary of the tactics discussed in this chapter. You can use as a memetic device the acronym TACTIC.

Establish **Trust**:
- Share weaknesses and uncertainties in your own position.
- Share your biases about your position.
- Share your social context and background as is relevant to the discussion.
- Vocalize curiosity and the desire to learn.
- Ask the other person to call you out if they think you're getting emotional or engaging in debate.

Set **Agreements**:
- Define relevant terms and establish shared evidence standards.
- Commit to the behaviors of the Pro-Truth Pledge in the conversation—this is an excellent way to establish trust and shared evidence standards.

- Go meta: agree to have a "conversation about the conversation"—how you will conduct the interaction.
- Agree on a clear "safe signal," a verbal or nonverbal signal for a meta-conversation.

Keep **Calm**:
- Use emotional management techniques to calm your emotions.
- Self-signal: signal to yourself that you want to engage in collaborative truth-seeking, not debate.
- Convey calm to help those you engage with keep calm.
- Be diplomatic: avoid anything that might cause defensiveness or aggression.

Watch how you **Talk**:
- Be specific: make your statements as close to the reality of sensory perception as possible.
- Use probabilistic language to help convey your view.
- Go slow: take the time needed to consider everything thoroughly and stay in the moment.
- Pause if you feel you need to gather your thoughts or deal with emotions.

Stay **Inquisitive:**
- Listen actively: focus on listening and convey that you are listening to your interlocutor.
- Echo: paraphrase the other person's ideas and check whether you've fully understood their thoughts.
- Empathize with the other person and check whether you've fully understood their feelings.

Practice **Collaboration**:
- Be open to changing your mind based on evidence.
- Steelperson: offer to help improve the other person's

points, rather than attack weak "straw man" versions of their positions.

- Charity mode: be more charitable to others than seems intuitive to you.
- Double crux: identify the crux of your mutual positions and examine it.
- Formal decision-making: to get closer to reality, use multiple attribute utility theory and weigh the strengths and weaknesses of various options.
- Mutual updating: during the conversation and especially at the end, describe how you updated your beliefs.
- Be grateful: express gratitude to each other for the hard effort of collaborative truth-seeking, throughout the conversation and particularly at the conclusion.

Important Terms Referenced in This Chapter

Bias blindspot: thinking that other people have more cognitive biases than oneself.

Reframing: intentionally changing our mindset on a topic, usually to adopt a perspective better aligned with our goals.

Priming: setting up a context, for example at the beginning of a conversation, that helps participants orient toward a certain outcome.

Steelpersoning: a collaborative truth-seeking tactic of strengthening your opponent's points into the strongest possible version.

Strawmanning: an underhanded debate tactic of attacking a very weak version of your opponent's point (a "straw man").

Charity mode: trying to be more charitable to others and their expertise than seems intuitive to you.

Double crux technique: when two parties who hold different positions each explicitly define the crucial reason—the crux—for their position, and then test whether or not the crux is true.

Probabilistic thinking: assigning probabilities to our understanding of reality, rather than thinking in black and white, true or false terms.

Conclusion

Building a Pro-Truth Movement

"I can't trust Obama. I have read about him and he's not...he's not...he's an Arab..."

A woman wearing a "McCain Palin" shirt said this to Republican presidential candidate John McCain at a campaign event in October 2008, during the last month of a bitterly fought election. McCain politely took back the microphone and shook his head.

"No, ma'am," he said. "He's a decent family man, citizen, that I just happen to have disagreements with on fundamental issues," McCain told the crowd. "That's what this campaign is all about."

This famous exchange showed the late senator at his best: as a pro-truth politician who chose not to profit by a lie, even one that could have given him an advantage in a presidential election.

A post-truth politician might observe that McCain still lost the election. But McCain had an answer to such cynicism. In his final speech on the Senate floor he said, "Our system doesn't depend on our nobility. It accounts for our imperfections, and gives an order to our individual striving that has helped make ours the most powerful and prosperous society on earth. It is our responsibility to preserve that, even when it requires us to do something less satisfying than 'winning.'"

McCain understood that prosperous and powerful societies don't simply exist because they are divinely blessed or have a robust constitution. It's the *system that gives order* that makes them so. Preserving that order is an active duty. It means upholding our democratic norms, including the norm of truth-telling. McCain knew that serving the order mattered more than winning. This is pro-truth politics in action.

This book began with a warning that the blatant lies of Trump and Brexit politicians have devastated the commons of public trust. As other politicians are adopting these post-truth tactics, we can anticipate that this tide of lies, authoritarianism, and corruption will continue. Unchecked, it will weaken and destroy our democracies. What gives us reason for hope are the successes of the environmental movement, as well as other movements, in fighting tragedies of the commons. We can rely on the successful examples provided by these movements to clean up the pollution of truth in politics.

Imagine with me what it would be like if even 5 percent of all citizens in the US, UK, and other democracies signed the Pro-Truth Pledge. How many elections are decided within that 5 percent margin? What if we get at least one candidate in each race to sign the pledge, so that other candidates must jump on the bandwagon for fear of being branded as untrustworthy?

Similarly, what if media figures who signed the pledge avoided clickbait headlines and commentary packaged as news? Would they find a substantially larger audience for truth-oriented reporting instead? What if civic activists and lobbying organizations of all sorts found their support melting away if they refused to make a commitment to honesty? Would they begin to rely more on accurately presenting the facts in order to have influence? Remember, organizations and public figures who sign the pledge with the intent to hack the system would face rigorous fact-checking by the pro-truth community, and would be called out if they refused to correct their lies. Once they signed, it would be difficult to backtrack. Who would trust such people ever again?

If politicians, media figures, and civic activists lived in a political environment where lies were not tolerated, how might our democracy evolve? Might we see more rational communications that relied on affirmation of values and empathy? Might politicians learn to practice collaborative truth-seeking, rather than grandstanding and smearing in their campaigns, debates, and hearings?

If there's one main message for readers of this book, it is that the change required to pull back from the post-truth precipice needs to start with you. Our age-old thinking and feeling patterns that evolved on the African savannah have left us vulnerable in the twenty-first century to misinformation and fake news spread via social and online media. Our thinking errors—*rosy retrospection, horns effect, group attribution error, confirmation bias,* the powerful *illusory truth effect,* and the host of others detailed in this book—are the weaknesses that make our minds easy to exploit. In this new and uncertain information environment, post-truth politicians like Trump have flourished like super-predators arriving on the savannah, hacking the system and winning elections.

Like our primate ancestors who first came down from the trees and walked on the savannah, we face again the imperative: evolve or die. *They* did. They outpaced their predators not by growing claws and fast legs, but by outthinking them, by creating tools to compensate for their weaknesses: chipping flint into spearheads, controlling fire, and hunting in collaborative bands. Thus, our ancestors transformed humankind's place from near the bottom of the food chain to the very top.

We face the same struggle today, not for dominance on the grasslands, but for control of the territory of our own minds. For this purpose, this book has taken the insights of behavioral science research and forged them into a set of tools you can use for spotting lies and thinking errors, and learning to resist them. And it has provided you with collaborative actions you can take: signing the Pro-Truth Pledge, and as a next step, joining the Pro-Truth Movement.

The Pro-Truth Movement, centered around the Pro-Truth Pledge, offers us the opportunity to work across partisan boundaries, uplifting actual facts over alternative facts and real news over fake news. It is crucial to remember we are not engaging in resisting Trump or any other politician or faction; we are simply targeting problematic behaviors that are fatal to democracy, and doing so in a way that unites people from all sides of the political divide around a common cause of fighting lies and promoting truth. In fact, we would welcome Trump or any other politician who decides to forswear deception and join us in rebuilding the commons of public trust. Most of all, we need to become intentional activists, citizens willing to work and think and strategize together for the long term.

I invite you to join us and become a pro-truth activist, to dedicate a portion of your time, money, and other resources to help build the world in which you want to live. For anyone who wants to get involved in the Pro-Truth Movement, I encourage you to sign the pledge at www.protruthpledge.org, and indicate that you would like to volunteer. We will then help get you plugged into the effort to turn back the downward spiral of deceit and help us put truth back in politics. You can also download the pro-truth activist PDF from the website for free at www.protruthpledge.org/handbook.

The fight for truth is a marathon, not a sprint. It will require building up an infrastructure of various truth-maintenance organizations and networks of pro-truth activists that will advocate for truth on the local, regional, national, and international levels. The marathon is long, yet you and I have no time to waste. The longer we delay action, the more likely our democracy will pass the point of no return and descend into authoritarianism, corruption, and abuse of power. But if you start now, and join the Pro-Truth Movement, together we have a good shot at reversing the downward slide. With this book, and the chance to join the broader Pro-Truth Movement by taking the pledge, you have everything you need to be part of the pragmatic plan to put truth back into politics.

Glossary of Cognitive Biases, Mental Errors, and Other Important Terms

Ten Lies

1. *Vagueness*: a generality that can't be pinned down as a lie, but gives an overall misleading sense.
2. *Glittering generality*: an emotional appeal to valued concepts (such as love of country) that distracts from a lack of relevant supporting information.
3. *Willful ignorance*: sharing incorrect information by purposefully choosing not to learn or understand the relevant facts.
4. *Lie by omission*: deceiving by deliberately omitting relevant information.
5. *Confabulation*: making false statements due to incorrect memories, without a deliberate intent to deceive.
6. *Deceptive hyperbole*: distorting reality by deliberately exaggerating or minimizing some aspect of it.
7. *Obfuscation*: deliberately making information unclear and confusing without actually lying.
8. *Blatant lie*: knowingly spreading false information.
9. *Gaslighting*: when confronted by evidence you lied, attacking the veracity of the truthful source (or purposefully causing someone to doubt their accurate perceptions of reality).
10. *Paltering*: using a small truth to cover a big lie.

Cognitive Biases and Mental Errors

Anchoring: the tendency to rely too heavily on an initial piece of information (the "anchor") when making decisions. Once we make an initial judgment about what something means, we tend to get fixed on it, and it's hard to change our minds.

Availability heuristic: a mental shortcut that inclines us to rely on immediate examples that come to mind when evaluating a specific topic, concept, method, or decision.

Backfire effect: happens when people are presented with information that challenges their beliefs. People tend to defend their positions, and by arguing for them they get more convinced their beliefs are true.

Bandwagon effect: when people do something primarily because other people are doing it, regardless of their own beliefs.

Black swan event: an unimaginable and very impactful event that radically transforms our society. The mental error is that because these events are rare, we mistakenly think they are impossible, and fail to plan for them; the solution is to anticipate rare events, thus turning them into 'grey swans' that we can plan for.

Bias blindspot: thinking that other people have more cognitive biases than oneself.

Cognitive biases: problematic thinking patterns that can easily lead us into error.

Confirmation bias: the tendency to look for and interpret new information in a way that conforms to our existing beliefs, and ignore or reject new information that goes against our current beliefs.

Curse of knowledge: the fact that most of us often forget that others do not have the knowledge and understanding that we do.

Dunning-Kruger effect: the tendency of people who have less expertise and skills in any given area to have an inflated perception of their abilities. (More bluntly, this describes people who are too stupid to know how stupid they are, so they falsely think they know more than they do.)

False consensus effect: a tendency to overestimate the extent to which other people share our opinions and predispositions.

False equivalence: the intention to evaluate all sides of an issue as equal; this undermines fairness, honesty, and accuracy in cases where one side of the story is actually correct and the others are false.

Group attribution error: assuming one person's attitudes and behavior accurately represent the attitudes and behavior of a group to which the person belongs.

Halo effect: when we positively evaluate one thing about a person (or ethnicity, political party, or nation), we tend to make positive evaluations about other unrelated characteristics of the person (or ethnicity, political party, or nation). For example, if we like or respect a person, we may be more willing to accept the information they tell us is true, even in an area of expertise where they are not knowledgeable.

Horns effect: when we dislike one aspect of a whole, we let this dislike color other aspects of that whole. This dislike may apply to a person, an ethnicity, a political party, or a nation.

Illusion of explanatory depth: an overconfidence in one's understanding of reality.

Illusion of superiority: a bias that causes a person to overestimate their own qualities and abilities in relation to the same qualities and abilities of other persons.

Illusion of transparency: our tendency to believe that other people understand us better than they really do.

Illusory truth effect: a mental error that causes us to perceive something to be true when we hear it repeated frequently and persistently, regardless of whether it is objectively true, or whether or not we are presented with evidence supporting it.

Interpersonal empathy gap: a tendency to make mistakes about the intensity of other people's emotions, usually underestimating it.

Narrative fallacy: our tendency to want to fit whatever information we have available into a story that makes intuitive sense to us.

Optimism bias: the belief things will turn out well.

Pessimism bias: the belief things will turn out poorly.

Primacy effect: when presented with a lot of information, we tend to remember best what we are exposed to first.

Processing fluency: the more comfortable we become with a statement through hearing it repeatedly, the more truthful it seems to us on a gut level.

Publication bias: when a scholar publishes a study with a successful experiment, while hiding the fact that he conducted 50 of the same experiments that failed, until by random chance one finally worked.

Rosy retrospection: our tendency to remember the past as much better than it actually was.

Single cause fallacy: assuming that a single, simple cause created an outcome, when in reality the outcome may have happened due to a number of causes.

Other Important Terms

Charisma: the ability to convey your own emotions to other people in a way that attracts or "charms" them, and thus more easily influence them (also known as *personal magnetism*).

Charity mode: trying to be more charitable to others and their expertise than seems intuitive to you.

Debiasing: with motivation and training, we can learn to detect and avoid the costly errors of our mental blindspots and cognitive biases.

Demagogue: a dictator who initially rises to power with support from the public.

Echoing: in a conversation, paraphrasing what the other person has said in a short summary using your own words.

Emotional intelligence: the ability to monitor one's own and others' feelings and emotions, to discriminate among them and to use this information to guide one's thinking and actions.

Expressive voting: a way of voting that accepts all that a favored politician says as true because one would be uncomfortable doing otherwise (voting with one's "gut" rather than one's head).

Filter bubble: the way social media algorithms distort reality by showing us news that fits our preferences and feeding us more posts from the people and organizations we "follow," "friend," and "like," rather than the diversity of viewpoints within our society.

Gaslighting: when confronted by evidence one lied, attacking the veracity of the truthful source (or purposefully causing someone to doubt their accurate perceptions of reality).

Hitchen's Razor: an aphorism useful for resisting claims made without evidence: "That which can be asserted without proof can be dismissed without proof."

Ideologically informed deception: where an ideologue pushes a favored agenda despite the actual evidence.

Meta-conversation: the implicit, unspoken interaction in a conversation.

Priming: setting up a context, for example at the beginning of a conversation, that helps participants orient toward a certain outcome.

Probabilistic thinking: assigning probabilities to our understanding of reality, rather than thinking in black and white, true or false terms.

Race to the bottom: what happens when trust starts to break down in a "commons" situation.

Rational communication: communication that uses accurate information to make wise decisions about how to communicate, and thereby to reach your goals by getting your message across.

Reframing: intentionally changing our mindset on a topic, usually to adopt a perspective better aligned with our goals.

Social intelligence: the ability to understand and manage people.

Steelpersoning: a collaborative truth-seeking tactic of strengthening your opponent's points into the strongest possible version.

Strawmanning: an underhanded debate tactic of attacking a very weak version of your opponent's point (a "straw man").

Tragedy of the commons: when a group of people share a common resource—the commons—without any controls on the use of this resource, individual self-interest may lead to disaster ("tragedy") for all involved.

Tribal epistemology: a perverse situation in which people believe that whatever their side says is true, and whatever the other side says is false.

References

Chapter 1

Haidt, Jonathan. *The Righteous Mind: Why Good People Are Divided by Politics and Religion*. Vintage, 2012.

Signer, Michael. *Demagogue: The Fight to Save Democracy from Its Worst Enemies*. Macmillan, 2009.

Frijda, Nico H., Antony S.R. Manstead, and Sacha Bem, eds. *Emotions and Beliefs: How Feelings Influence Thoughts*. Cambridge University Press, 2000.

Baron, Jonathan. "Philosophical impediments to citizens' use of science." Paper presented at the Annenberg Public Policy Center conference on "Science of Science Communication," October 17, 2014.

Taylor, Luke E., Amy L. Swerdfeger, and Guy D. Eslick. "Vaccines are not associated with autism: an evidence-based meta-analysis of case-control and cohort studies." *Vaccine* 32.29 (2014): 3623–9.

Marks, Gary, and Norman Miller. "Ten years of research on the false-consensus effect: an empirical and theoretical review." *Psychological Bulletin* 102.1 (1987): 72–90.

Institute of Medicine. *Priorities for Research to Reduce the Threat of Firearm-Related Violence*. The National Academies Press, 2013.

Ludwig, J., and P.J. Cook. "Homicide and suicide rates associated with implementation of the Brady Handgun Violence Prevention Act." *JAMA* 284(5) (2000): 585–91.

Vars, Fredrick E. "Self-Defense Against Gun Suicide (September 23, 2014)." *Boston College Law Review*, 2015; University of Alabama Legal Studies Research Paper No. 2500291.

Fleegler, E.W., L.K. Lee, M.C. Monuteaux, D. Hemenway, R. Mannix. "Firearm legislation and firearm-related fatalities in the United States." *JAMA Internal Medicine* 173.9 (2013): 732–40.

Levitt, Justin. *The Truth About Voter Fraud*. Brennan Center for Justice at New York University School of Law, November 9, 2007: http://www.brennancenter.org/sites/default/files/legacy/The%20Truth%20About%20Voter%20Fraud.pdf

Taleb, Nassim Nicholas. *The Black Swan: The Impact of the Highly Improbable*. Penguin, 2007.

US Customs and Border Protections. "U.S. Border Patrol Monthly Apprehensions (FY 2000–FY 2018)": https://www.cbp.gov/sites/default/files/assets/documents/2019-Mar/bp-total-monthly-apps-sector-area-fy2018.pdf

Chapter 2

Verwoerd, Johan, et al. "'If I feel disgusted, I must be getting ill': emotional reasoning in the context of contamination fear." *Behaviour Research and Therapy* 51.3 (2013): 122–7.

Alkozei, Anna, Peter J. Cooper, and Cathy Creswell. "Emotional reasoning and anxiety sensitivity: associations with social anxiety disorder in childhood." *Journal of Affective Disorders* 152 (2014): 219–28.

Evans, Jonathan St. B.T., and Keith E. Stanovich. "Dual-process theories of higher cognition: advancing the debate." *Perspectives on Psychological Science* 8.3 (2013): 223–41.

Kahneman, Daniel. *Thinking, Fast and Slow*. Macmillan, 2011.

Dennett, Daniel. "Intentional systems theory." *The Oxford Handbook of Philosophy of Mind* (2009): 339–50.

Heath, Chip, and Dan Heath. *Decisive: How to Make Better Choices in Life and Work*. Random House, 2013.

Arkes, Hal R. "Costs and benefits of judgment errors: implications for debiasing." *Psychological Bulletin* 110.3 (1991): 486.

Haselton, Martie G., Daniel Nettle, and Damian R. Murray. "The evolution of cognitive bias." *The Handbook of Evolutionary Psychology* (2005).

Mullen, Brian, et al. "The false consensus effect: a meta-analysis of 115 hypothesis tests." *Journal of Experimental Social*

Psychology 21.3 (1985): 262–83.

Gigerenzer, Gerd, and Reinhard Selten. *Bounded Rationality: The Adaptive Toolbox*. MIT Press, 2002.

Schuessler, Alexander A. "Expressive voting." *Rationality and Society* 12.1 (2000): 87–119.

Hatfield, Elaine, John T. Cacioppo, and Richard L. Rapson. "Emotional contagion." *Current Directions in Psychological Science* 2.3 (1993): 96–100.

Rodriguez, Barrera, Oscar David, Sergei M. Guriev, Emeric Henry, and Ekaterina Zhuravskaya. "Facts, alternative facts, and fact checking in times of post-truth politics." SSRN Paper (July 18, 2017).

Mitchell, Terence R., et al. "Temporal adjustments in the evaluation of events: the 'rosy view.'" *Journal of Experimental Social Psychology* 33.4 (1997): 421–48.

Katz, Sidney. "The importance of being beautiful." *Down to Earth Sociology* 8 (1995): 301–7.

Burton, Scot, et al. "Broken halos and shattered horns: overcoming the biasing effects of prior expectations through objective information disclosure." *Journal of the Academy of Marketing Science* 43.2 (2015): 240–56.

Shevlin, Mark, et al. "The validity of student evaluation of teaching in higher education: love me, love my lectures?" *Assessment & Evaluation in Higher Education* 25.4 (2000): 397–405.

Nadeau, R., E. Cloutier, and J.H. Guay. "New evidence about the existence of a bandwagon effect in the opinion formation process." *International Political Science Review* 14.2 (1993): 203–13.

Allison, Scott T., and David M. Messick. "The group attribution error." *Journal of Experimental Social Psychology* 21.6 (1985): 563–79.

Mackie, Diane M., and Scott T. Allison. "Group attribution errors and the illusion of group attitude change." *Journal of*

Experimental Social Psychology 23.6 (1987): 460–80.

Nickerson, Raymond S. "Confirmation bias: a ubiquitous phenomenon in many guises." *Review of General Psychology* 2.2 (1998): 175.

Lord, Charles G., Lee Ross, and Mark R. Lepper. "Biased assimilation and attitude polarization: the effects of prior theories on subsequently considered evidence." *Journal of Personality and Social Psychology* 37.11 (1979): 2098.

Ask, Karl, and Pär Anders Granhag. "Motivational sources of confirmation bias in criminal investigations: the need for cognitive closure." *Journal of Investigative Psychology and Offender Profiling* 2.1 (2005): 43–63.

Taber, Charles S., and Milton Lodge. "Motivated skepticism in the evaluation of political beliefs." *American Journal of Political Science* 50.3 (2006): 755–69.

Chapter 3

Dechêne, Alice, Christoph Stahl, Jochim Hansen, and Michaela Wänke. "The truth about the truth: a meta-analytic review of the truth effect." *Personality and Social Psychology Review* 14.2 (2010): 238–57.

Arkes, Hal R., Catherine Hackett, and Larry Boehm. "The generality of the relation between familiarity and judged validity." *Journal of Behavioral Decision Making* 2.2 (1989): 81–94.

Fazio, Lisa K., Nadia M. Brashier, B. Keith Payne, and Elizabeth J. Marsh. "Knowledge does not protect against illusory truth." *Journal of Experimental Psychology* 144.5 (2015): 993–1002.

Sundar, Aparna, Frank R. Kardes, and Scott A. Wright. "The influence of repetitive health messages and sensitivity to fluency on the truth effect in advertising." *Journal of Advertising* 44.4 (2015): 375–87.

Polage, Danielle. "Making up history: false memories of fake news stories." *Europe's Journal of Psychology* 8.2 (2012): 245–50.

Baron, Jonathan. "Why teach thinking?—an essay." *Applied Psychology* 42.3 (1993): 191–214.

Gino, Francesca. "There's a word for using truthful facts to deceive: paltering." *Harvard Business Journal*. October 5, 2016.

Taylor-Wynn, Heaven. "Donald Trump misleads on US defense spending, NATO budget." *Politico*. July 12, 2018.

Harwood, John. "Pay attention to the man behind the curtain: Trump is no wizard of government." *CNBC*. April 28, 2017.

Chapter 4

Presidential newspaper endorsements: http://www.presidency. ucsb.edu/data/2016_newspaper_endorsements.php

Lewis, Charles. *935 Lies: The Future of Truth and the Decline of America's Moral Integrity. PublicAffairs*, 2014.

Republican National Lawyers Association (RNLA) "Vote Fraud Survey": http://www.rnla.org/survey.asp; http://www.gao. gov/assets/670/665966.pdf

Christensen, Ray, and Thomas J. Schultz. "Identifying election fraud using orphan and low propensity voters." *American Politics Research* 42.2 (2014): 311–37.

Levitt, Justin. *The Truth About Voter Fraud*. Brennan Center for Justice at New York University School of Law, November 9, 2007: http://www.brennancenter.org/sites/default/files/ legacy/The%20Truth%20About%20Voter%20Fraud.pdf

Willnat, Lars, and David H. Weaver. "The American Journalist in the Digital Age: Key Findings." School of Journalism, Indiana University, 2014.

Sarnov, Benedikt. *Our Soviet Newspeak: A Short Encyclopedia of Real Socialism*. Moscow, 2002.

Crankshaw, Edward. *Khrushchev*. A&C Black, 2011.

Morrow, James D. *Game Theory for Political Scientists*. Princeton University Press, 1994.

Camerer, Colin. *Behavioral Game Theory: Experiments in Strategic Interaction*. Princeton University Press, 2003.

Cimaglio, Christopher. "'A tiny and closed fraternity of privileged men': the Nixon–Agnew anti-media campaign and the liberal roots of the US conservative 'liberal media' critique." *International Journal of Communication* 10 (2016): 1–19.

Feldstein, Mark. *Poisoning the Press: Richard Nixon, Jack Anderson, and the Rise of Washington's Scandal Culture.* Macmillan, 2010.

Ladd, Jonathan M. *Why Americans Hate the Media and How It Matters.* Princeton University Press, 2011.

Becker, Jonathan. "Lessons from Russia: a neo-authoritarian media system." *European Journal of Communication* 19.2 (2004): 139–63.

Translation of *Kommersant* article "The Reform of the Administration of the President of the Russian Federation": http://miamioh.edu/cas/_files/documents/havighurst/english-putin-reform-admin.pdf

Freedom House Reports on Freedom of the Media in Russia: https://freedomhouse.org/report/freedom-press/2002/russia

Freedom House Reports on Freedom of the Media in Turkey: https://freedomhouse.org/report/freedom-press/2015/turkey

Shin, Jieun, and Kjerstin Thorson. "Partisan selective sharing: the biased diffusion of fact-checking messages on social media." *Journal of Communication* 67.2 (2017): 233–55.

Hamilton, James T. "Subsidizing the watchdog: what would it cost to support investigative journalism at a large metropolitan daily newspaper?" *Duke Conference on Nonprofit Media*, 2009.

Walton, Mary. "Investigative shortfall: many news outlets are doing far less accountability reporting than in the past, bad news indeed for the public. New nonprofit investigative ventures have emerged, but they can't pick up the slack by themselves." *American Journalism Review* 32.3 (2010): 18–34.

Bagdikian, Ben H. *The New Media Monopoly: A Completely Revised and Updated Edition with Seven New Chapters.* Beacon Press, 2014.

Bednarski, Anastasia. "From diversity to duplication: mega-mergers and the failure of the marketplace model under the Telecommunications Act of 1996." *Fed. Comm. LJ* 55 (2002): 273.

Noam, Eli. *Media Ownership and Concentration in America.* Oxford University Press on Demand, 2009.

Champlin, Dell, and Janet Knoedler. "Operating in the public interest or in pursuit of private profits? News in the age of media consolidation." *Journal of Economic Issues* 36.2 (2002): 459–68.

"Code of Ethics" for the Society of Professional Journalism: https://www.spj.org/ethicscode.asp

Barnett, Steven. "Broadcast journalism and impartiality in the digital age." *Regaining the Initiative for Public Service Media* (2012): 201–18.

Koomey, Jonathan. "Separating fact from fiction: a challenge for the media [soapbox]." *IEEE Consumer Electronics Magazine* 3.1 (2014): 9–11.

Gans, Herbert J. "The American news media in an increasingly unequal society." *International Journal of Communication* 8 (2014): 12.

Pickard, Victor. "Media failures in the Age of Trump." *The Political Economy of Communication* 4.2 (2017).

Turner, Nikki M., Deon G. York, and Helen A. Petousis-Harris. "The use and misuse of media headlines: lessons from the MeNZB (TM) immunisation campaign." *The New Zealand Medical Journal* (online) 122.1291 (2009).

Andrew, Blake C. "Media-generated shortcuts: do newspaper headlines present another roadblock for low-information rationality?" *Harvard International Journal of Press/Politics* 12.2 (2007): 24–43.

"How Americans Get Their News." 2014 survey by the American Press Institute: https://www.americanpressinstitute.org/publications/reports/survey-research/how-americans-get-news/

Rasmussen poll on March 8, 2017, on Obama administration wiretapping Trump Tower: http://www.rasmussenreports. com/public_content/politics/trump_administration/ march_2017/did_obama_wiretap_trump_voters_react

CBS News poll on March 29, 2017 on US government deliberately surveilling Trump Tower: https://www.scribd.com/ document/343392363/Cbs-Poll-7am-Toplines

Chapter 5

Pew Research Center. "News Use Across Social Media Platforms 2016": http://www.journalism.org/2016/05/26/news-use-across-social-media-platforms-2016/

Pariser, Eli. "Beware Online 'Filter Bubbles,'" 2011 Technology, Entertainment, and Design (TED) talk: https://www.ted.com/ talks/eli_pariser_beware_online_filter_bubbles

Resnick, Paul, et al. "Bursting your (filter) bubble: strategies for promoting diverse exposure." *Proceedings of the 2013 Conference on Computer Supported Cooperative Work Companion.* ACM, 2013.

Wojcieszak, Magdalena. "False consensus goes online: impact of ideologically homogeneous groups on false consensus." *Public Opinion Quarterly* 72.4 (2008): 781–91.

Bauman, Kathleen P., and Glenn Geher. "We think you agree: the detrimental impact of the false consensus effect on behavior." *Current Psychology* 21.4 (2002): 293–318.

2015 Nielsen Global Trust in Advertising Report: http://www. nielsen.com/us/en/press-room/2015/recommendations-from-friends-remain-most-credible-form-of-advertising.html

Nisbett, Richard E., and Timothy D. Wilson. "The halo effect: evidence for unconscious alteration of judgments." *Journal of Personality and Social Psychology* 35.4 (1977): 250–5.

Borah, Abhishek, and Gerard J. Tellis. "Halo (spillover) effects in social media: do product recalls of one brand hurt or help rival brands?" *Journal of Marketing Research* 53.2 (2016): 143–60.

"The Value of Influencers on Twitter." 2016 study by Twitter and Annalect: https://blog.twitter.com/2016/new-research-the-value-of-influencers-on-twitter

Allcott, Hunt, and Matthew Gentzkow. "Social media and fake news in the 2016 election." No. w23089. National Bureau of Economic Research, 2017.

American Press Institute 2016 survey on trust in media: https://www.americanpressinstitute.org/publications/reports/survey-research/news-trust-digital-social-media/

Stanford University History Group. "Evaluating Information: The Cornerstone of Civic Online Reasoning," November 22, 2016: https://sheg.stanford.edu/upload/V3LessonPlans/Executive%20Summary%2011.21.16.pdf

van der Linden, Sander, et al. "Inoculating the public against misinformation about climate change." *Global Challenges* 1.2 (2017): 1–7.

Society of Professional Journalists Code of Ethics: https://www.spj.org/ethicscode.asp

The First Amendment Center — Ethics in Journalism. 2007 report on journalism ethics scandals: http://catalog.freedomforum.org/FFLib/JournalistScandals.htm

Baum, Matthew A., and Tim Groeling. "New media and the polarization of American political discourse." *Political Communication* 25.4 (2008): 345–65.

Chapter 6

Barclay, Pat. "Trustworthiness and competitive altruism can also solve the 'tragedy of the commons.'" *Evolution and Human Behavior* 25.4 (2004): 209–20.

Fehrler, Sebastian, and Wojtek Przepiorka. "Charitable giving as a signal of trustworthiness: disentangling the signaling benefits of altruistic acts." *Evolution and Human Behavior* 34.2 (2013): 139–45.

Liang, Jianping, Zengxiang Chen, and Jing Lei. "Inspire me to donate: the use of strength emotion in donation appeals." *Journal of Consumer Psychology* (2015): http://doi.org/10.1016/j.jcps 1.

Trump, Donald J., with Tony Schwartz. *Trump: The Art of the Deal*. Random House, 1987.

Hosmer, Larue Tone. "Trust: the connecting link between organizational theory and philosophical ethics." *Academy of Management Review* 20.2 (1995): 379–403.

Hardin, Garret. "The tragedy of the commons." *Science* 162.3859 (1968): 1243–8.

Vogler, John. *The Global Commons: Environmental and Technological Governance*. 2nd Edition, John Wiley & Sons, 2000.

Hanley, Nick, and Henk Folmer. *Game Theory and the Environment*. Edward Elgar Publishing, 1998.

Smith, Robert J. "Resolving the tragedy of the commons by creating private property rights in wildlife." *Cato Journal* 1 (1981): 439–68.

McWhinnie, Stephanie F. "The tragedy of the commons in international fisheries: an empirical examination." *Journal of Environmental Economics and Management* 57.3 (2009): 321–33.

Bhagwat, S., X. Zhang, and H. Fan. "Estimation of coal cleaning costs: a spreadsheet based interactive software for use in estimation of economically recoverable cost reserves." Final Report Submitted to US Geological Survey, Reston, VA (2000).

Epstein, Paul R., et al. "Full cost accounting for the life cycle of coal." *Annals of the New York Academy of Sciences* 1219.1 (2011): 73–98.

U.S. Energy Information Administration (EIA), "Count of Electric Power Industry Power Plants, by Sector, by Predominant Energy Sources within Plant, 2005 through 2015": https://www.eia.gov/electricity/annual/html/epa_04_01.html (retrieved on July 6, 2017).

Hardin, Russell. *Trust and Trustworthiness*. Russell Sage

Foundation, 2002.

Newton, Kenneth. "Trust, social capital, civil society, and democracy." *International Political Science Review* 22.2 (2001): 201–14.

Braithwaite, Valerie, and Margaret Levi, eds. *Trust and Governance*. Russell Sage Foundation, 2003.

McCabe, J. Terrence. "Turkana pastoralism: a case against the tragedy of the commons." *Human Ecology* 18.1 (1990): 81–103.

Berkes, Fikret. "Fishermen and 'the tragedy of the commons.'" *Environmental Conservation* 12.3 (1985): 199–206.

Chapter 7

Hardin, Garret. "The tragedy of the commons." *Science* 162.3859 (1968): 1243–8.

Vogler, John. *The Global Commons: Environmental and Technological Governance*. 2nd Edition, John Wiley & Sons, 2000.

Ostrom, Elinor. *Governing the Commons*. Cambridge University Press, 1990.

Feeny, David, Fikret Berkes, Bonnie J. McCay, and James M. Acheson. "The tragedy of the commons: twenty-two years later." *Human Ecology* 18.1 (1990): 1–19.

van Vugt, Mark. "Averting the tragedy of the commons: using social psychological science to protect the environment." *Current Directions in Psychological Science* 18.3 (2009): 169–73.

Milinski, Manfred, Dirk Semmann, and Hans-Jürgen Krambeck. "Reputation helps solve the 'tragedy of the commons.'" *Nature* 415.6870 (2002): 424–6.

Barclay, Pat. "Trustworthiness and competitive altruism can also solve the 'tragedy of the commons.'" *Evolution and Human Behavior* 25.4 (2004): 209–20.

King, Andrew, Michael J. Lenox, and Michael L. Barnett. "Strategic responses to the reputation commons problem." *Organizations, Policy and the Natural Environment: Institutional and Strategic Perspectives* (2002): 393–406.

Santos, Francisco C., and Jorge M. Pacheco. "Risk of collective failure provides an escape from the tragedy of the commons." *Proceedings of the National Academy of Sciences* 108.26 (2011): 10421–5.

Thaler, Richard, H., and R. Sunstein Cass. *Nudge: Improving Decisions About Health, Wealth, and Happiness*. Penguin Group, 2009.

Selinger, Evan, and Kyle Whyte. "Is there a right way to nudge? The practice and ethics of choice architecture." *Sociology Compass* 5.10 (2011): 923–5.

Johnson, Eric J., Suzanne B. Shu, Benedict G.C. Dellaert, Craig Fox, Daniel G. Goldstein, Gerald Häubl, Richard P. Larrick, et al. "Beyond nudges: tools of a choice architecture." *Marketing Letters* (2012): 1–18.

Camerer, Colin, Samuel Issacharoff, George Loewenstein, Ted O'Donoghue, and Matthew Rabin. "Regulation for conservatives: behavioral economics and the case for 'asymmetric paternalism.'" *University of Pennsylvania Law Review* 151.3 (2003): 1211–54.

Korobkin, Russell. "Libertarian welfarism." *California Law Review* 97.6 (2009): 1651–85.

Boyd, Robert, Herbert Gintis, and Samuel Bowles. "Coordinated punishment of defectors sustains cooperation and can proliferate when rare." *Science* 328.5978 (2010): 617–20.

Gino, Francesca, Michael I. Norton, and Dan Ariely. "The counterfeit self: the deceptive costs of faking it." *Psychological Science* 21.5 (2010): 712–20.

Mazar, Nina, and Dan Ariely. "Dishonesty in everyday life and its policy implications." *Journal of Public Policy & Marketing* 25.1 (2006): 117–26.

Mazar, Nina, On Amir, and Dan Ariely. "The dishonesty of honest people: a theory of self-concept maintenance." *Journal of Marketing Research* 45.6 (2008): 633–44.

Mazar, Nina, On Amir, and Dan Ariely. "More ways to cheat—

expanding the scope of dishonesty." *Journal of Marketing Research* 45.6 (2008): 651–3.

Katzev, Richard D., and Anton U. Pardini. "The comparative effectiveness of reward and commitment approaches in motivating community recycling." *Journal of Environmental Systems* 17.2 (1987): 93–113.

Mann, Heather, Ximena Garcia-Rada, Daniel Houser, and Dan Ariely. "Everybody else is doing it: exploring social transmission of lying behavior." *PloS One* 9.10 (2014): e109591.

Ariely, Dan. *The Honest Truth About Dishonesty: How We Lie to Everyone — Especially Ourselves*. HarperCollins, 2012.

Krippendorff, K. *Content Analysis: An Introduction to Its Methodology*. Sage, 2004.

Kray, Laura J., and Adam D. Galinsky. "The debiasing effect of counterfactual mind-sets: increasing the search for disconfirmatory information in group decisions." *Organizational Behavior and Human Decision Processes* 91.1 (2003): 69–81.

Hirt, Edward R., and Keith D. Markman. "Multiple explanation: a consider-an-alternative strategy for debiasing judgments." *Journal of Personality and Social Psychology* 69.6 (1995): 1069.

Fernbach, Philip M., Todd Rogers, Craig R. Fox, and Steven A. Sloman. "Political extremism is supported by an illusion of understanding." *Psychological Science* 24.6 (2013): 939–46.

Kruger, Justin, and David Dunning. "Unskilled and unaware of it: how difficulties in recognizing one's own incompetence lead to inflated self-assessments." *Journal of Personality and Social Psychology* 77.6 (1999): 1121.

Van Lange, Paul A.M., Ellen De Bruin, Wilma Otten, and Jeffrey A. Joireman. "Development of prosocial, individualistic, and competitive orientations: theory and preliminary evidence." *Journal of Personality and Social Psychology* 73.4 (1997): 733.

Zimmerman, Rick S., and Catherine Connor. "Health promotion in context: the effects of significant others on health behavior change." *Health Education Quarterly* 16.1 (1989): 57–75.

van Vugt, Mark. "Community identification moderating the impact of financial incentives in a natural social dilemma: water conservation." *Personality and Social Psychology Bulletin* 27.11 (2001): 1440–9.

Kerin, Roger A., P. Rajan Varadarajan, and Robert A. Peterson. "First-mover advantage: a synthesis, conceptual framework, and research propositions." *Journal of Marketing* (1992): 33–52.

Hurley, Terrance M., and Jason F. Shogren. "Environmental conflicts and the SLAPP." *Journal of Environmental Economics and Management* 33.3 (1997): 253–73.

Connelly, Brian L., S. Trevis Certo, R. Duane Ireland, and Christopher R. Reutzel. "Signaling theory: a review and assessment." *Journal of Management* 37.1 (2011): 39–67.

McCabe, Donald L., and Linda Klebe Trevino. "Academic dishonesty: honor codes and other contextual influences." *Journal of Higher Education* 64.5 (1993): 522–38.

Bearman, Peter S., and Hannah Brückner. "Promising the future: virginity pledges and first intercourse." *American Journal of Sociology* 106.4 (2015): 859–912.

Surowiecki, James. *The Wisdom of Crowds*. Anchor, 2005.

Tsipursky, Gleb, Fabio Votta, and Kathryn M. Roose. "Fighting fake news and post-truth politics with behavioral science: the Pro-Truth Pledge." *Behavior and Social Issues* 27.2 (July 2018): 47–70.

Tsipursky, Gleb, Fabio Votta, and James A. Mulick. "A psychological approach to promoting truth in politics: the Pro-Truth Pledge." *Journal of Social and Political Psychology* 6.2 (July 2018): 271–90.

Chapter 8

Kuklinski, James H., Paul J. Quirk, Jennifer Jerit, David Schweider, and Robert F. Rich. "Misinformation and the currency of democratic citizenship." *Journal of Politics* 62.3

(2000): 790–816.

Nickerson, Raymond S. "Confirmation bias: a ubiquitous phenomenon in many guises." *Review of General Psychology* 2.2 (1998): 175.

Lord, Charles G., Lee Ross, and Mark R. Lepper. "Biased assimilation and attitude polarization: the effects of prior theories on subsequently considered evidence." *Journal of Personality and Social Psychology* 37.11 (1979): 2098.

Nyhan, Brendan, and Jason Reifler. "When corrections fail: the persistence of political misperceptions." *Political Behavior* 32.2 (2010): 303–30.

Wood, Thomas, and Ethan Porter. "The elusive backfire effect: mass attitudes' steadfast factual adherence." SSRN Paper (August 5, 2016).

Peter, Christina, and Thomas Koch. "When debunking scientific myths fails (and when it does not): the backfire effect in the context of journalistic coverage and immediate judgments as prevention strategy." *Science Communication* 38.1 (2016): 3–25.

Nyhan, Brendan, and Jason Reifler. "The roles of information deficits and identity threat in the prevalence of misperceptions." Manuscript submitted for publication (2015).

Trevors, Gregory J., Krista R. Muis, Reinhard Pekrun, Gale M. Sinatra, and Philip H. Winne. "Identity and epistemic emotions during knowledge revision: a potential account for the backfire effect." *Discourse Processes* 53.5–6 (2016): 339–70.

Thorndike, Robert L., and Saul Stein. "An evaluation of the attempts to measure social intelligence." *Psychological Bulletin* 34.5 (1937): 275.

Salovey, Peter, and John D. Mayer. "Emotional intelligence." *Imagination, Cognition and Personality* 9.3 (1990): 185–211.

Goleman, Daniel. *Emotional Intelligence: Why It Can Matter More Than IQ*. Bantam, 1995.

Goleman, Daniel. *Social Intelligence: The New Science of Human*

Relationships. Bantam, 2006.

Ariely, Dan, and George Loewenstein. "The heat of the moment: the effect of sexual arousal on sexual decision making." *Journal of Behavioral Decision Making* 19.2 (2006): 87–98.

Loewenstein, George, and Jennifer S. Lerner. "The role of affect in decision making." *Handbook of Affective Science* 619.642 (2003): 3.

Kabat-Zinn, Jon. *Full Catastrophe Living: Using the Wisdom of Your Body and Mind to Face Stress, Pain, and Illness*. Delacorte Press, 1990.

Marks, Gary, and Norman Miller. "Ten years of research on the false-consensus effect: an empirical and theoretical review." *Psychological Bulletin* 102.1 (1987): 72.

Bauman, Kathleen P., and Glenn Geher. "We think you agree: the detrimental impact of the false consensus effect on behavior." *Current Psychology* 21.4 (2002): 293–318.

Haidt, Jonathan. *The Righteous Mind: Why Good People Are Divided by Politics and Religion*. Vintage, 2012.

Lakoff, George. *Moral Politics: What Conservatives Know That Liberals Don't*. University of Chicago Press, 1997.

Ekman, Paul. *Emotions Revealed: Recognizing Faces and Feelings to Improve Communication and Emotional Life*. Times Books, 2003.

Van Boven, Leaf, George Loewenstein, David Dunning, and Loran F. Nordgren. "Changing places: a dual judgment model of empathy gaps in emotional perspective taking." *Advances in Experimental Social Psychology* 47 (2013): 117–71.

Nordgren, Loran F., Kasia Banas, and Geoff MacDonald. "Empathy gaps for social pain: why people underestimate the pain of social suffering." *Journal of Personality and Social Psychology* 100.1 (2011): 120.

Gutsell, Jennifer N., and Michael Inzlicht. "Intergroup differences in the sharing of emotive states: neural evidence of an empathy gap." *Social Cognitive and Affective Neuroscience* 7.5 (2011): 596–603.

Rosenberg, Marshall. *Nonviolent Communication: A Language of Life*. PuddleDancer Press, 2003.

Gilovich, Thomas, Kenneth Savitsky, and Victoria Husted Medvec. "The illusion of transparency: biased assessments of others' ability to read one's emotional states." *Journal of Personality and Social Psychology* 75.2 (1998): 332.

Birch, Susan A.J. "When knowledge is a curse: children's and adults' reasoning about mental states." *Current Directions in Psychological Science* 14.1 (2005): 25–9.

Cabane, Olivia Fox. *The Charisma Myth: How Anyone Can Master the Art and Science of Personal Magnetism*. Penguin, 2013.

Heath, Chip, and Dan Heath. *Made to Stick: Why Some Ideas Survive and Others Die*. Random House, 2007.

Broockman, David, and Joshua Kalla. "Durably reducing transphobia: a field experiment on door-to-door canvassing." *Science* 352.6282 (2016): 220–4.

Interview: Gleb Tsipursky interview with Douglas Coleman on July 17, 2017. Retrieved from https://www.youtube.com/watch?v=Vkyu538T4ts

Chapter 9

Lakoff, George, and Mark Johnson. *Metaphors We Live By*. University of Chicago Press, 1980.

Kurzban, Robert. *Why Everyone (Else) Is a Hypocrite: Evolution and the Modular Mind*. Princeton University Press, 2012.

Stanovich, Keith E., and Richard F. West. "On the relative independence of thinking biases and cognitive ability." *Journal of Personality and Social Psychology* 94.4 (2008): 672.

West, Richard F., Russell J. Meserve, and Keith E. Stanovich. "Cognitive sophistication does not attenuate the bias blind spot." *Journal of Personality and Social Psychology* 103.3 (2012): 506.

Perkins, David, Barbara Bushey, Michael Faraday. "Learning to Reason." Unpublished manuscript, Harvard Graduate School of Education, Cambridge, MA, 1986.

Niederle, Muriel, and Lise Vesterlund. "Do women shy away from competition? Do men compete too much?" *The Quarterly Journal of Economics* 122.3 (2007): 1067–101.

Baron, Jonathan. "Citizenship and morality." *Current Opinion in Psychology* 6 (2015): 6–9.

Woolley, Anita Williams, Christopher F. Chabris, Alex Pentland, Nada Hashmi, and Thomas W. Malone. "Evidence for a collective intelligence factor in the performance of human groups." *Science* 330.6004 (2010): 686–8.

Nyhan, Brendan. "Why the 'death panel' myth wouldn't die: misinformation in the health care reform debate." *Politics* 8.1 (2010): 5.

Flynn, D.J., Brendan Nyhan, and Jason Reifler. "The nature and origins of misperceptions: understanding false and unsupported beliefs about politics." *Political Psychology* 38.S1 (2017): 127–50.

Ray, Rebecca D., K.N. Ochsner, J.C. Cooper, E.R. Robertson, J.D.E. Gabrieli, and J.J. Gross. "Individual differences in trait rumination and the neural systems supporting cognitive reappraisal." *Cognitive, Affective & Behavioral Neuroscience* 5 (2005): 156–68.

Alter, Adam L., Joshua Aronson, John M. Darley, Cordaro Rodriguez, and Diane N. Ruble. "Rising to the threat: reducing stereotype threat by reframing the threat as a challenge." *Journal of Experimental Social Psychology* 46.1 (2010): 166–71.

Stanovich, Keith E., and Richard F. West. "On priming by a sentence context." *Journal of Experimental Psychology* 112.1 (1983): 1–36.

Noam, Gil G., and Kurt W. Fischer. *Development and Vulnerability in Close Relationships*. Psychology Press, 2013.

Goleman, Daniel. *Emotional Intelligence*. Bantam, 2006.

Goleman, Daniel. *Social Intelligence*. Random House, 2007.

Rosenberg, Marshall B. *Nonviolent Communication: A Language of*

Compassion. PuddleDancer Press, 1999.

Butler, Andrew C., Jason E. Chapman, Evan M. Forman, and Aaron T. Beck. "The empirical status of cognitive-behavioral therapy: a review of meta-analyses." *Clinical Psychology Review* 26.1 (2006): 17–31.

Shapiro, Shauna L., and Roger Walsh. "An analysis of recent meditation research and suggestions for future directions." *The Humanistic Psychologist* 31.2–3 (2003): 86.

Smith, Jerome C., and James B. Crabbe. "Emotion and exercise." *International Journal of Sport Psychology* 31.2 (2000): 156–74.

Butler, John, Douglas J. Morrice, and Peter W. Mullarkey. "A multiple attribute utility theory approach to ranking and selection." *Management Science* 47.6 (2001): 800–16.

Surowiecki, James. *The Wisdom of Crowds*. Anchor, 2005.

About the Authors

Dr. Gleb Tsipursky is a passionate advocate for using behavioral economics and cognitive science to advance truth-oriented behavior, rational thinking, and wise decision-making. A civic activist, he serves as the president of Intentional Insights, a nonprofit devoted to popularizing these topics. Its main focus is the Pro-Truth Pledge, a project that aims to reverse the tide of misinformation, fake news, and post-truth politics sweeping over democracies around the globe. A social entrepreneur, Dr. Tsipursky is the CEO of Disaster Avoidance Experts, a consulting and training firm that helps leaders and organizations avoid disasters. As a scholar, he has a strong research background with over 15 years at the Ohio State University and the University of North Carolina-Chapel Hill and dozens of peer-reviewed publications, in venues such as *Journal of Political and Social Psychology* and *Behavior and Social Issues*. He is the author of four books, and has also contributed over 400 articles that range across the liberal/conservative divide to publications such as *Time, Scientific American, Psychology Today, Newsweek, The Conversation, Inc. Magazine, CNBC, New York Daily News, The Dallas Morning News, The Daily Caller, The Plain Dealer*, and given over 350 interviews to TV stations such as CBS News, ABC, and NBC and FOX affiliates, and radio stations such as NPR, WBAI, KGO 810, 700WLW, KRLD, AM980. In his free time, he makes sure to spend abundant quality time with his wife to avoid disasters in his personal life. To learn more, visit his website, *GlebTsipursky. com*, and you can email him at gleb@intentionalinsights.org.

Tim Ward is co-owner of Intermedia Communications Training, Inc., and his driving passion is how communications creates transformation. He has designed and led hundreds of communications workshops in more than 40 countries around the world, working with organizations such as WWF, the World Bank, the International Monetary Fund, the Asian and African Development Banks, the Green Climate Fund, and the Bipartisan Policy Center. He is a former print journalist, and the author of nine books. Tim is also publisher of Changemakers Books. He lives in Bethesda, Maryland, with his wife and business partner Teresa, and spends his free time kayaking on the Potomac, hillwalking in Scotland, and struggling to learn French.

Books by Gleb Tsipursky

Never Go With Your Gut: How Pioneering Leaders Avoid Business Disasters and Make the Best Decisions
Want to avoid business disasters, whether minor mishaps such as excessive team conflict or major calamities that threaten bankruptcy or doom a promising career? Fortunately, behavioral economics studies show that such disasters are preventable. They stem from poor decisions due to our faulty mental patterns, what scholars call cognitive biases. Unfortunately, the typical advice for business leaders to go with their guts plays into these cognitive biases and leads to disastrous decisions that devastate the bottom line. By combining practical case studies with cutting-edge research, *Never Go With Your Gut* will help you make the best decisions and prevent these business disasters.

The Blindspots Between Us: How to Overcome Unconscious Cognitive Bias and Build Better Relationships
We all have hidden blindspots in our minds that often ruin our relationships, what scholars term cognitive biases. The resulting misconceptions, misunderstandings, and mistakes result in severely damaged or completely broken relationships with our romantic partners, friends, families, work colleagues, as well as within community groups, civic and political engagement. This is the first book that helps you recognize cognitive biases in relationships. However, its true pay-off comes from helping you solve these dangerous judgment errors by drawing on the very latest groundbreaking research to help this book's readers build better relationships in all life areas.

The Truth Seeker's Handbook: A Science-Based Guide
How do you know whether something is true? How do
you convince others to believe the facts? Research shows
that the human mind is prone to making thinking errors—
predictable mistakes that cause us to believe comfortable lies
over inconvenient truths. These errors leave us vulnerable to
making decisions based on false beliefs, leading to disastrous
consequences for our business, personal lives, relationships,
and civic engagement. This book presents a variety of research-
based tools for ensuring that our beliefs are aligned with
reality. With examples from daily life and an engaging style,
the book will provide you with the skills to avoid thinking
errors and help others to do so.

Books by Tim Ward

The Master Communicator's Handbook
(with Teresa Erickson)

This book is for people who want to change the world. Here's the challenge: it's impossible to change the world all by yourself. To have an impact, you need to communicate. In these pages, the authors share what they've learned over 30 years as professional communicators and advisors to leaders of global organizations. The book covers: how to create powerful messages, how to speak with authority, how to avoid the tics and quirks that create a negative impression, how to answer questions effectively, how to develop rapport, how to persuade and motivate others, how to use visuals, how to frame the issues, and how to tell a transformational story. In short, the book gives you the tools you need to become the most effective and powerful communicator you can be—a catalyst for transformation, capable of changing the world.

Indestructible You: Building a Self that Can't be Broken
(with Shai Tubali)

Indestructible You is a practical guidebook for making yourself so strong inside that life's relentless ups and downs cannot shake you and cannot break you. It will help you uncover the powerful, driving force of your true self, and let go of everything that holds you back. The book is based on exercises and practices developed by Shai Tubali through his research and work guiding several hundred individuals through psycho-transformational processes. In essence: life is like an eternal seesaw. At every given moment you're either up—getting what you want and feeling powerful, or down—finding yourself rejected, weakened and frustrated. We are forever hoping to bend the laws of this 'unfair game' so that we stay on the up-side of life. But this unrealistic insistence is why we suffer. *Indestructible You* reveals the way to step down from the eternal seesaw and build an unbreakable self, a self that remains fearless and strong no matter what life throws at you.

Zombies on Kilimanjaro: A Father/Son Journey Above the Clouds

A father and son climb Mount Kilimanjaro. On the journey to the roof of Africa they traverse the treacherous terrain of fatherhood, divorce, dark secrets and old grudges, and forge an authentic adult relationship. The high-altitude trek takes them through some of the weirdest landscapes on the planet, and the final all-night climb to the frozen summit tests their endurance. On the way to the top father and son explore how our stories about ourselves can imprison us in the past, and the importance of letting go. The mountain too has a story to tell, a story about climate change and the future of humankind—a future etched all too clearly on Kilimanjaro's retreating glaciers.

CHANGEMAKERS
BOOKS

TRANSFORMATION

Transform your life, transform your world - Changemakers
Books publishes for individuals committed to transforming their
lives and transforming the world. Our readers seek to become
positive, powerful agents of change. Changemakers Books
inform, inspire, and provide practical wisdom and skills to
empower us to write the next chapter of humanity's future.
If you have enjoyed this book, why not tell other readers by
posting a review on your preferred book site.

Recent bestsellers from Changemakers Books are:

Integration
The Power of Being Co-Active in Work and Life
Ann Betz, Karen Kimsey-House
Integration examines how we came to be polarized in our dealing
with self and other, and what we can do to move from an either/
or state to a more effective and fulfilling way of being.
Paperback: 978-1-78279-865-1 ebook: 978-1-78279-866-8

Bleating Hearts
The Hidden World of Animal Suffering
Mark Hawthorne
An investigation of how animals are exploited for
entertainment, apparel, research, military weapons, sport, art,
religion, food, and more.
Paperback: 978-1-78099-851-0 ebook: 978-1-78099-850-3

Lead Yourself First!
Indispensable Lessons in Business and in Life
Michelle Ray
Are you ready to become the leader of your own life? Apply
simple, powerful strategies to take charge of yourself, your
career, your destiny.
Paperback: 978-1-78279-703-6 ebook: 978-1-78279-702-9

Burnout to Brilliance
Strategies for Sustainable Success
Jayne Morris
Routinely running on reserves? This book helps you transform
your life from burnout to brilliance with strategies for sustainable
success.
Paperback: 978-1-78279-439-4 ebook: 978-1-78279-438-7

Goddess Calling
Inspirational Messages & Meditations of Sacred Feminine
Liberation Thealogy
Rev. Dr. Karen Tate
A book of messages and meditations using Goddess archetypes
and mythologies, aimed at educating and inspiring those with
the desire to incorporate a feminine face of God into their
spirituality.
Paperback: 978-1-78279-442-4 ebook: 978-1-78279-441-7

The Master Communicator's Handbook
Teresa Erickson, Tim Ward
Discover how to have the most communicative impact in this
guide by professional communicators with over 30 years of
experience advising leaders of global organizations.
Paperback: 978-1-78535-153-2 ebook: 978-1-78535-154-9

Meditation in the Wild
Buddhism's Origin in the Heart of Nature
Charles S. Fisher Ph.D.
A history of Raw Nature as the Buddha's first teacher, inspiring
some followers to retreat there in search of truth.
Paperback: 978-1-78099-692-9 ebook: 978-1-78099-691-2

Ripening Time
Inside Stories for Aging with Grace
Sherry Ruth Anderson
Ripening Time gives us an indispensable guidebook for growing
into the deep places of wisdom as we age.
Paperback: 978-1-78099-963-0 ebook: 978-1-78099-962-3

Striking at the Roots
A Practical Guide to Animal Activism
Mark Hawthorne
A manual for successful animal activism from an author with
first-hand experience speaking out on behalf of animals.
Paperback: 978-1-84694-091-0 ebook: 978-1-84694-653-0

Readers of ebooks can buy or view any of these bestsellers by
clicking on the live link in the title. Most titles are published
in paperback and as an ebook. Paperbacks are available in
traditional bookshops. Both print and ebook formats are available
online.

Find more titles and sign up to our readers' newsletter at
http://www.johnhuntpublishing.com/transformation
Follow us on Facebook at
https://www.facebook.com/Changemakersbooks